The Theory of Income and Wealth Distribution

The Theory of
Income and Wealth
Distribution

Edited by

Y.S. Brenner
J.P.G. Reijnders
A.H.G.M. Spithoven

The University of Utrecht,
The Netherlands

WHEATSHEAF BOOKS · SUSSEX

ST. MARTIN'S PRESS · NEW YORK

First published in 1988 by
Wheatsheaf Books Ltd
16 Ship Street, Brighton, BN1 IAD
A Division of
Simon & Schuster International Group
and in the USA by
St. Martin's Press, Inc.
175 Fifth Avenue, New York, NY 10010

Printed and bound in Great Britain by
Billing & Sons Ltd, Worcester

British Library Cataloguing in Publication Data

The Theory of income and wealth distribution.
1. Wealth
I. Brenner, Y.S.   II. Reijnders, J.P.G.
III. Spithoven, A.H.G.M.
339.2   HB251
ISBN 0-7450-0479-2

Library of Congress Cataloging-in-Publication Data

The Theory of income and wealth distribution / edited by
Y.S. Brenner, J.P.G. Reijnders, A.H.G.M. Spithoven.
p.   cm.
Bibliography: p.
Includes index.
ISBN 0-312-01965-3 (St. Martin's Press) : $30.00 (est.)
1. Income distribution. 2. Wealth. I. Brenner, Y.S.
II. Reijnders, J. (Jan) III. Spithoven, A.H.G.M.
HB523/T45 1988
339.2—dc19   87-35308
                                                      CIP

Contents

v

Editorial Preface

The contributions to this volume were selected out of twenty-five papers presented at two meetings in the summer of 1986. The first of these meetings was the conference on Income and Wealth Distribution in Historical Perspective, held at the University of Utrecht (August 20–2); the second, on Income and Wealth Distribution and Economic Development at the Ninth International Economic History Congress, in Bern (August 24–9). The papers cover a wide spectrum of issues related to the functional aspect of distribution theory. Another selection of papers, dealing with the historical aspects of the problem, is published separately.

The papers are introduced by J. Tinbergen with a survey of the essential concepts required for the collection of income distribution data and for the description and analysis of the mechanism by which income is formed and with which the factors entering into that mechanism can be studied.

The first two papers provide an outline of various distribution theories and elements of an empirical examination of the neoclassical and Post-Keynesian approaches. They are followed by two papers dealing with the relationship between wages, productivity and employment in the 1930s and with the share distribution between investment and consumption in the 1970s and early 1980s. The link between the periods is discussed in the next paper by a long-wave concept which is explained by means of a modified version of Hick's model of constrained business cycles. Then three kinds of trade-off are considered in succession. The trade-off between growth and distribution in general; the trade-off between economic growth and the relative diminution of the incomes of the poorest in developing countries; and the trade-off between efficiency and equity in the welfare state. After this the discussion shifts to the effects of distribution on the selection of production technologies and to the distributional consequences of concentration and collusion between giant corporations. The last paper restores the problem to its cultural and social context. Some ancient views on how an economic surplus ought to be distributed are presented. The ancient Greeks are cited to caution us that the distribution of the economic surplus must be guided by public policy 'where serious faults in the distribution of bargaining power' may divert it from the path of equity.

THE THEORY OF DISTRIBUTION

After a brief review of various theories of distribution in the *social surplus* and the *supply and demand* traditions, and a survey of the modifications introduced into them with the passage of time, Y.S. Brenner focuses attention in Chapter 3, 'The Tricky Problem of Distribution', on the distributive effects of the expanding public sector and oligopoly. He maintains that the expansion of the public sector is a natural concomitant of industrialization and indispensable for sustaining effective demand; and that if an essential part of an economy is controlled by oligopolies, production targets are scaled down in prolonged depressions and profits kept up by cost reductions which are not passed on to consumers. He concludes that without further expansion of the public sector, industrial progress will grind to a halt, and that distributive effects in an economy with a large oligopolistic component must lead to unemployment and, in the long run, to self-sustained economic decline.

In Chapter 2, 'Recent Trends in Labour's Share', J.E. King and P. Regan review the development of the relative magnitudes of labour and property income in the United

Kingdom, the United States, Australia and Japan. They outline three theoretical models of the development of relative shares, which originate from the neoclassical, Post-Keynesian and Marxian point of view, and confront their empirical findings with the predictions which derive from these theoretical models. Their conclusion is that the empirical findings support none of them.

DISTRIBUTION, EMPLOYMENT AND ECONOMIC POLICY

Apart from providing alternative explanations for the mechanisms of distribution, the neoclassical and (Post-) Keynesian theories have widely different policy implications. On the whole, the neoclassical approach tends toward *laissez-faire* and suggests that distribution policies may subvert the economic self-adjustment mechanisms. The adherents to this approach fear that the implementation of such policies may lead in the national context to unemployment and insurmountable financial difficulties. In contrast, followers of the (Post-)Keynesian approach tend toward active intervention and suggest that in the absence of an adequate distribution policy there will be no escape from the actual economic difficulties of our time. The next three papers relate to these issues.

S.M. Bonnell and R.J. Rimmer in Chapter 3, 'Trends and Cyclical Changes in Wages, Productivity and the Distribution of Income during the 1930s', try to assess the degree to which between 1929 and 1938 employment was affected by changes in real unit labour costs, which they define as equivalent to labour's share. On the basis of a survey of eleven countries, they find the diversity of economic experiences too vast to draw definite conclusions about the existence or non-existence of a causal link.

In 'A Case Study on Functional Income Shares and the Distribution of Income between Investment and Consumption 1965–85', Chapter 4, A.H.G.M. Spithoven addresses himself to a similar question. Analysing recent Dutch statistics, he examines the proposition that low profits are causally related to rising unemployment. Taking account of the unreliable statistical methods employed to calculate relative income shares and of the fact that savings and investment do not depend on the share of profits alone, he investigates the development of actual savings and of the actual distribution of income between investment and consumption. He finds no lack of savings in the Netherlands but huge capital transfers abroad (mainly by giant corporations) and indications that domestic investments were mainly cost reducing. His conclusion is that policies of wage restraint to raise profits do not necessarily induce domestic investment.

J.Reijnders in Chapter 5, 'Economic Stability and Political Expediency', discusses the Keynesian application of distribution theory. The difficulty he encountered in studying this problem on the basis of the available empirical evidence was that most governments which adopted such policies paid little more than lip-service to the Keynesian approach. Employing a modified version of Hick's model of constrained business cycles, he arrives at the provisional conclusion that on the whole public policy in the welfare state was improperly phased. From a long-run point of view it had been pro-cyclical. He believes that from the perspective of a long-wave approach the contradiction between 'Keynesian' and 'Anti-Keynesian' policy prescriptions may well be resolved by correct timing.

TRADE-OFF: THE POLICY-MAKERS', THE POOR MEN'S AND THE RICH MEN'S CHOICE

Economists are accustomed to the idea that all economic decisions involve choice — perhaps too accustomed. In chapter 6, 'Trade-off between Economic Growth and Income Equality: A Re-evaluation', J.W. Lee and S.M. Koo investigate the long-run trade-off between income equality and the level of income — the Kuznets curve relation, and the short-run trade-off between income equality and the growth rate of income. Their empirical findings do not confirm the long-run trade-off suggested by the Kuznets curve but lend support to a short-run trade-off relation. On the basis of these results they caution governments to pay more attention to the redistribution effects of accelerated growth promoting policies.

In Chapter 7, 'IMF Policies: The Dilemma of Their Effect on Growth and Income Distribution in Developing Countries, 1980-5', J.K. Verkooijen discusses the poverty variant of the trade-off between growth and distribution in the Third World. According to Verkooijen, the Kuznets hypothesis (that income inequality increases during the early stages, reaches a peak and then declines in the later stages of development) does not necessarily affect the generally positive influence of growth on actual incomes. Verkooijen pleads for a policy combining growth with distribution. He argues that during the first half of the 1980s the process of adjustment to the generally poor performance of the world economy was characterized by a negative growth of GNP in most low-income countries. In many countries debt rescheduling seems therefore inevitable because further reductions in investment and lower consumption will not only be economically harmful but politically infeasible. A modification of the adjustment process is required to improve long-term growth prospects. In his opinion, debt rescheduling and debt servicing should be linked to and restricted by export earnings, and redistribution effects should be taken into account in fund-supported adjustment programmes.

J.Hartog and J.G. Odink in Chapter 8, 'Equity and Efficiency in Holland: An Overview', concentrate on another aspect of the trade-off between growth and income distribution, namely the equity–efficiency trade-off in the welfare state. Their study is formulated in terms of the Paretian welfare theory: if initial-wealth policies are incapable of satisfying the objectives of distributive justice, this goal can only be reached at the cost of loss of efficiency. They use four measures of income inequality and measure the costs of loss of efficiency by a redistributive linear income tax. This cost they attribute to leisure preference and to the magnitude of inequality reduction. By this method they discover a reduction in income inequality and a rise in welfare costs since 1914.

POWER AND DISTRIBUTION

Following the three papers on the trade-off between growth and distribution, A. Manders in Chapter 9, 'Production Technology and Distribution Theory', deals with the too often neglected problem in this context, namely with technological innovation. Manders elaborates some elements of the degree of monopoly theory and claims that the share of wages in the national income is determined by the average degree of monopoly which itself is, among other things, influenced by the collusion between giant corporations. He investigates the developments of new production techniques and concentration. From a close study of a Dutch multinational giant he reaches the conclusion that through concentration the new production techniques and modes of organization affect income distribution.

In the final chapter, 'Insights from Ancient Views on Distribution', S. Todd Lowry shows the relevance of the ancient views for modern times with regard to trade when the trading partners are unequal in bargaining power or when they 'march to a different drummer'. Next to this he also relates distributive justice to its cultural background by indicating how the meaning of such apparently simple ideas like 'to each according to his needs' vary with the environment in which they are conceived. The ancient Greeks considered fair a tripartite distribution of goods or income to the members of the household in accordance with their needs. The goods for sustenance, for the satisfaction of physical wants, were shared by all. The external goods and amenities, were shared by the artisans or specialized craftsmen but not by the agricultural labourers or slaves who had no use for them. The 'goods of the soul', which provide the leisure and aesthetic values necessary for the cultivation of the mind for the performance of the duties of the free citizen, were reserved for the free citizen alone. This is hardly what Karl Marx had in mind when he wrote in *Criticism of the Gotha Programme*, 'From each according to his abilities, to each according to his needs'.

The sequence in which the papers are presented was chosen to make the book also accessible to readers who have not previously delved deeply into the distribution problem. It begins with a review of the familiar theories and of the empirical evidence which either supports or casts doubt upon these theories. This is followed by several papers which indicate the relevance of distribution theory for macroeconomic policy decisions with regard to growth, stability and equity. Then the relationship between distribution and innovation and the choice of technologies in oligopolistic environments is considered. And finally the problem is presented in its cultural setting by relating it to ancient views and practices.

Readers who are well familiar with the distribution problem may of course prefer to read the papers in another sequence. They may wish to begin from the modified Keynesian model presented at the end of Brenner's paper and judge its validity by comparing it with the results obtained by Manders, which tend to support it, and by Spithoven, which supports it in some points but contradicts it in others. Other readers may be interested mainly in the empirical studies and the doubts they raise about the validity of all the familiar distribution theories. These readers would be well advised to begin with the papers by King and Regan and by Bonnell and Rimmer. They should then move to Reijnders and decide whether his long-wave approach can resolve some of these doubts. Readers interested in the Kuznets curve should turn to the papers by Lee and Koo and by Verkooijen, of whom the last mentioned deserves particular attention by those whose main interest lies with the development of Third World countries. In the neoclassical tradition is the paper of Hartog and Odink. It is best read in conjunction with the papers by King and Regan and by Bonnell and Rimmer, in which grave doubts are raised against the neoclassical approach, and with the paper by Lee and Koo, whose paper tends at least in parts to support it. Finally, Todd Lowry's contribution to this volume should be of interest to every reader not only for its contribution to the better understanding of the problem at hand but also for the sheer pleasure of reading it.

Y.S.Brenner
J.P.G.Reijnders
A.H.G.M.Spithoven

Introductory Remarks

J. Tinbergen

In order to analyse effectively the history of income
distribution a number of concepts have to be introduced
necessary to describe the mechanism of income information
and the factors entering into that mechanism. It seems
appropriate to pay attention to at least the following aspects
of income.

SOURCES OF INCOME

Incomes can be derived from various sources, of which the
most important ones are *labour, capital* and *transfers.*
Income from *labour* is called wage or salary and considerable
differences exist between wages or salaries received by
labour of different quality. Broad subdivisions are those
between skilled and unskilled labour. This is a crude way
to take into account the amount of schooling the workers
considered have completed. A more refined way is to
specify the length and type of schooling, in particular
subdivided into three levels (primary, secondary and
tertiary) and two types: general and vocational schooling.
But this refers to formal schooling only and in addition we
have informal schooling (i.e. the education received at
home, in the neighbourhood and the training on the job).
A recent tendency is to add, later in one's life, retraining,
in order to adapt oneself to rapid technological development.
Income from labour also depends, of course, on the number
of hours worked. Income from *capital* originally meant

1

income from physical or financial capital and was called profit or interest. In contrast to income from labour it has also been called 'labourless' income (*arbeitsloses Einkommen*), which quality it shares with rent (from land), but also with transfers. More recently the capital concept has been broadened and we also speak of human capital, which is the schooling or education paid with the money amounts spent on them. This redefinition simultaneously reduces labour to pure or raw (i.e. unskilled), labour in the strictest sense. Labour income is then reduced to the wage of unskilled labour and the income of skilled labour consists of a pure labour income (the wage of unskilled labour), plus the yield of invested human capital. This method has the advantage that it doesn't require the 'quality of labour' concept.

Income from financial capital is identical, in a sense, to income from physical capital, since the buildings and machines (the assets) bought with financial capital at the moment of buying have a money value equal to that financial capital. Income from financial capital depends on the *conditions* on which the capital has been made available by its owners. If a loan is made, some interest rate has been conditioned and a repayment scheme agreed upon. If the capital owner participates in the risk incurred, the yield will depend on the profits made and a variable *dividend* is the income obtained. The level of the dividend is decided upon in a shareholders meeting. There are some intermediary forms, as is well known.

Income from *transfer* is income—positive or negative—resulting from systems of social security, that is, systems to provide income to people unable to work because of illness or accident or old age, income to unemployed and so on. Those who, at some time, benefit from the system receive positive transfer incomes and those who pay the contributions experience negative transfer incomes. Among the contributors we find employees and employers in one type of system, or all citizens below some age in another type, the social insurance systems for all citizens. The expression 'insurance' is used in a more general sense than in insurance proper, where contributions are made by the person who benefits, as is the case in private insurance.

NATURE OF INCOME-RECEIVING UNIT

A further aspect of income is the nature of the receiver of income. This may be the income *earner*, that is the person whose labour or capital has been supplied and paid for. In many problems it is relevant to know whose living has to be paid for out of the income considered. Then the *income of a family* may be the better yardstick. In such a case the composition of the family is important: it may be a 'normal natural' family, consisting of a couple and some children. In developing countries it may be an extended family, of which also one or two grandparents are members. The extended family may also have other relatives as its members. Finally, the family concept may be extended in another way, to the concept of 'household', of which also non-relatives are members. The criterion of whether some non-relative must be included may be that the meals are taken jointly or that the persons considered as a household live in one dwelling. In all these cases two further data are relevant, namely the *number of persons* and the *number of earners* among these persons. When counting the number of persons, a child may be counted as part of an adult man and even an adult woman may be counted as, for instance, 0.9 adult man. In this example the figure 0.9 in the past was based on the observed consumption of a female member of the household. Today we have alternative methods of estimating such *weights*, based on welfare estimates, or on an evaluation of the labour supplied in the household, and not usually paid for. The hours of work in the household often are many and this will have to be reflected in such an evaluation.

However, we are not here discussing norms, but facts and the facts often deviate from the norms as seen by different scholars or citizens. A last remark on the composition of families or households is that they may be incomplete: as a consequence of death or divorce there may be only one parent.

STAGE OF REDISTRIBUTION

A third aspect of income measurement depends on the stage of redistribution we consider. Usually a distinction is made between primary, secondary and tertiary income. *Primary* income, then, is the income from labour or other sources before direct taxes have been paid (income and wealth taxes, for instance). *Secondary* income is what is left after direct taxes have been deducted. In modern developed countries this may be, for high incomes, a considerable deduction. *Tertiary* income is secondary income augmented by what is sometimes called *profit from the state* or from the political system; it is not the amounts of income received as transfers, discussed before. By profit from the state we mean the advantage derived from collective goods, made available by public authorities below the cost of their production. (The missing amount is paid for by the authorities out of the taxes collected). Examples are the use of roads, of railways, of local transportation, of police services and those of the fire brigade, of the schooling system, of information services such as radio and television.

Some collective goods are called *quasi-collective*, if their availability in fact is not collective, for instance the health service. Medical treatment by a nurse is given to one person at a time and cannot simultaneously be given to somebody else. Schooling to a very large extent belongs to this category.

Another subcategory is that of *semi-collective* goods. These are goods available publicly, but only in a restricted area, for instance municipal police as distinct from national police.

A last subcategory is *part-collective*. These goods (or services) are available to all who want them, *most of the time*, but occasionally are not available. One example is the road system at a moment of congestion (in case of an accident, or on a national holiday). Another example is the police in case of unexpected riots, or of an exceptional event, when they have to concentrate on one task and temporarily are not available to solve a case of theft.

These various remarks illustrate the difficulties arising when tertiary income must be estimated. Even so, the concept of tertiary income makes sense, since in some countries more collective goods are made available than in others; and in a given country the extent of public goods available has varied over time.

MARKET FORM OF FACTOR MARKETS

Labour and capital are called production *factors* and so are the subcategories of each, mentioned in the first section. The markets of these factors may be perfectly competitive, but they may also have another 'form', such as monopolistic (on one or both sides) or oligopolistic. This form affects the price of the factor considered: a monopolist is able to raise the price above the level of a competitive market. Strictly speaking, part of the income of some factor is due to the market form. Highly specialized labour may be able to claim an excessive income. This may be due to a natural monopoly, which it is hard to distinguish from a situation of scarcity; or it may be due to an organized monopoly, against which measures can be taken.

Trade unions came into existence as a defence of low wages paid by employers whose abilities or whose capital made them oligopolists on the labour market.

NOMINAL VERSUS REAL INCOMES

Incomes are usually measured in terms of money units, but a given amount of money does not represent the same quantity of goods (or buying power) in different countries, or in the same country at different times. In order to compare incomes earned in different countries or at different times we therefore need information about the price levels.

MEASURES OF INCOME DISTRIBUTION

If only two incomes have to be compared, a measure of income distribution can easily be found: the ratio is a sufficient measure. Sometimes no other information than two incomes is available and still relevant as well; an example being the average incomes per capita for two countries. Another example may be the income of a well-defined type of worker in two countries or at two points of time. The larger the number of incomes we want to study, the more complicated their distribution is and the more difficult it is to express income inequality in one figure. There are some well-known measures which each have their own advantage. Simplest to explain is perhaps the ratio of incomes in two deciles: the upper and the lower, or the upper and the third from below. More complicated but quite useful are the Gini coefficient and the Theil coefficient. The Gini coefficient must always be between 0 for no inequality and 1 for maximal inequality. The Theil coefficient has no fixed upper value but is able to decompose inequality of grouped incomes into the inequalities between and within groups.

FACTORS AFFECTING INCOME DISTRIBUTION

For a complete analysis of changes in income distribution it is desirable not only to observe income distributions in various periods (for historical research) or countries (to compare social systems, for instance), but also to explain them, that is to identify the main causes, or to investigate how income distributions can be changed in a preferred direction. (The present author prefers a reduction in income inequality.)

There are many theories that either try to explain income inequality or try to indicate how income inequality can be affected. The theories can be listed by listing the instrument variables that determine income inequality. An instrument variable is a variable that can be changed by government. Some examples of instrument variables are:

(1) taxes on income or wealth or both,
(2) social insurance systems: level of contribu,
    benefits,
(3) schooling: fees, fellowships, training facilities,
(4) nationalization of wealth components: land, capit,

Part I

The Theory of Distribution

1 The Tricky Problem of Distribution*

Y.S. Brenner

Theories of income distribution are theories which explain the mechanisms by which the national income is distributed between groups and individuals in the economy. Normally, a distinction is made between functional and personal distribution theories. Functional distribution theories are concerned with the division of the national income between factors of production, that is with the distribution of the national product between the providers of labour and the suppliers of land and capital. Personal distribution theories are concerned with the determination of individual, family and household incomes regardless of the factor from which the income is derived.

This paper deals with functional distribution alone. Next to exploring the mechanisms by which income is distributed between factors of production, this study is concerned with the following questions: are long-run changes in the functional distribution of income possible and, if so, can such changes influence investment, the rate of economic growth and the pace and character of technological innovation. The study examines the possibility that it is *not* technological innovation or economic growth which determines the level of employment and real wages, but that the latter, together with transfer payments for social security, determine technological innovation and, within limits, the rate of economic growth.

---

* An earlier, more extensive Dutch version of this paper appeared in Y.S. Brenner *et al. Visies op Verdeling* (Perspectives on Distribution), 's-Gravenhage: Vuga, 1986.

1.1   THE 'SOCIAL SURPLUS' APPROACH.

Two approaches to the theory of distribution can be distinguished: the *social surplus* approach and the *demand-and-supply* approach. The former found expression in the works of the English classical economists and Marx; the latter in the theories which relate distribution to the interaction of supply and demand through price variations.

The social surplus is the difference between the output of an economy and the cost of producing it, where cost means the outlay for wages, raw materials and the replacement of depreciated capital. The adherents of this approach, Ricardo in particular, stressed the antagonistic relationship between a subsistence wage, the rate of profit on capital, population accretion and what may be called the marginal productivity of labour. Ricardo suggested that 'profits depend on high or low wages, wages on the price of necessaries, and the price of necessaries chiefly on the price of food'. The exchange value of food depends on the labour cost of producing it at the margin of land utilization; in the long run, wages tend toward a minimum set by this exchange value of food, and wage rates are equalized by competition. Profits get the remainder of the marginal product, and rates of profit are also equalized by competition. In the more productive land uses, rent arises. Marx improved on this by elaborating the interdependence of class structure, changes in technology, population growth, the organization of workers and class struggle, and the extension of capitalist production into new areas.

The classical economists and Marx treated profit as a residue—that part of the social product which remains after labour's share is subtracted. Labour's share, in their view, was the volume of output necessary for the workers' subsistence, that is for 'reproduction'. However, neither the classics nor Marx considered this 'subsistence' or 'reproduction' wage constant through time. They believed it to be subjected to a kind of ratchet effect which relates it to changes in the volume of the social product. In the words of Ricardo,[1] 'It is not to be understood that the natural price of labour estimated even in food and necessaries, is absolutely fixed and constant. It varies at different times in the same country, and very materially differs in different countries. It essentially depends on the habits and customs of the people' (Ricardo 1962: 54–5). The classics and Marx did not deny the influence of technological progress and other factors on the level of real wages but treated real wages as an independent variable—independent in the sense that only after the share which goes to wages is deducted from the entire social product can the remainder be determined. They did also not deny that profits exert an important influence on real wages through their impact on accumulation and investment and on the choice of technologies. But unlike recent economic theories, in which all major distributive values are assumed to be determined simultaneously, the classical economists and Marx maintained that the level of real wages determines the volume of the other shares and thereby investment and the size of the social product available for distribution in the historical progress of the economic process. In a modern form this approach has been revived and developed further by the Post-Keynesian and radical schools.

1.2   THE DEMAND-AND-SUPPLY APPROACH

The other approach, which relates distribution to the supply of and demand for factors of production, assumes that the volume of output, its distribution and real wages are all determined simultaneously. The factors which influence these variables, such as consumers' tastes, the availability of factors of production and the level of technological efficiency, are all assumed 'given'. 'Given' in the sense of being determined outside the core of the interdependent economic system. It explains the price of goods and of factors of production by their relative scarcity. It does so less in terms of production costs than in terms of what people are willing to pay for them. It considers the determination of the rewards received by the providers of the various factors of production a matter of supply and demand, where the demand determines supply.[2] In other words, the demand-and-supply approach is concerned with the allocation of scarce resources in an essentially static economic situation in which market prices ensure the equality of supply and demand. It is not concerned with class conflict and exogenous influences on income distribution but with what for all intents and purposes is a closed, almost perfectly competitive, equilibrium—seeking harmonious economic system in which the distribution of income is determined by the Law of Diminishing Returns, and 'marginal productivity'.[3] Accordingly, for example, the reward of the factor of production labour is taken to be determined in the following manner: Because of 'diminishing returns', at a certain point the employment of an addditional unit of labour will only add to total output the value of the wages paid to that unit. Another unit of labour would add less to the value of output than the wage received by it. It would therefore not be employed. Similarly, if one unit less were engaged, profit would be reduced below the maximum which could be realized. The total amount of labour employed by a profit-maximizing employer is therefore determined by the contribution made by the wage paid to that last unit which brings the wage paid to it into equality with the expected revenue from its contribution to the total output. As all units of labour are assumed to be identical and interchangeable, the wage paid to the last employable unit—the marginal unit—is the wage paid to all. This is 'the marginal revenue productivity theory of wages'. It follows that for a firm the level of wages is given—is determined exogenously, while for the economy as a whole it is determined by the system's tendency towards full employment equilibrium. Ignoring the intricacy of the aggregation problem, the overall demand for labour is then explained in similar terms as the demand for labour of an individual firm.[4] It is regarded as varying inversely with the movement of real wages.[5] Consequently, in the absence of rigid money wages, real wages and the level of employment are determined simultaneously by the supply of and the demand for labour. Assuming that an economy is in full employment equilibrium and for one reason or another autonomous spending is reduced, the volume of output sold will be less than the volume of output produced with full employment. As the firms will only gradually become aware of this, they will at least initially continue producing the full employment output. Supply will continue to exceed demand, and prices will fall. With money wages at this point still unaffected, real wages will be higher than before. Consequently, the demand for labour will diminish while the supply of labour will increase. With flexible wages in a downward direction this will cause money wages to fall. The fall in prices and in money wages will reduce the demand for money and so raise bond prices and diminish interest rates. In turn this will increase investment-spending and once again raise both output and employment. Before long, full employment equilibrium will be restored with prices, money wages and interest rates lower than they had been before and real wages at their old level. This is a perfect model of a self-correcting system in which deviations from equilibrium are not impossible but short-lived—a system in which the level of output is determined by technological efficiency and its distribution by a socially neutral mechanism based on utility and scarcity. The demand for labour is varying inversely, and the supply of labour positively, with the movement of real wages. Firms maximize profits at all times and switch from the employment of labour to the employment of capital and from capital to labour without much difficulty and delay when labour or capital price variations indicate that this is desirable.

1.3 ASSUMPTIONS BEHIND THE DEMAND-AND-SUPPLY APPROACH

The problem with this approach is that it requires several assumptions which can hardly be accepted without considerable modifications: first, that the supply of and the demand for labour react to wage movements in the suggested manner; second, that labour and capital are homogeneous; third, that the entire economic system is naturally gravitating towards full employment equilibrium and that several important factors are left exogenous which may well be endogenous.

In order to be satisfied with the assumption concerning the variations in the demand for and supply of labour as a result of rising or falling wages, one would have to accept that firms are always maximizing their profit; that the supply of labour is totally elastic—that as wages rise, more labour would immediately be offered and as wages fall, workers prefer to increase their leisure rather than try to make up their lost income. Second, one would have to be satisfied that firms are able to substitute capital for labour and labour for capital at will; that both labour and capital are homogeneous, malleable and exchangeable in spite of restrictions on vertical and lateral mobility; and one would have to ignore that capital, once installed, can usually not be abandoned in the short run without considerable cost. Third, one would have to forget the lessons from the 1930s and 1970s, or explain them away by reference to exogenous forces, in order to believe that the entire economic system tends to gravitate towards full employment equilibrium. One would also have to accept that what applies to an individual firm is equally applicable to an industry and to the entire economy. Finally, one would have to ignore the influence of income effects on social conditions and historical developments. All this would make the model more precise and suitable for quantification but, by and large, also irrelevant.

1.4   THE DEMAND-AND-SUPPLY APPROACH AND J.M.KEYNES

Keynes showed the assumption that the supply of labour is elastic at all levels of income, to be dubious (Keynes 1936: 5). He showed that the idea that 'the utility of the wage when a given volume of labour is employed is equal to the marginal disutility of that amount of employment', is a fallacy. But in spite of his belief that the demand for labour is related to its marginal productivity, he was critical of the proposition that changes in wages necessarily lead to changes in the demand for labour. Keynes believed that changes in nominal wages affect effective demand and hence prices. This is the essence of his explanation for rigidities in real wages. More important, however, he challenged the idea that the entire economic system is tending towards full employment equilibrium. He did not believe that wages adjust to the level at which all labour finds employment, and he denied that the rate of interest determines investment in the manner suggested by his predecessors. In his opinion, wages were on the whole inflexible in a downward direction, and increases in the money supply were just as likely to augment idle balances as to reduce interest rates. Whether or not his denial of the automatic readjustment mechanism to full employment equilibrium was well founded (Hicks), or whether it was only true with rigid wages and prices (Modigliani), or whether even given rigid money wages an unemployment equilibrium remains an impossibility (Patinkin), the empirical evidence of sticky wages called for an explanation. Keynes provided a wage theory, but it related alone to _real_ wages. The gap he left was filled by a variety of exogenous, mainly institutional theories. These explained the determination of wages by sociological and political factors and led to important amendments in the so-called Neoclassical Synthesis.

Labour economics showed the role of institutional arrangements in the adjustment processes which are taking place in the labour markets. Wage-bargaining theories improved on bilateral monopoly analysis and introduced game theory, risk evaluation and cost–benefit techniques into the study of wage determination. Human capital theories explained wage differentials and other things by transforming the types of training and education which are capable of increasing a person's labour productivity into 'human capital'. Information economics explained 'market failures' as the product of imperfect information. And the dual market hypothesis explained the absence of full employment equilibrium in the labour market by the impediments on mobility which separate the 'good jobs' from the 'bad jobs' due to discrimination, lack of 'human capital', institutional rigidities and restrictive practices exercised mainly by labour unions. The most interesting contributions in this vein were probably made by labour economics and by the theories of wage bargaining, human capital, information economics, and by the theory of the dual labour market. All of these provided some useful insight into the ways in which wages are determined, but they did not provide the link which could explain the determination of wages from within the equilibrium system itself. They presented a list of factors which had to be taken into account if reasonable predictions were to be made on the basis of the equilibrium theories, but they did not show how these factors could themselves be the product of the system. Although these theories throw considerable light on the effect of institutional and other factors on the behaviour of the economic system; and although they led to certain modifications in the demand-and-supply approach, they did not provide the necessary link between the entire economic system as it is conceived in the neoclassical approach and the development of the institutional framework.

1.5 PARADIGM SAVED

To account for the influence of the structural and frictional forces which affect the labour market, the amended version of the demand-and-supply approach allowed for rigidities. Milton Friedman, for example, defined full employment as the volume of employment which cannot be increased by raising aggregate demand—as the level of unemployment which none the less remains at 'full employment'. The name given to this level of unemployment is the 'natural rate of unemployment'. Friedman described this 'natural' rate as:

the level that would be ground out by the Walrasian system of general equilibrium equations provided there is embedded in them the actual structural characteristics of the labour and commodity markets, including market imperfections, stochastic variability in demands and supplies, the cost of gathering information about job vacancies and labour availabilities, the cost of mobility and so on. (Pearce 1981:302)

Given this carefully hedged definition of full employment, the demand-and-supply approach could, so it seemed, continue to regard unemployment as a transitory phenomenon —as a temporary deviation from equilibrium. However, the questions regarding what percentage of the labour force can be considered as 'naturally' unemployed; how long it takes for equilibrium to be restored and at what level of real income, remained unanswered. Sustained massive unemployment was simply defined out of existence.

The conception of an eternally equilibrium-seeking competitive economic system was preserved. Keynes's interpretation of the causes of unemployment was not regarded as a disequilibrium model but as a correction to allow for some peculiarities such as inflexible wages—no disequilibrium but equilibrium with less than full employment. Even if Keynes was right in claiming that effective demand affects the level of investment and the level of investment determines the volume of employment, the belief in the 'general equilibrium' was not entirely wrong. Assuming that consumption is a relatively constant proportion of aggregate expenditure and that an equilibrium level of employment exists for every level of investment, though full employment occurs only at one of them, and assuming that, for example, wage cuts cannot increase overall employment because they reduce effective demand, and reduced effective demand diminishes investment, and diminished investment increases unemployment, in the event of price rigidity the sources of the Keynesian unemployment equilibrium would still remain outside the system, namely rigid wages and diminished occupational mobility and so on and would therefore not invalidate the belief in a world ruled by equilibrating forces. The discussion simply shifted from the validity of the Keynesian criticism of the neoclassical model to 'unemployment equilibrium' and the rigidity of money wages. The discussion did not focus on the validity of the Marshallian or Walrasian ideas but on the universality of Keynes's. The

orthodox view that 'price tends to equal marginal cost' and
'wages equal the marginal product of labour' was retained.
Keynesian unemployment was interpreted as a special case
of equilibrium with rigid money wages and a liquidity trap
(the latter being a situation in which an increase in the
money supply will not result in a fall in the rate of interest
but in increasing idle balances). Given this interpretation,
the Keynesian solutions appeared to be of applicability only
under specific exceptional circumstances. What Keynes had
called a 'General Theory', and was a critique of the
neoclassical approach, was reduced to a special case in the
neoclassical tradition. That the neoclassical conception did
not conform with reality did not cause it to be abandoned
but to be corrected to allow for rigid money wages and for
interest inelasticities of investment. These modifications
legitimized state intervention (which in the post-war era of
democratic euphoria was in any event unavoidable for
political reasons) but left the essential tenets of the general
equilibrium dogma untouched. Practical suggestions, such
as demand management, were adopted in isolation from
each other, but the theoretical lessons to be learnt from
Keynes's General Theory were pushed into the background.
Couched in neoclassical terms, the Keynesian approach to
value and distribution was no longer recognizable as a
fundamental critique of mainstream economic thought. The
theoretical critique was simply ignored and the establishment
could sing in harmony that 'we are all Keynesians now'.
All that was left to separate the Keynesian from the
neoclassical approach was the role of expectations and the
role of money (which conflicted with the classical theory
of money as reflected in Say's Law). Yet while the
neoclassical assumption of perfect competition can be
relaxed without too much damage to the demand-and-supply
approach, the assumption about the inherent tendency of
the economic system to gravitate towards full employment
equilibrium cannot. It provides the link between the micro
and the macro aspects of income distribution. It is therefore
at this juncture where Post-Keynesians and modern mainstream economists go their separate ways.

1.6 THE MODERN DEMAND AND SUPPLY APPROACH: THE MAINSTREAM VERSION

Modern mainstream distribution theory no longer denies that unemployment can be caused and sustained by a shortage of effective demand and by a shortage, or surfeit, of capital goods. It also abandoned the assumption of perfect substitutability of capital and labour, and it made room for the role of expectations in investment decisions. It recognized the influence of institutional factors, even of power in economics, and introduced them as *data* into the amended model. It acknowledged that workers may derive part of their income from property, or from transfer payments provided by the state, and it modified the assumption that the remuneration of work is equal to its marginal product. Even 'mark-ups' or profits (which in the pure neoclassical approach cannot exist except as a Marshallian 'quasi rent') are sometimes incorporated in the modern versions of the demand-and-supply approach. But essentially the marginalist conception of distribution remained as before. It continues to ignore the point made by Piero Sraffa and Joan Robinson that capital cannot be measured in separation from prices without circular reasoning and that prices depend on income distribution; and it continues to uphold the view that competition is sufficiently lively to regulate distribution in the expected manner by price variations.[6]

Essentially, the macroeconomic conception of mainstream economics is like this: investment, autonomous or induced, creates employment and incomes. The incomes raise consumers demand, and this induces further investment. Competition between producers encourages innovation, and innovation reduces production costs. The lower production costs are passed on to consumers because of market competition. Real incomes rise and induce even more investment. Ignoring here (to make this exposition less complex) the complications introduced by government expenditure and foreign trade, the main flaw in this is that they explain lack of harmony by exogenous factors. The most frequently cited factor in this context is labour, though the oil shocks of the 1970s are also regularly mentioned. In the same way that cost reductions, which are brought about by technological innovation, are passed on to consumers, so, on the macro level, are the cost increases due to wage hikes in excess of productivity also passed on to consumers. The result is inflation. At the same time the high cost of labour makes machines relatively cheaper. More machines are employed and workers are dismissed. With unemployment spreading, demand also diminishes. There comes a point when the higher wages of those workers who remain employed no longer suffice to make up the lost demand for goods and services of those who lost their jobs, and prices stabilize or fall. The least efficient firms go out of business and unemployment increases even further. Consequently, government expenditure rises but government revenue falls. If the state resorts to borrowing or to creating more money to fill the gap, inflation accelerates. If it borrows, a 'crowding out effect' will cause a shortage of loanable funds and interest rates will rise. The higher interest rates will discourage investment or will add to production costs. In spite of unemployment and diminished demand, consumer prices will not fall. If the government creates more money, the value of the currency depreciates and lenders will pass on to borrowers the expected future diminution in the value of their money. Interest charges will rise and the result will be similar to the one which must be expected when the government is borrowing excessively. Firms with few financial reserves go out of business and firms with large reserves exacerbate unemployment by purchasing more labour-saving capital. Eventually, the spreading unemployment will make workers in the less successful firms realize that their jobs are at risk—that their employers simply cannot survive in business unless labour cost is reduced. The trade unions' powers of 'monopoly' will weaken, and real wages will revert to their equilibrium level. By this time it will once again become profitable to employ workers, and the economy will be set on the path to recovery.

In conclusion, on the macro level, wage increases which

are 'forced' on employers and do not reflect the true demand-and-supply relationship, cannot raise workers' real incomes. Such wage increases raise prices and eliminate the workers' ostensible advantage. Actually, this means no more than changes in the nominal sphere of prices and incomes. The volume of employment and production remains unaltered. For these reasons, capital accumulation—not efforts to redistribute the social product—is still 'the worker's friend'; it leads to greater productivity and hence to prosperity and employment. In the end, 'we all share in the blessings of technology by cheaper products, higher incomes, greater prosperity' (Pen 1971:198, 201).

1.7 THE NEOCLASSICAL SYNTHESIS AND ITS CRITICS

With the introduction of the concept of 'elasticity of substitution' and its application to aggregate production functions, the neoclassical approach became more sophisticated. But, again, it introduced several questionable assumptions. Technical change needed to be assumed neutral with regard to distribution; inputs needed to be assumed homogeneous and perfectly divisible and substitutable; and aggregation from the microeconomic to the macroeconomic level needed to be regarded as no more than summation. That technical change is not neutral is fairly obvious, for else how could some of the 'temporary deviations' from the normal equilibrium trend which, according to the neoclassical theory, reflect the 'dynamic character' of the economy be explained? That inputs, say capital goods, are neither homogeneous nor perfectly divisible and substitutable, is also fairly obvious. Capital goods are designed for specific purposes and for specific combinations and are produced in a time-consuming process with the help of other factors of production whose prices do not remain unaffected during the 'switching' processes, that is during changes in the production techniques. Therefore, capital goods are neither neutral with regard to rising wages nor promptly available for the replacement of labour when rising wages indicate that this may be more profitable. The possibility that the principle of substitution may not operate in the manner assumed by the neoclassical approach was only recognized following Sraffa's publication of *Production of Commodities by Means of Commodities*, and even then ignored together with the likelihood that substitution effects may well be only secondary to income effects. But most violence was done to aggregation from the micro to the macro level. The point is that all efforts to derive macroeconomic demand functions from individual consumer preferences run up against the Impossibility Theorem, and the Composite Commodity Theorem. The former relates to Kenneth Arrow's well-known problem of decision theory where a person or group of persons are faced with several alternative courses of action with only incomplete information about the true state of affairs and about the consequences of each possible choice (Suppes 1967: 310- 13; Hicks 1939) and the latter to the requirement that the prices of all commodities involved in firms' aggregation remain, relative to each other, the same throughout the entire process, and that the possibility of 'reswitching' or 'double switching' is ignored (Kaldor and Mirrlees 1962; Kaldor 1972; Kaldor, 1966)[7] In a nutshell: only if the elasticities of all inputs are the same, which is seldom the case, will some change not cause some factors to be better and others less well rewarded then they ought to be according to the values of their marginal products. To be sure, it is as Kaldor says: 'Economic theory went astray when the theory of value took over the centre of the stage and when attention was focusing on the *allocative* functions of markets to the exclusion of their *creative* functions—as an instrument for transmitting impulses to economic change' (Kaldor 1972:1240)

The point was forcefully made by Anwar Shaikh in his article 'Laws of Production and Laws of Algebra' (Shaikh 1980: 80–96). The most widely used distribution model in both the theoretical and empirical literature is the aggregate production function model. This model, which is an aggregated version of the general equilibrium, explains, or more precisely attempts to explain, wage rates and rates of profit as 'scarcity prices' determined by efficiency considerations. The wage rate and the rate of profit move inversely to the supply of labour and capital and are equal to and determined by their respective marginal products. But, as Garegnani was able to show, the rate of profit varies inversely with the supply of capital, and the wage rate with the supply of labour, only if prices in all possible equilibria are proportional to labour values—that is, when all industries have the same capital–labour values (Garegnani 1970: 407–36). It is, of course, possible to define the inputs and outputs of some imaginary industry working under conditions of perfect competition if one assumes that all firms that make up this industry produce an identical product and use the same inputs, but even under such assumptions it would be difficult to aggregate because at least the 'condition' of an identical product would have to be abandoned.

1.8 SUBSTITUTION EFFECTS AND INCOME EFFECTS

In spite of all the earlier mentioned adjustments the fundamental facets of the demand-and-supply approach remained unaltered. The approach continued to be based on the Walrasian model, which as A. Eichner correctly claims, encompasses little more than the substitution effect:

Within the logic of the model the demand for one good can increase only at the expense of the demand for another good, and then only because the relative price of the former has fallen. Similarly, one type of input, such as capital goods, can be used more intensively in the production process only at the expense of another type of input, such as labour, and again only because the relative price of the former has fallen. This approach usually eliminates by assumption the possibility that the demand for all goods and the use of all types of inputs may increase together—at different rates, to be sure—as a result of the higher income and level of demand which economic growth brings with it . . . .
In the more sophisticated versions of the neoclassical theory, some income effects . . . are allowed for. But still, it is the substitution effects arising from a change in relative prices which provide the impetus for

the shift from one static equilibrium position to another, and thus it is only the substitution effects which make any real difference in the models. (Eichner 1979: 169)

But this is simply not enough: 'It is also necessary to recognise that the income effects generally swamp the substitution effects—if they do not eliminate them altogether'. (*ibid.*)

The point is that, for example, a decline in wages is more likely to reduce effective demand and business confidence and consequently investment and employment than increase the demand for labour as the neoclassical model postulates. Seen in this way, it becomes 'the level and composition of investment, together with the income effects which derive from that investment, which are the principal operative factors, not any change in relative prices' (*ibid.*). But the emphasis on income effects, again according to Eichner, has also a disadvantage: 'It makes neat solutions difficult to obtain' (*ibid.*). It disturbs the scientists' deep-rooted urge to obtain precision by quantification. The results become open-ended. In Eichner's own words:

When the scope of the analysis is restricted to substitution effects, as it is in the neoclassical approach, there is always some new equilibrium position which a change in relative prices will bring about, and that new position can be determined simply by solving the set of mathematical equations that define the new system (or, in a partial analysis, by examining the point of intersection between the new supply and demand curves). However, when the income effects are fully allowed for, . . . there need not be any new equilibrium position. Rather, the change in investment or whatever else has produced the income effects is likely to initiate a process (or, more accurately, modify a process already under way) without a determinable end state . . . . The analysis shifts from logical time to historical time in which the future cannot be predicted because of the complex nature of the interaction among the different social subsystems that comprise the larger system. (Eichner 1979: 168–79) [8]

The puzzling thing about the neoclassical school's approach is that in spite of its positivistic search for mathematical precision, it even now totally ignores the normative basis of the Walrasian vision of the general equilibrium upon which it is founded. As W. Jaffe was able to show: 'Walras' latent purpose in contriving his general equilibrium model was not to describe or analyse the workings of the economic system as it existed . . . . It was . . . rather to demonstrate the possibility of formulating axiomatically a rationally consistent economic system' (Jaffe 1979: 386). Therefore, according to Jaffe, Walras' purpose was *not* to describe or to analyse a real world system, not even under stringent assumptions. His goal was not positivistic but essentially normative: 'Walras was attempting to find out whether an economic system based upon conditions that to his mind constituted economic justice both in exchange and distribution could exist at any given time. (ibid.). His 'aim was prescriptive or normative not positive or descriptive. His object was to formulate (invent?) an economic system in conformity with an idea of social justice' (Chase 1979: 84).

1.9 THE POST-KEYNESIAN APPROACH

The Post-Keynesian approach introduces 'imperfect competition' into the regulating mechanism of prices; relates changes in the productivity of labour to the rate of gross investment and technological progress; and stresses that changes in output are functionally related to the division of the social product between profits and wages.

Beginning from Keynes's notion of uncertainty, Post-Keynesians reject the neoclassical theory of price determination. Investment is directed towards the future and the future is notoriously uncertain; it is done on the basis of expectations which may or may not come true. But as investment generates output and output may exceed or fall short of future demand, it is in the end investment and not demand which plays the major role in price determination. Moreover, Post-Keynesians distinguish between markets in which output is fairly fixed (raw materials and foodstuffs may serve as examples), in which prices are determined by demand, and markets for which commodities are produced by means of commodities (i.e. markets for manufactured and 'finished' goods), where changes in demand engender changes in production capacity (or changes in the use of production capacity) while prices remain unaffected. In the private sector of a highly industrialized capitalist economy the last-mentioned markets are of greater importance. In them oligopoly is strongest and, within limits, prices are administered in accordance with planned investment targets. Unlike mainstream economics, which examines the rewards of the various factors of production on the basis of some imagined terminal state of equilibrium, that is from the point of view of how resources would come to be allocated under different degrees of competition when the adjustment process between demand and supply comes to its end, Post-Keynesian economics examines distribution as an ongoing process. From this point of view, profit maximization is not an end but a means for survival in an environment in which firms are relentlessly forced to increase their market shares in order not to be eliminated by others. In this way, the maximization of the growth in sales revenue over time, subject to a minimum profit constraint, becomes the end of their endeavours (Kenyon 1979: 37–8). Consequently, in the sector which uses commodities to produce commodities, oligopolies set prices with an eye to financing their investments out of internal funds. These funds, which account for more than three-quarters of investments in this sector (Eichner 1976: 13), reflect profits which cannot be explained by the conventional 'quasi rents'. Their presence shows firms as 'price setters' not 'price takers'—it shows their capacity to mark up prices above what is conventionally called the cost of the factors of production. While the neoclassical theory, which focuses attention on an imaginary terminal state of interaction between demand and supply, has no room for profit and has therefore little if anything to say about oligopoly and trade-union power, Post-Keynesian analysis claims to have no difficulty with either. In Post-Keynesian analysis, prices do not reflect current demand alone but a combination of current demand with prices administered to meet the funding requirements of firms for future investment. But future investment targets depend on expectations, and these are influenced by the level of aggregate demand which itself reflects the level of aggregate income and hence the level of output, which is again dependent on investment—on entrepreneurial expectations. In other words, the key to the system is investment. Investment generates output, but being based on expectations this output may be too large or too small to meet demand at current prices, and prices rise or fall. It can therefore be argued that investment, not demand, plays the major role in price determination.

Post-Keynesian economics may be said to study a system in unstable equilibrium—a dynamic system moving along some secular trend, in which changes in demand are more closely related to changes in income than to relative price movements. It stresses that as long as there is net investment, the economy must be growing. The disequilibrium arising out of the possible disparity between saving and investment, which Keynes suggested in his *Treatise on Money*, is transformed into a theory of growth. And it reintroduces the conceptual world of classical economics with the idea of the 'social surplus' and the antagonistic relationship between wages and profits.

In this world, which is here described in Kaleckian terms (simplified for the sake of clarity), there are two sources of income, namely wages and profit; and two types of expenditure, namely consumption and investment. Wages are earned by workers, and profit by capitalists. Workers spend their income on consumer goods, and capitalists on consumption and investment. As workers are employed to produce both consumer goods and investment goods, but spend their entire income on consumption, investment is what remains of the social product after consumption is deducted. In physical terms, therefore, the part of profit which capitalists do not spend for their own consumption is investment. The greater the share of profit, whether it is consumed or invested, the smaller will be the share of wages. Hence real wages are determined by the rate of investment. For if the share of investment goods in the social product increases, while total income remains unchanged, the share of consumer goods diminishes. But as the income from work in both sectors remains the same, the claim on wage goods (i.e. goods mainly bought out of

wages) will be met by a diminished supply. Wage good
prices will rise and real wages fall.[9]

In the preceding, no notice was taken of changes in total
income. In a more dynamic analysis, economic growth is
taken into account. This implies that the earlier-mentioned
effects on relative wages remain but the changes in real
wages do not necessarily follow. Another point is that
workers may well save part of their earnings, but most of
workers' savings go into housing, and dwelling houses
cannot be properly defined as 'capital' in the economic
sense of the term. But even if the condition that all wages
are consumed is relaxed, this will not invalidate the theory
(Pasinetti 1962: 267–79). The reason for this is that any
increase in savings out of wages is offset by a diminution
of savings out of profit. Consequently, aggregate saving
remains unaffected and the same is true for aggregate
demand. Even if it is assumed that workers' savings
are substantial, with regard to entrepreneurs' investment
requirements it does not invalidate the propositions. By
saving and investing their savings in profit-yielding stock,
workers' incomes become a combination of wages and
profit. For this reason some economists prefer, when they
discuss the distribution of the social product, to use the
terms 'income from work' and 'income from property' as
the basic categories rather than 'wages' and 'profit'. In this
way, the Gross National Product is defined as the sum
of gross investment, capitalist consumption and workers
consumption; and the national income is defined as the
sum of income from property (profit, depreciation, rent
and interest) and income from work (wages and salaries)
(Cowling 1982: 43). This reformulation of the Kaleckian
division avoids confusion between the economic and the
sociological categories involved in the analysis but does not
alter the general proposition (Pasinetti 1962: 267–79).

All this refers, of course, to capitalists as a class. An
individual capitalist may very well receive less than his
outlay in return for his investment, but this loss will
automatically be offset for the class as a whole by an equally
increased return received by others. Similarly, the term
'worker' does not necessarily exclude, in this context,

workers who also have earnings from dividends and rent. If a worker is able and willing to invest, then part of his total earnings—the income he receives from his investments—makes him to that extent also a capitalist. The entire problem does in fact disappear when a distinction is made between the economic and the sociological definition of the terms.

The importance of stressing the distinction between 'income from work' and 'income from property' (or between wages and profit), and the distinction between consumers' expenditure and investors', is that it illuminates the mechanisms by which the distribution of the social product determines prices, employment and the rate of economic growth. It shows *how* investment determines employment and technological innovation and hence the rate of economic growth (Kaldor 1960; Kaldor and Mirrlees 1962; Pasinetti 1962; Pasinetti 1972); how under one set of circumstances investment will cause real incomes and employment to rise and under another it will not. It shows how in the latter event investment may raise consumer good prices and thereby cause effective demand to fall and after some time also the rate of investment and employment. It highlights the 'trade-off' between investment and consumption and explains how in an economy in which prices are administered in some important sectors and output is managed accordingly, a rise in investment affects demand and employment. It shows the dynamic character of the economic system and incorporates *time*, or 'historical time' as some authors prefer to call it, into the analysis—something which is neglected in mainstream economic theories. It shows why in a less than perfectly competitive economy only continual adjustments in the distribution of the social product between the share of wages and the share of profit can assure full employment and a measure of stability and economic growth. It indicates that there is both an upper and a lower limit to investment and exhibits that, because investment raises productivity when prices are not allowed to fall or wages to rise in line with productivity, effective demand cannot suffice to induce further investment. It shows that under such circumstances workers previously employed in the production of new investment goods will be dismissed and that the shortfall in demand will be exacerbated and spread throughout the entire economic system. Eventually, profit expectations may become so low that sometimes even depreciated capital will not be replaced. It shows that even with flexible prices and wages there is a limit to investment, namely when, because of the relative diminution of the share of wage goods in the social product, real wages fall below the level that workers can accept and money wages rise which causes inflation (Robinson 1962: 23–9, 51–74).[10]

This type of approach is far from new. The division of the national output into consumer and producer goods sectors, of which the latter is taken as the growth producing element, underlay all Soviet Five Year Plans since 1928 and most development plans in the Third World since 1963. In Russia the consumer goods sector was held at the lowest pitch possible in order to allow for a maximum surplus of savings to accelerate investment in the producer goods sector which was taken to be the one responsible for the augmentation of the capital stock and for the replacement of technologically outdated equipment (Domar 1957: 223–61). In the words of the Soviet textbook (Dutt 1964: 419)[11] 'Socialist industrialisation is the development of large scale industry, and primarily heavy industry, to a level where it becomes the key to the reorganisation of the entire national economy on the basis of advanced machine technology'. However, 'the creation of modern industry requires huge material and financial outlays and as these cannot be obtained through capitalist exploitation, the share of the national income previously devoted to the parasitical consumption of the exploiting classes is used for socialist accumulation'. In fact, it was not only the 'share of the national income previously devoted to the parasitical consumption of the exploiting classes' which Stalin aimed to transform into investment, but practically all that could be squeezed out of the population by restricting consumption, (that is by restricting what Kalecki called the workers' share, by means of maximum taxation and price fixing. In a nutshell, Stalin stimulated accumulation by holding consumers' expenditure as low as it was practicable and so increased the share of capital (though not of the capitalists) in the national income at the cost of consumption. All this was of course done in the hope that at some later date the higher productivity generated by the additional capital would allow him to raise consumption too, at an accelerated rate.

Not dissimilar ideas about the distribution of the national product were entertained by the formulators of development plans in economically underdeveloped countries after the second World War. In this context (of a mixed rather than a 'centralized command economy') the antagonistic relationship between the share of capital and the share of labour in the national income was the issue.[12]

In conclusion:

the orthodox justification of income inequality in terms of productivity differences finds no support in the Post-Keynesian approach as was emphasized by Edward Nell in his 1973 paper. Neither can profits be explained in terms of a return to a 'productive' factor, 'capital'. This was demonstrated by both Garegnani and Sraffa in 1960. Nor, finally, is inequality required to provide incentives for higher rates of growth as Paul Davidson notes in a 1973 article. (Kregel 1979: 59)

What the Post-Keynesian approach does suggest is that investment gives rise to technological innovation and hence to rising per capita output and that in order to maintain full employment the system must grow and real wages must rise in line with productivity. It does *not* suggest that profit ought to or can be eliminated but that it must neither exceed nor fall below certain limits.

Essentially, the 'social surplus' school of income distribution maintains that the distribution of wealth and income can better be explained by political and social factors than by economic laws. Its followers prefer a social theory of distribution to an economic theory. Tugan-Baranovsky already claimed that non-economic factors interfere in the market, for 'factors of production' which do not play an equally important role in the market for consumer goods. This caused him to separate the problem of distribution from the general study of value and prices. But this is not the Post-Keynesian approach, although they too believe that they can show that 'the incomes earned in society can be explained independently of any direct relation to individual or class productivity' and that for this reason unequal incomes cannot be justified by reference to differences in productivity. They claim, in other words, that income differences are 'neither natural nor economic facts, but the result of social and political customs and decisions, as well as market power'. (Kregel 1979: 58). Their point of departure is Keynes's opinion that 'given the psychology of the public, the level of output and employment as a whole depends on the amount of investment' (p. 46). But they extend this by arguing that investment is not only the determinant of the 'level of output' but also of the distribution between income from work and from property. They deny that the demand for labour is necessarily related to its marginal productivity (Weintraub 1956) and that the determination of prices requires the concepts of 'marginal utility' or 'marginal disutility' (Sraffa 1960). They believe that capital cannot be measured in separation from prices and hence not in separation from the distribution of income by which prices are determined (Robinson 1962: 31–3)

Looking in this way at the problem of income distribution it suggests that investment decisions and the productivity of new investment determine the prices of consumer goods and hence the distribution of the national income between capital and labour. But this assumes that investment is mainly 'autonomous'—the product of Stalin's or capitalist entrepreneurs' 'animal spirits'. Kalecki went further than that. Insisting that entrepreneurs have a degree of freedom to 'mark up' prices in accordance with the 'degree of monopoly', he examined the influence of prices on invest-ment. Distinguishing between 'demand-determined' and 'cost-determined' processes,[13] and claiming that the former are more or less determined in the manner suggested by the neoclassical school but the latter differently, and rejecting the notions of equilibrium and perfect competition, he claimed that firms normally neither operate at the summit of productive capacity nor set prices at the level at which their marginal revenue is equal to their short-run marginal cost. In fact, he claimed that firms apply a 'mark up' to their average variable cost, which reflects the degree of monopoly (and which is only influenced by the most drastic changes in demand) and that it is this 'mark up' (i.e. the degree of monopoly) which influences prices. In other words, he concluded that the share of wages in the national income is inversely related to the degree of monopoly and to the prices of raw materials, but has little if anything to do with labour's marginal efficiency.

Both his theoretical construction and his interpretations of historical statistics did not go unchallenged. The most damaging criticism of his work appears to be to the effect that he did not provide answers to questions like how overhead and net profit components of gross non-wage income are related to each other—whether they move in the same or in opposite directions; how international competition affects the degree of monopoly; if the ratio of total expenditure on raw materials to the total wage bill is wholly independent of the degree of monopoly; and how, say, a rise in the expenditure on raw materials affects the 'mark up' (King and Regan 1976: 55). King and Regan therefore conclude (though only tentatively) 'that market imperfection is no more satisfactory as an explanation of changes in factor shares than the neoclassical theories of market perfection' (P. 56).

1.10 INCOME FROM WORK AND INCOME FROM PROPERTY

All seem to be in agreement that it is no longer possible, if ever it was, to identify social groups with particular sources and levels of income. Although the great majority of earners (perhaps 90 per cent) have no other sources of income than their salaries or wages, the rest also receive dividends, interest and rent. In addition, there are self-employed, whose income is 'mixed'—from work and from property—and 'not gainfully employed', who draw very diverse levels of income from a wide variety of sources (Kravis 1962). The income and life-style of some salaried managers of corporations certainly defies the conventional stratification or classification of persons by their sources of income. Too many exogenous factors blur the picture: among them the consequences of an ageing population, the height of pensions, changes in the years of schooling, preferences for part-time work as the level of income rises, tax laws and other state regulations. All these add to the difficulties in making interpersonal and intertemporal comparisons.

John King and Philip Regan in their succinct and lucid discussion of relative income shares (King and Regan 1976) stress that neither income from employment nor from property represents a homogeneous category. They define wages as income from manual labour, and salaries as income from non-manual work. They divide income from property between rent, interest and profit, with the last mentioned being the reward of entrepreneurship. To this they add 'human capital' as part of workers' income. Supported by the studies of A.B. Atkinson (1972: 120), they show that in the course of time the difference between income from wages and from salaries has diminished considerably while the difference between the income of a substantial minority of wage earners and average salary-earners greatly increased; and the difference between the income of high salary earners and the highest of wage earners widened. But the classification problem is even more confounded: the ambiguity of the concept 'entrepreneurship' and the term 'human capital' can serve as illustrations. The former may either be regarded as a separate factor of production, or as no more than the 'difference between total and contractual property incomes which arises in an uncertain world' (Bronfenbrenner 1971: 25–43);[14] the latter is inseparable from its owner and therefore not capital in the normal sense in which the term 'capital' is employed by economists. Finally, there are many people, like farmers, who are self-employed and obtain an income from both work and ownership of property.[15] On the whole, however, it remains true that most working people receive very little income from property, though an increasing number have become property owners by purchasing their own homes. If the classification of income from work causes difficulties, so does the identification of the 'capitalist class'. The control of large businesses no longer coincides with their ownership (Brenner 1984: 10–19)—'Power does not necessarily coincide with property', and top managers' salaries and 'perks' often reflect their 'power'. Another problem arises out of the growth of state sectors: 'As all incomes in this sector are conventionally treated as earnings from work, inter-country comparisons are distorted by the varying sizes of the state sectors in different countries'. Consequently, there is 'an upward bias in the share of labour over time, since the relative economic importance of the state has been increasing' (King and Regan 1976: 12). Finally, it is also difficult to determine what share of the decline in property income was at one time or another due to a decline in self-employment.

The methodological solutions suggested by King and Regan are as follows: to focus attention on the corporate sector alone or to exclude those sectors where self-employment remains very influential; alternatively, to allocate the income of the self-employed between its assumed labour and property components (King and Regan 1976: 13–14). This, they suggest, can be done in several ways: by imputing to the self-employed the average income from employment in the corporate sector, and treating their property income as a residual (the 'labour basis'); or by reversing this procedure, imputing to them the average rate of profit on capital in the corporate sector and treating the remainder of their income (if any) as employment income (the 'asset basis'); or by dividing income from self-employment between labour and property in the same ratio as it is distributed in the corporate sector (the 'proportional basis'); or by applying some other, arbitrary, ratio; or by ignoring completely the property ownership of the self-employed and regarding their entire income as labour income. Another possibility,

which deals with the whole economy rather than the corporate sector alone, but . . . dispenses with the need for any of these methods of 'imputation' is to express the observed share of salaries and wages as the product of two ratios. The first is the ratio of employees, n, to the total occupied population including the self-employed, $N > n$. The second is the ratio of the average income of employees, w, to national income per head of occupied population, y. Thus,

$$\frac{W}{Y} = \frac{w}{y} \cdot \frac{n}{N}$$

where W is total 'employee compensation', and Y is national income (King and Regan 1976: 14).

Expecting n/N to rise over time, *ceteris paribus*, W/Y will also rise: 'Whether there has been a shift away from property to labour income *independently* of the decline in self-employment depends on the movement of w/y, the "wage income ratio". Changes in w/y thus reflect "pure" distributional shifts between labour and property income' (*ibid.*). This method for determining the course of the income-shares-distribution is of course closer to the 'social surplus' and neo-Keynesian way of thinking than to the demand-and-supply approach.

A fairly wide consensus of opinion holds with Kuznets that 'the share of compensation of employees in the national income, like the share of employees in the labour force, generally rises with a country's economic growth' (Kuznets 1959). Alas, the evidence is far from unambiguous (Solow 1958). At least in the short-run, that is in the course of the familiar business cycle, the total share of employee compensation has, during the last eight decades, undergone clear counter-cyclical movements and the total share of profits pro-cyclical movements (Phelps Brown and Hart 1952; St Cyr, 1972; Kuh 1965). But even here a distinction needs to be made between the shares of salaries and rent on the one hand, which rose with recessions and declined during the periods of revival, and, on the other hand, the shares of wages and profit which rose in the course of the revivals and fell during recessions. The net result of the contrary tendencies roughly corresponds with Kalecki's observation that the share of wages in the aggregate income is fairly constant over the cycle (Kalecki 1971: 62–77). However, Kuznets's observation seems to hold only in the long-run. The question which remains unanswered is, how long is 'the long-run'? Therefore, the only thing which may be said with certainty is that labour's share in the national income is not constant. This conclusion is contrary to Pareto's Law and to the premise upon which many of the explanations for the distribution patterns in the neoclassical tradition are founded.

1.11 TRADE UNIONS AND WAGE LEGISLATION

Two related problems which also do not provide an unambiguous answer to the question of whether 'class' distribution of income can or cannot be influenced by 'market imperfection', are the problems of trade-union interference and of state legislation.

There can be no doubting the fact that at times unions can raise the incomes of their members and that when this happens it often causes a spill-over to non-union workers. Less certain is whether in the long run such improvements are nominal or real, and if they are real, whether they benefit the workers in a single industry and at the expense of other workers' real incomes or if they are obtained at the expense of capitalists' profits. Nor is it clear how such increases are related to other factors, for example to technological innovations, which workers may or may not have enjoyed even without union pressure due to the operation of the price mechanism.

One thing, however, is fairly certain, namely that some unions have obtained for their membership, at least for the duration of spells of full employment, better wages and work conditions than were prevalent among non-union workers. Another fairly well established fact is, again during periods of high employment, that real incomes (including non-salary advantages) of both union and non-union employees have risen considerably more in large corporations with oligopolistic powers than in highly competitive firms.

An important argument in favour of unions with regard to income distribution is that when competition fails to reduce prices and raise incomes in line with productivity, the unions restore the necessary effective demand to clear the markets of the growing output by raising wages. But this still does not show if in the long run capitalists compensate this loss in their share of the national income by productivity improvements or by meeting the increased effective demand for consumers goods and services by price hikes which re-establish the old ratios.[16]

The conclusion about unions' impact on distribution can therefore only be that without their intervention the tendency towards monopoly might well have led to a fall in labour's relative share in the national income. The oligopolistic 'mark up' would have been retained by adjustments of output targets in line with stagnating or falling consumers' demand, and investment in depth to save labour cost would have made an even greater impact than it did in the 1980s on employment and distribution. Even without unions there is a starvation floor below which wages cannot fall while there is almost no floor below which the demand for labour cannot be reduced by technological innovations.

The position is a little clearer with regard to the distribution of income within the working class itself. At least in the short run unions can and do create income differentials. These are generally positively related to the degree of workers' organization. Yet the differences are often not long-lasting. On the one hand, spill over effects and, on the other hand, changes in the modes of production and in the composition of the output basket, frequently eliminate advantages gained by successful unions, though at the same time other workers in other industries may be gaining advantages they previously did not enjoy.

Also inconclusive is the role of government in the redistribution of income between classes. In spite of extensive research, the effects of, say, minimum wages and efforts to reduce income differentials, have not yielded unambiguous results. Though in other spheres, such as the abolition of child labour, government legislation has certainly been effective.

Minimum-wage legislation is sometimes introduced to raise the living standard of the lowest paid workers. The intention then is to increase both wages and the level of employment by reducing monopsonistic practices in the labour market. By the logic of the 'marginal productivity theory of labour', all such attempts are of course either unnecessary or *a priori* doomed to fail. In practice, such legislation seems usually unworkable in times of labour shortage and unnecessary in times of high employment. The only sector of the labour market where this kind of legislation has shown positive results is with regard to teenagers during their training period. A different matter is a state-imposed general prices and wages policy. So far such policies have usually failed to reduce inflation and maintain full employment. One reason for this is that such policies were normally not introduced to reduce income differentials but to contain inflation by means of reducing organized labour's wage gains. In addition, no distinction was made between profits retained by firms to finance investment and profits paid out as dividends (i.e. as additions to capitalists personal income), which would have been the reasonable way to approach an incomes policy. This is so because it is only the share going to dividends which needs to be adjusted in line with wages to meet changes in productivity. This, however, would involve the acceptance of the 'social surplus' approach as the best premise for economic legislation by all concerned.

1.12 SOME GENERAL OBSERVATIONS

Whether one chooses the demand-and-supply approach or prefers the social surplus approach to explain the processes by which income is distributed, it is obvious that at least in a closed economy investment cannot exceed (at any given time) certain limits. It is restricted by the level of technology, by the overall supply of available resources and by the share of these resources which is required to meet the immediate needs of the community for physical survival. One will also find it reasonable to assume that investment tends to raise productivity and that a trade-off exists between its present and future effects on consumers' welfare; that the larger the share of the national income which is devoted to investment, the higher will be the rate of economic growth and the greater the national product available for distribution at some future date. This, however, raises the problem of the determination of the path of growth. From the point of view of the demand-and-supply approach, the path is determined by the price mechanism. Investment, particularly innovating investment, reduces production costs; under the pressure of competition the reduced costs are passed on to consumers by price reductions. The lower prices raise real wages more or less in line with productivity. As real incomes rise, the share of savings rises with them and provides the necessary funds for further investment and growth. Seen in this way, serious deviations from the growth path are exogenously induced. They are the result of stochastic shocks, government intervention and interference with the self-adjusting mechanisms by monopolies and trade unions. Barring such deviations, the division of the national income between investment and consumption depends on the technological coefficient, that is on the ratio of the amount of capital to the amount of output produced by that capital. The price of money—the rate of interest—regulates the adjustment of saving and investment. In the short run the technological coefficient can be taken as given, but the cost of money varies with the supply of and the demand for savings. As savings are the share of the national income which is not consumed, the supply of savings is inversely related to consumption. It follows that saving increases the supply of funds and therefore reduces interest rates. Low interest rates reduce production costs and encourage investment. At the same time, however, saving reduces the effective demand for consumer goods and discourages investment. This gives rise to the oscillations in the major economic indicators known as the familiar business cycle. In the course of the cycle the necessary balance between the share of the social product for consumption and the share which goes to investment is restored. Alone, as investment tends to raise productivity, it is restored at a level at which output is greater than it had been before. The 'cake' which can be distributed, has 'grown'. This is, in its simplest form, the idea of the multiplier and accelerator interacting along a technologically determined secular growth path. It implies that if wages or profits rise above their shares in the national income, as they are determined by the technological coefficient, a mechanism is set in motion to restore the right proportions. If wages are too high, high production costs are passed on to consumers in higher prices, and real wages remain unaffected. When higher costs cannot be passed on, the high wages discourage net investment, workers previously engaged in the production of investment goods are dismissed, and the increased demand for consumer goods which was the result of the wage hike is offset by the diminished purchasing power of those whose jobs are lost. The diminished purchasing power spreads unemployment to the rest of the economy and the wage rise is reversed. Alternatively, high wages may induce workers to save a greater proportion of their income and the loss in business savings will to a certain degree be made up by workers' savings. The difference between the last- and the earlier-mentioned alternatives is that it affects the personal distribution of income. Similar adjustment processes take place when, instead of wages, profits rise above the technologically determined level. Demand for consumer goods diminishes, prices fall and subsequently so do profits.

All this appears to be logical. Stochastic shocks may occur and cause some temporary disturbance, but in time their effects are corrected by the system. Governments do interfere but their efforts cannot really influence the course of events, at least not in the long run. Monopolies and labour unions do exert an influence, but it is restricted by the self-correcting mechanisms which are inherent in the system. Even the assumption of the closed economy can be relaxed by allusion to Ricardo's Law of Comparative Advantages or to J.S. Mill's Law of Reciprocal Demand. One may even be tempted to believe that as economic relations between nations grow closer, the same adjustment mechanism which in one country distributes the national product in line with the technologically determined coefficient of expansion, will be internationalized.

The problem with this perception is that it rests upon a

great many uncertain assumptions and that, by ignoring sociological factors, it is far too deterministic to reflect reality. In addition, it takes scientific discoveries to be exogenous. It treats science as if it has an independent existence—that it influences the system but is not itself influenced by economic events. Another difficulty is that it assumes price competition to be effective in spite of monopolistic interference, if not immediately then in the long run. It ignores the possibility that with a large monopolistic sector falling demand for consumer goods may lead to adjustments in the volume of production rather than to price adjustments. Finally, the conception does not take the possibility into consideration that there may be several equilibrium positions at various levels of employment—as Keynes apparently believed; or that the system may be tending towards unstable equilibrium and that under certain circumstances dislocation will tend to increase—as Sidney Weintraub seems to suggest.

The objections to the theoretical underpinnings of both the supply-and-demand and the Post-Keynesian approaches have been dealt with earlier in this discussion. A few words are in order now concerning the place of scientific discovery, the power of multinational oligopolies, and the place of institutional factors in relation to economic growth and distribution. If it could be shown that scientific discovery is not independently determined and that monopolies can and do set prices, it would also be possible to show that there is no cause to believe in the existence of an in-built mechanism which necessarily adjusts investment and consumption in the direction of full employment growth.

Kondratieff, who identified a wave-like movement in the long-term path of several crucial economic indicators and concluded that long waves in the development of the capitalist economy are 'at least very probable', apparently believed that scientific discovery is endogenous. Kuznets identified twenty-year-long growth cycles and related them to variations in the rates of population accretion, to the stability of the ratio of consumption to income, and to the falling quantity of real capital required to produce a given volume of goods. Juglar explained his cycles by psychological factors affecting bank credit. In various degrees all of them considered some factor or factors endogenous which modern mainstream economics regards exogenous. More in line with the mainstream approach, in spite of his acknowledgement of the existence of long waves, was Schumpeter. His explanation is essentially exogenous. He explained their presence as a reflection of technological innovations, which he believed to come in clusters. In his opinion, new products, new production techniques, new modes of organization and new markets stir some entrepreneurs to action. Their actions are imitated by others and give rise to a general economic upturn. Eventually, the process of adaptation which accompanies the upturn and the boom turns the tide towards depression. The depression lasts until equilibrium is restored and the next cluster of innovations turns the tide anew. This suggests that, contrary to the received view of mainstream economics, prolonged recessions or lasting depressions exist and may not be terminated by self-correcting wage and price adjustments. Therefore the existence of 'long-waves' is either denied by many mainstream scholars or explained by exogenous factors.

The denial of the existence of long waves has usually led to the questioning of the statistical methods employed for their identification or to the doubting of the reliability of the time series—of the data. Their explanation by exogenous factors has mainly involved either a sequence of *ad hoc* interpretations—bad harvests, wars, etc., or the declaration of all factors which cannot be accounted for by the model as independent variables such as state intervention, sticky wages and other institutional arrangements. Schumpeter regarded inventions as such a positive independent variable. From time to time they appear, and when equilibrium is restored they generate impulses to which the whole economic system then readjusts. The entrepreneurs take over and the rest follows in the familiar sequence of events. If this was true, the question would still need to be answered why sometimes inventions raise entrepreneurs' 'urge to action' and 'animal spirits' and other times they do not; why modern technology is employed in one part of the

world and not in another; and why several inventions which
later became crucial for industrial societies were known for
decades and even centuries before they were industrially
exploited on a massive scale.[17] In other words, even if
innovating investment could be an independent variable,
Schumpeter's ideas about the spreading of innovation
remain, to say the least, incomplete.

An alternative explanation would be that innovation does
not precede economic revival but that it follows in its wake.
Such an hypothesis involves an examination of the role of
several factors in the economic process, namely the role of
expectations, of intensities of business competition, of
the division of the national income between saving and
consumption and of the differing effects of product and
process innovation. In the first place, such an examination
may show that in a capitalist environment, incentives,
'animal' or otherwise, are influenced by profit expectations
which have an affinity to entrepreneurs' experience (i.e. to
the recent past). Second, that unless they are driven to do
so by the threat of competition, entrepreneurs normally
tend to shun the risks involved in innovating as long as
their tried methods of production and customary markets
continue to yield reasonable returns. Third, that entrepreneurs behave differently in periods of general economic
expansion and in periods of contraction, and that they
behave differently when they operate in highly competitive
sectors of the economy and in sectors in which oligopoly
predominates.

Normally, an expanding demand for consumer goods
raises entrepreneurial expectations and induces investment
in *product innovation*. When the market for some of this
type of good approaches saturation,[18] and competition for
market shares is increasingly influencing profit margins,
entrepreneurs become increasingly more interested in new
labour-cost-reducing equipment, though they will also not
abandon the search for new marketable products. But then
the division between process innovating investment and
product innovation is determined by the intensity of
competition and by the changes in consumers' marginal
propensities to consume and to save. The situation is

different, however, during prolonged recessions or depressions when business prospects seem dim. The entrepreneurs are more inclined in favour of process innovation alone. This is particularly so in sectors of the economy where oligopolies have, within limits, the power of determining prices by scaling down production targets. At such times entrepreneurs in these sectors try to maintain their customary rates of profits by adjusting production targets and attempting to make good the loss of customers by greater efforts to reduce production costs. They concentrate on *process innovation* to obtain increasingly more efficient labour-cost-reducing equipment. The competition for markets yields prime of place to a scramble for finance. Unemployment and interest-rates rise and add impetus to other economically debilitating processes. These tendencies can perhaps be gleaned from the observation that during the 1960s, when almost in all industrial countries wages rose more or less in line with productivity, markets were practically flooded with new products (from silly-putty to electric toothbrushes); while in the 1970s, when unemployment, wage restraint and cuts in social-security-restricted demand for consumer goods, few goods of this type were added while the demand for labour-saving investment goods (robots, computers, etc.) burgeoned. The 1960s were the years of the 'false wants' and the 1970s of the job-devouring silicon chips.

If this is a true account of the modern economic process, a drastic revision of the neoclassical foundations of mainstream economic theory would be unavoidable, and the Post-Keynesians' link between autonomous investment and the economic system would need to be reversed. It would not give rise to a new underconsumption theory but to a theory which takes into account power in economics. Such a theory would stress the need for state intervention—state intervention to bridge the gap between the micro mechanisms and the macro requirements for attaining and sustaining economic equity, stability and growth.[19] The verification, or falsification, of this account of the economic process would depend on evidence that the long waves in the historical development of the capitalist economic system are not a statistical illusion, or coincidental—the product of a concatination of unrelated events; that government intervention can be effective and can go beyond the humanitarian (but not economically necessary) task of supporting those members of society who, for one reason or another, cannot care for themselves; that the causes of the long waves are endogenous and not exogenous; and that if they are not exogenous, this is visible from the analysis of the historical sequences of events; that changes in the personal distribution of the national product have a crucial influence on the economic system's long-term stability; that price rigidities play a much greater role in the economic process than they are credited with in conventional economic theories, and that prices do not adjust supply to demand in the way mainstream economic theories suggest; that even in the long run, prices can be insensitive to variations in demand and that, at least in a number of crucial economic sectors, diminutions in effective demand engender reduced production targets; that the substitution of depreciated capital by more labour-cost-reducing equipment in periods of depression is a widespread practice; that business concentration is increasing—that the power of oligopoly is rising; and that a fall in real wages is followed by a decline in the output of consumer goods and not in prices, interest rates and demand for labour-saving capital goods. Finally, it would also be necessary to show that changes in managerial attitudes towards product and process innovations and changes in management practices accompany the upswings and downswings of the long waves.

The implication of all this for government economic policy, if it can be shown to be true, would be that state intervention in the functional and personal income distribution is necessary to correct the system by income policies designed to maintain the division between consumption expenditure and savings in such a manner that any fall in the rate of demand for consumer goods would be made good by an equivalent rise in public demand, and that any rise in the rate of demand for consumer goods which is in excess of productivity increases would be reduced by an equivalent increase in savings. The question which would then still have to be answered is how far governments are capable of influencing the economy and how far they may be willing and able to do so within the framework of a democratic free-enterprise system.

NOTES

1. According to Ricardo, 'An English labourer would consider his wages under their natural rate and too scanty to support a family if they enabled him to purchase no other food than potatoes and to live in no better habitation than a mud cabin; yet these moderate demands of nature are often deemed sufficient in countries where man's life is cheap. . . Many of the conveniences now enjoyed in an English cottage would have been thought luxuries at an earlier period of our history' (Ricardo 1962: 53–5).
2. More precisely in this case it is a matter of supply and 'derived demand'. The need to stress the distinction between 'demand' and 'derived demand' arises out of the effect it has on demand elasticities and on the degree to which one factor of production can be substituted by others.
3. The Law of Diminishing Returns stipulates that beyond a certain point, the more of one factor of production is applied to a fixed amount of another factor of production, the smaller the additional output will be.
4. Consider the figure below:

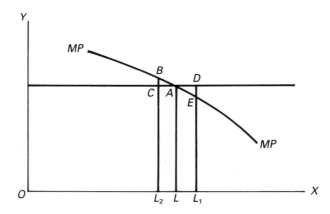

Axis *OY* measures the value of output and the cost of labour (wages), and *OX* measures the units of labour engaged. The downward sloping curve *MP* shows the marginal value of output added by each additionally employed unit of labour beyond the point of full-capacity utilization. The area below the *MP* curve shows the total value of output. An employer who engaged OL_1 units of labour will lose money equal to the area *ADE* An employer who restricts production to OL_2 units of labour will lose the potential gain equal to the area *ABC*. An employer who engages OL units of labour will be maximising profits and be in equilibrium.

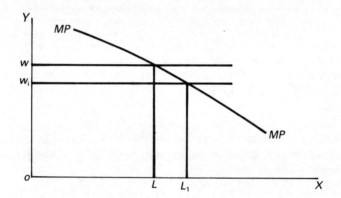

If wages fall from W to W_1, the volume of employment will increase from L to L_1 and if wages rise from W_1 to W then employment will be reduced from L_1 to L.

5. Real wages are wage rates measured in terms of the goods and services they can buy. They are obtained by dividing the nominal (money) wages by the retail price index. In neoclassical theory real wages are measured by the slope of the budget constraint relating hours of leisure to the amounts of goods for which these hours can be exchanged.

6. A good example of this perception can be found in Professor van den Beld's interview with the *de Volkskrant*, 6 June 1984. Professor van den Beld is the recently retired head of the Centraal Planbureau. According to the reporter he said, 'ook de huidige werkloosheid kan worden opgelost als de prijs van de arbeid zich aanpast aan de situatie op de arbeidsmarkt; als de lonen maar laag genoeg zijn'. In his own words, 'Bij energie weet iedereen, dat de vraag daalt als de prijs stijgt. Dat staat op de eerste pagina van het economieboekje'. ('The present unemployment too can be resolved if the price of labour adjusts to the situation in the labour market; if the wages are low enough . . . . With regard to energy everyone knows that demand diminishes when the price rises. That's on the first page of the economics book.')

7. According to Pearce, 'The point is that a technique of production abandoned when the rate of profit is low may be introduced when the rate of profit rises to much higher levels, with an alternative, more profitable technique being used in the interim. It is a problem which arises from heterogeneous capital. When the capital to output ratios in each technique are not equal, the factor price frontiers of the individual techniques exhibit varying degrees of curvature' (Pearce 1981: 376).
8. Perhaps the clearest of the early neoclassical formulations of distribution theory can be found in J.B. Clark, *The Distribution of Wealth (1899)*. The competition among the providers of various inputs equates the values of their marginal products where profit is interest on capital and wages the reward of work. Under static equilibrium all agents of production are justly rewarded. There can be no profit, only a remuneration of entrepreneurs according to the marginal productivity of their services. If profits do arise, they merely reflect temporary deviations from the normal trend; that is, they reflect the dynamic character of the economy. Labour and capital are entirely divisible and homogeneous. Competitive long-run equilibrium sees to it that all are rewarded 'fairly' for their contributions. The question about the meaning of 'fair'—a normative proposition which served to legitimize Clark's prejudices in favour of the ruling social system and which comes, perhaps not surprisingly, close to Pareto's, remains unanswered.
9. By combining elements from Keynes's *Treatise on Money* (1930) with Kalecki's *Studies in the Theory of Business Cycles 1933–39* (1969), they propose the following alternative: 'National income, as is well known, can be measured in two ways, namely from the side of income and from the side of expenditure, as follows:

Income	Expenditure
Profits (income of capitalists)	Investment
+ wages (income of workers)	+ capitalists' consumption
	+ workers' consumption
= national income	= national product

'Following Kalecki, the national income can be divided into the profits received by capitalists and the wages received by the workers. The national product, on the other hand, can be divided into investment and the consumption by the capitalists and the consumption by the workers. Investment includes the purchase of fixed capital (machinery, buildings, etc.) and any change in inventories.

With the workers assumed to spend all their earnings on consumption, the wages they receive as income must necessarily be equal to the value of workers' consumption goods produced since all their income is spent on them. This means that the income of the capitalists, profits, will be equal to the value of the goods purchased by the capitalists with their profits, both for investment and for consumption. Two striking conclusions emerge from this simple classification of the economic system. The first is that the capitalists can increase the share of national income they receive as profits simply by increasing the amount they spend on investment, with the higher level of investment leading, of course, to an increase in aggregate output based on the multiplier. On the other hand, even if the capitalists consume their profits in 'high living' rather than investing, they do not suffer a reduction in their profit income. As far as the capitalists' income is concerned, it is maintained independently of how it is spent'(Kregel 1979: 52).

10. The discussion here centres on the difference between Sir J. Harrod's 'knife edge' equilibrium and Joan Robinson's parameters within which the system is confined.

11. This is the G.A. Feldman model (Domar 1957: 223–61).

12. This can be illustrated by the following example: Let it be assumed that the total of the wages earned in the production of consumer goods and of capital goods together amounts to $100m. Half of this ($50m) is earned by workers engaged in the production of consumer goods and the other half ($50m) by workers engaged in the production of capital goods. By the end of the period the workers in both sectors would be able to spend $100m on consumer goods. But the supply of consumer goods was produced by only half the work-force, i.e. at the cost of $50m. Ignoring depreciation, taxes and workers' savings, capitalists would therefore soon be in the possession of the $100m from the sale of consumer goods, and in addition possess capital goods equivalent to the value of the $50m paid to the workers who produced them.

If then, in the next period the capitalists or the state decide to increase their outlay on the production of capital goods so that three-quarters of the work-force is employed in the production of capital goods and only one quarter in the production of consumer goods, the result would be as follows: The capitalists or the state would receive $100m from the sale of consumer goods (which cost them $25m in wages to the quarter of the work-force which produced them) and they would possess additional capital goods to the value of another $75m (paid to the workers who produced them). The diminished supply of consumer goods would force workers to vie for them. Consequently consumer goods' prices would rise in precisely the measure which would return to capitalists the entire $100m spent on wages in both sectors, unless of course workers' consumption is reduced by the price increases, or productivity in the consumer goods producing sector rises so steeply that competition between capitalists brings down prices to a level where workers save more of their earnings (Brenner, 1971: 9–19).

13. See 'Functional Distribution'.

14. Quoted here from King and Regan (1976: 10).

15. King and Regan (1976: 12) write that in Britain 1 per cent of the
    population own more than a quarter of all *personal* wealth and 5
    per cent at least half; and that 5 per cent receive over 92 per cent
    of all property income (See Atkinson 1972: 14, 36, for details).
16. For a historical account of union influence on incomes and prices,
    see Brenner (1969: 204–37) and Brenner (1984).
17. I discussed the first problem in Brenner (1971: 9–19) and provided
    examples for the second in Brenner (1969: 145–95);
18. For examples, see Brenner (1984: 71, 73, 230–1).
19. I have elaborated this in Brenner (1984: 184–210).

2 Recent Trends In Labour's Share

J.E. King and P.Regan

The purpose of this paper is to outline recent trends in the relative income shares of labour and property in the United Kingdom, the United States, Australia and Japan and to offer some tentative explanations for them.

Section 2.1 outlines the neoclassical, Post-Keynesian and Marxian theories of relative income shares, and considers their empirical implications. In section 2.2 we present the evidence for each of the four countries, while section 2.3 offers some simple tests of the theories already outlined and summarizes our conclusions.

2.1 THEORIES OF RELATIVE SHARES

Neoclassical Theory
Modern neoclassical theory dates from Hicks [1932] and centres on the elasticity of substitution. In long-run equilibrium under perfect competition with two inputs (K, L) only, the elasticity of substitution can be used to predict movements in relative shares. Elasticity of substitution can be defined as:

$$= \frac{\% \text{ change in } K/L}{\% \text{ change in MRTS } (L/K)} \tag{1}$$

Under long-run equilibrium in perfect competition, the marginal rate of technical substitution (MRTS) can be replaced by the factor price ratio:

$$= \frac{\% \text{ change in } K/L}{\% \text{ change in } P_L/P_K} \qquad (2)$$

If $\sigma > 1$ a rise in the relative price of a factor will reduce its share, since the factor ratio will be adjusted by more than in proportion to the relative price change. Similarly, a rise in the relative quantity of an input will raise its share if $\sigma > 1$. Exactly opposite conclusions follow if $\sigma < 1$. Shares are unchanged if $\sigma = 1$.

The problem with this model is not its logic but its application. It only predicts under conditions of long-run equilibrium in perfect competition, with two inputs and neutral technical progress which leaves relative factor productivities unchanged. If these conditions prevail and the technology of a whole economy can be represented by a two-input aggregate production function, then knowledge of σ allows the prediction of changes in relative shares. We have argued elsewhere that it is extremely unlikely that such conditions can be met, since perfect competition does not hold and it may be impossible to construct an appropriate aggregate production function. The problems of applying an aggregate production function arise both in the construction of aggregate indices of capital, labour and output and in the restrictions which must be placed on the form of individual sector production functions in order to generate a given aggregate function [see Harcourt, 1972; Fisher, 1969].   In the unlikely event that all the preconditions can be met, the model predicts relatively stable shares. This is because, over a considerable range of elasticities of substitution, shares are not highly sensitive to the relative prices or quantities of factors [Bronfenbrenner, 1960]. Following Bronfenbrenner, labour's share can be written as:

$$S = \frac{Lp_L}{Lp_L + Kp_K} \qquad (3)$$

and the sensitivity of S to changes in the output ratio may be defined in terms of S and the elasticity of substitution:

$$\frac{\% \text{ change in labour share } (S)}{\% \text{ change in L/K}} = \frac{(1 - S)(\sigma - 1)}{\sigma} \qquad (4)$$

This expression will be small for a considerable range of values of σ, and particularly if S is large and $\sigma > 1$. For example, if $\sigma = 2$ and $S = 3/4$, a rise in the L/K ratio of 40 per cent is required to generate a 5 per cent rise in labour's share. S is more sensitive if $\sigma < 1$, but even with $\sigma = 1/2$ and $S = 3/4$, L/K has to fall by 20 per cent to generate a 5 per cent rise in labour's share. Symmetrical results follow for changes in relative factor prices. Furthermore, most empirical estimates of σ lie well within this range [see Arrow *et al*. 1961: Fuchs 1963: Ferguson 1969].

It is only in disequilibrium that relative shares are expected to change much [see Morley 1979]. In this case, counter-cyclical fluctuations in the wage share are not inconsistent with perfect competition. On an upswing, for example, firms will be forced on to upward-sloping sections of their short-run marginal cost curves, with the result that prices rise relative to wages [see Hahn 1972, Ch. 8]. But pro-cyclical fluctuations in the profit share can be predicted from an explicitly non-neoclassical model, as is demonstrated in Appendix I.

We conclude that, for a single perfectly competitive firm or sector with two easily defined inputs, simple predictions of relative shares can be made by using elasticity of substitution. For a whole economy, no clear long-run predictions follow from the neoclassical model. If our reservations are dismissed and the model employed with an aggregate production function, then in the long-run relatively stable shares are predicted, while in the short-run there may be counter-cyclical variations in labour's share.

Post-Keynesian Theory

The central feature of Post-Keynesian macroeconomic theories of relative shares is that entrepreneurs' own spending decisions determine their share (Kaldor 1955–6; Pasinetti 1962). If aggregate supply is fixed at full employment, an aggregate demand function in which investment is chosen by capitalists and consumption depends on the distribution of income can be made to predict shares. The

model is most simply expressed in terms of the equality of
savings and investment:

$$I = s_p P + s_w W \qquad (5)$$

Where: I = investment
$\quad\quad P$ = total profits
$\quad\quad W$ = total wages
$\quad\quad s_p$ = average propensity to save of capitalists
$\quad\quad s_w$ = average propensity to save of workers

If $s_p = 1$ and $s_w = 0$, the familiar result follows that
capitalists get what they spend and workers spend what
they get. This is illustrated in Figure 2.1, where real income
is constrained to $Y_f Y_f$, $I\,I$ indicates points where
savings equal investment, and equilibrium is at point a. If
capitalists invest more, say $I'I'$, profits rise by exactly the
same amount and wages fall in order to maintain the
equality of savings and investment at a'. Given the full
employment income level Y_f, any rise in real wages, perhaps
through trade-union pressure, must be at the expense of
profits and investment. The key assumption of the model
is that entrepreneurs' investment decisions have priority.
Their 'animal spirits' drive the model through the choice
of how much to invest. Wages are passive, since workers
are either deluded by price changes which alter real wages
or simply powerless to resist.

The full employment assumption restricts the application
of the model and is at odds with Keynesian unemployment.
Goodwin (1983) proposes a Post-Keynesian model where
spare capacity exists and output can respond to changes in
demand. It amounts to saying that distribution is no longer
a zero-sum game, as increases in aggregate demand can
call forth increased output. Goodwin also allows a much
more positive role for real wages. If there is spare capacity,
the relative shares of profits and pay will be less sensitive
to changes in investment or real wages than if output is
constrained at the full employment level. In Figure 2.2,
when investment rises to I', real wages are unaffected since
ouput and profits rise exactly in line with the increased
investment; the new equilibrium is at a'', with output equal

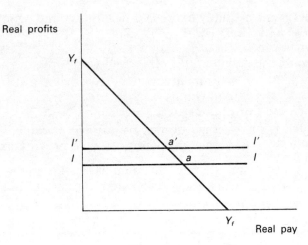

Figure 2.1

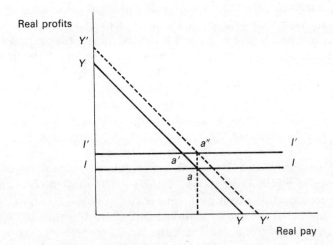

Figure 2.2

to $Y'Y'$. The profit share rises but by less than in Figure 2.1 as the increase in profits is not now at the expense of wages. Similarly, if real wages rise, consumption and output increase by an equal amount. The wage share rises, but again the increased wages are not gained at the expense of profits, since output expands.

This very simple analysis suggests that relative shares are much more likely to change rapidly during periods of full employment than when an economy is demand-constrained away from its aggregate supply function. Goodwin's analysis is more sophisticated in assuming fixed coefficient technology and mark-up pricing, but his conclusions are similar. He employs a neo-Marxian reserve army hypothesis to argue that upward pressure on real wages will be at a maximum at the peaks of trade cycles and at a minimum in deep depression when union power is broken. He expects rapid share changes at peaks when shares are most sensitive and wage pressure greatest, and also in deep depression when real wages are most likely to fall.

Our conclusion that shares are more likely to be responsive to real wage changes under full employment assumes that capitalists maintain a constant level of investment. The model can be extended by including a simple theory of investment. It would be Keynesian in spirit to assume that investment is positively related to the level of consumption (so that the construction of breweries, for example, is encouraged by increased consumption of beer). If investment is a positive function of consumption, and if capitalists do not respond greatly to consumption changes when they have spare capacity, then similar conclusions follow. In fact, a small increase in investment following a rise in wages and consumption merely damps its effect on the wage share. In Figure 2.3, when wages rise from W to W', ouput rises from Y to Y' and the wage share rises. If investment now rises to I', the increase in the wage share is somewhat reduced at the new equilibrium of a''. In the event that investment increases greatly in response to the increased consumption of workers, real wages and the wage share may move inversely. If investment responds inversely to rises in real wages, the sensitivity of the wage share to real wage changes is increased, since investment declines as real wages rise. These results are demonstrated formally in Appendix II. Relaxing the assumption that $s_p = 1$ and $s_w = 0$ does not alter these conclusions.

The predictions that follow from this highly simplified Post-Keynesian analysis are precisely the reverse of those

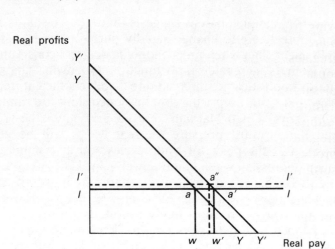

Figure 2.3

suggested by the neoclassical model: shares are likely to be fairly stable during Keynesian unemployment, and will change rapidly only when the economy is constrained by supply. If investment is allowed to depend on consumption, these conclusions still stand, as investment will not be highly responsive to consumption when there is spare capacity, and may well be inversely related to real wages in the presence of a capacity constraint. In contrast, the neoclassical analysis predicts stable shares at full employment and rapid changes only in short-run disequilibrium.

Marxian Theory
The closest approximation in Marxian theory to the ratio of property income to labour income is the rate of exploitation:

$$e = \frac{s}{v} = \frac{\text{surplus value}}{\text{variable capital}} = \frac{\text{unpaid labour}}{\text{paid labour}} = \frac{\text{surplus labour}}{\text{necessary labour}}$$

Since net output is defined as total living labour performed (paid plus unpaid), it can be written as $v + s$, so that the labour share of net income is $v/(v+s)$, an inverse function of s/v. There are however several problems inherent in moving from conventional to Marxian categories, of which two are serious enough to mention here. First, the Marxian aggregates are expressed in labour values while the national accounts are in market prices. Even if, as Marx claimed, total surplus value is equal to the sum of profits, interest and rent (which is itself controversial), there is no reason to suppose that total variable capital will be equal to aggregate wages and salaries. Second, the incomes of unproductive labourers constitute for Marx payments out of surplus value rather than a component of variable capital, so that estimates of the property share in national income (which ignore the distinction between productive and unproductive labour) will understate the Marxian concept $s/(v+s)$, to an extent which depends upon one's formulation of the distinction itself (Moseley 1985). Although W/Y is a rough approximation to $v/(v+s)$, and P/Y to $s/(v+s)$, then, there are important differences of unknown magnitude between the two pairs of concepts (Howard and King 1985: Chs 7–8).

Subject to these reservations, changes in the rate of exploitation can be regarded as corresponding to inverse variations in labour's share. Marx himself wrote at considerable length on the determinants of the rate of exploitation (Marx, 1969:Chs 7–18), showing it to depend upon the length of the working day, the level of real wages and the intensity of labour. But he did not provide an unambiguous prediction as to its secular trend. The question arises most clearly in his discussion of the long-run tendency for the rate of profit to fall, since the rate of exploitation is one of the latter's two fundamental components. Where c represents constant capital; k ($= c/v$) is the ratio of constant to variable capital, the so-called 'organic composition of capital'; and r is the rate of profit, that is the ratio of surplus value to total capital (constant plus variable), we can write:

$$r = \frac{s}{c + v} = \frac{s/v}{c/v + 1} = \frac{e}{k + 1}$$

Marx expected k to rise due to the use of increasingly machine-intensive technology. In many of his numerical examples he holds the rate of exploitation constant, which would imply a constant labour share and real wages which rose at the same rate as labour productivity. This, however, may have been no more than a provisional simplifying assumption. Elsewhere Marx suggests that the rate of exploitation is a function of the class struggle, since there is no effective minimum to the level of profits in the way that physical subsistence requirements set a floor to real wages: 'The matter resolves itself into a question of the respective powers of the combatants' (Marx, 1962: 443).

Until recently most Marxian writers held the rate of exploitation constant in their formal models of capital accumulation and economic crises, in effect renouncing any interest in the relative shares of labour and capital. In the most sophisticated of such models to appear before 1914, Otto Bauer adopted constancy as a supposedly provisional hypothesis which he nevertheless failed to reconsider (Bauer, 1913: 93). A generation later Henryk Grossmann's elaborate reformulation of the falling rate of profit theory managed to combine technical progress, constant or falling real wages and an unchanging rate of exploitation, apparently without realizing the inconsistency (Grossmann, 1929; Robinson, 1949:38–9; Meek, 1967). Not until the 1960s was there any serious Marxian interest in changes in the rate of exploitation as a factor which might significantly affect the rate of profit. Glyn and Sutcliffe's (1972) pioneering account of the 'profit squeeze', in which the property share was ground relentlessly between an aggressive labour movement and a 'hard' (i.e. increasingly competitive) global product market, was extremely influential. The relative bargaining strength of rank-and-file trade unionism came to be seen as a major determinant of the rate of exploitation, and thereby also of the rate of capital accumulation. For Ernest Mandel, for example, it represents one of the most important elements distinguishing long upswings from periods of protracted depression (Mandel, 1980, see also 1975).

By far the most ambitious empirical study of the issue from a Marxian viewpoint is Weisskopf's (1979) analysis of the declining profit rate in the United States. Using conventional rather than Marxian categories, Weisskopf writes the rate of profit as:

$$r = \frac{P}{K} = \frac{P}{Y} \cdot \frac{Y}{Z} \cdot \frac{Z}{K},$$

where K stands for the capital stock and Z is full-capacity output. Movements in r can thus be attributed to changes in the property share (P/Y); fluctuations in the degree of capacity utilization (Y/Z); and alterations in the output–capital ratio (Z/K), which Weisskopf interprets as a rough proxy for the Marxian organic composition of capital. In fact, the first of these was found to be by far the most important cause of the decline in the US profit rate since 1949. Weisskopf further decomposed the increase in the labour share into three components. One, reflecting the effect of changes in capacity utilization on relative shares, proved to be quite minor. The other two represented the 'rising strength of labour', which had both 'defensive' and 'aggressive' aspects. Labour's increasing defensive strength was mobilized to protect real wages against the increasing relative prices of natural resources and services. Its aggressive strength was used to give increases in real wages in excess of productivity growth. Weisskopf concluded:'the long-term decline in the rate of profit from 1949 to 1975 was almost entirely attributable to a rise in the true share of wages, which indicates a rise in the strength of labour. This rise, however, was largely defensive in nature. The working class did not succeed in making true real wage gains commensurate with the growth of true productivity; it merely succeeded in defending itself somewhat more successfully against a long-term deterioration in the terms of trade than did the capitalist class'.(Weisskopf, 1979: 370).

One further development, which is entirely consistent with Marxian theory without presupposing it, is the recognition that productivity is a social rather than a purely technical variable. The social relations of production may affect the intensity of labour in addition to impinging upon wages and hours of work (Hodgson, 1982). Weisskopf, Bowles and Gordon (1983) argue that work intensity depends both on the effectiveness of employer control of the workforce (reflected in the expected costs of dismissal for 'shirking' and in the intensity of supervision and surveillance), and on the motivation of the workers through wages and working conditions. Their empirical work suggests that much of the decline in US productivity growth in the post-war period resulted from a reduction in the intensity of work (but see Rees 1983). This contributed to the increase in labour's share over the same period. An elaborate Marxian model of changes in relative shares over the cycle, focusing on fluctuations in labour productivity as industrial conflict waxes and wanes, is presented by Hahnel and Sherman (1982). As empirical testing of their model requires quarterly data, however, we have not been able to assess its validity outside the United States.

To conclude, modern (if not classical) Marxian analysis emphasizes the distributional effects of the class struggle over wages and work intensity. It offers a perspective on labour's share which is quite distinct from those of neoclassical and Post-Keynesian theory. It is also, in our view, a plausible one: the relative strength of the labour movement can be expected to play a significant part in affecting the course of relative income shares.

2.2 THE EVIDENCE

The United Kingdom

The evidence for the UK is presented in Table 2.1 and Figure 2.4, which are derived from UK National Income and Expenditure Accounts (HMSO 1985 and 1986). Shares are expressed as a percentage of Gross Domestic Product at factor cost to allow comparison with Feinstein (1968). Figure 2.4 reveals a reasonably stable long-run trend in the share of employee compensation from 1952 to 1973, with more marked fluctuations thereafter. Corporate profits less stock appreciation fell steadily as a proportion of GDP from

1952 to 1973, while the self-employed share declined until the early 1960s and recovered by 1973. After the first oil shock of 1973, employee compensation rose rapidly at the expense of the corporate profit share, but since 1981 corporate profits have recovered and the employee compensation share has declined sharply.

In comparison with the pre-war period, the employee compensation share has been much higher since 1946. Up to 1973, the employee compensation share shows considerable stability, as in the inter-war period. Since 1973 both the employee compensation and corporate profit shares reveal a degree of instability not seen in the earlier post-war years or in the pre-war period. The only year with a change in the corporate profit share comparable to that of 1973–4 was the fierce recession of 1921. There is evidence of a sharp rise in real wages in 1974–5 and concern, as in Australia (see below, p. 70), about its effects on employment (see Andrews 1985). As expected, the labour share fluctuates counter-cyclically and the corporate profit share pro-cyclically; since 1973 the amplitude of cyclical fluctuations has been much larger than was previously the case.

United States

The evidence for the United States is summarized in Table 2.2 and Figure 2.5. Pre-1970 data were derived from B.J. Wattenberg's *Statistical History of the US from Colonial Times to the Present*, while data for 1971 onwards came from the *Statistical Abstract of the United States* for 1978 and 1985. Shares are expressed as a percentage of national income to allow comparison with Kravis (1968). Corporate profits are measured before tax but net of the inventory valuation adjustment.

The share of the self-employed has declined steadily since 1946 without (as in the United Kingdom) any recent sign of recovery. A sustained and substantial rise in the labour share came to an end at the beginning of the 1970s and has since been (rather weakly) reversed. The corporate profit share fell steadily until the early 1970s; there is no clear evidence of either an increasing or a diminishing trend thereafter. The first oil crisis appears to have coincided

Table 2.1: Shares of national income: United Kingdom, 1946–84 (%)

	Corporate profits	Self-employed income	Employee compensation
1946	15.5	13.1	65.8
1947	13.4	13.3	67.1
1948	14.3	12.9	66.0
1949	15.1	12.9	66.6
1950	13.1	12.5	67.4
1951	13.8	11.6	67.4
1952	16.3	11.0	66.5
1953	16.2	10.6	65.4
1954	16.1	10.3	65.9
1955	16.2	10.1	67.2
1956	15.2	9.6	67.4
1957	15.3	9.4	67.5
1958	15.1	9.1	67.2
1959	15.5	9.2	67.3
1960	16.2	9.1	67.8
1961	14.2	8.8	68.5
1962	13.8	8.7	69.5
1963	14.5	9.5	66.9
1964	14.6	9.2	66.9
1965	14.1	9.4	67.1
1966	12.9	9.5	68.1
1967	12.9	9.5	67.7
1968	12.5	9.7	67.4
1969	12.3	9.6	67.2
1970	11.3	9.4	68.6
1971	12.2	9.8	67.4
1972	12.2	10.4	67.1
1973	11.6	11.4	66.6
1974	7.2	10.9	70.2
1975	6.6	9.7	72.5
1976	7.3	9.9	70.6
1977	11.5	9.4	67.3
1978	12.4	9.3	66.9
1979	11.9	9.3	67.6
1980	11.2	8.8	68.9
1981	10.8	8.9	68.3
1982	12.5	8.9	66.5
1983	13.7	9.2	65.5
1984	15.3	9.6	64.4

Source: see text

Figure 2.4: UK shares of GDP, 1946–84

with a significant break in the trend of relative shares in the United States. It did not, however, affect the pro-cyclical fluctuations in the profit share, and counter-cyclical swings in the labour share, which can be observed throughout the post-war period.

Australia
The evidence for Australia is presented in Table 2.3 and Figure 2.6, which are derived from successive issues of *Australian National Accounts,* published by the Australian Bureau of Statistics in Canberra. The data are derived from the tables of Gross Domestic Product at factor cost. To permit approximate comparisons with the other countries studied, four components of GDP were omitted from the calculations. These were gross operating surplus of public enterprises and financial enterprises, the imputed bank service charge and the net income of persons from dwellings.

Table 2.2: Shares of national income: United States, 1946–83 (%)

	Corporate profits	Self-employed income	Employee compensation
1946	10.6	20.1	64.8
1947	12.9	17.8	64.8
1948	14.7	17.9	62.9
1949	14.2	16.2	64.8
1950	15.6	15.6	64.1
1951	15.4	15.1	65.0
1952	13.7	14.4	67.0
1953	13.0	13.3	68.6
1954	12.5	13.2	68.6
1955	14.2	12.6	67.8
1956	13.1	12.1	69.3
1957	12.5	12.1	69.9
1958	11.2	12.6	70.1
1959	12.9	11.6	69.8
1960	12.0	11.2	70.1
1961	11.8	11.3	70.8
1962	12.2	10.9	70.7
1963	12.2	10.6	70.8
1964	12.8	10.1	70.6
1965	13.5	10.1	69.8
1966	13.3	9.9	70.2
1967	12.0	9.5	71.5
1968	11.9	9.1	72.4
1969	10.4	8.8	73.9
1970	8.6	8.3	75.4
1971	9.0	7.9	75.8
1972	9.4	8.0	75.1
1973	9.1	8.7	75.1
1974	7.7	7.6	77.1
1975	8.5	7.0	76.4
1976	9.9	6.5	76.0
1977	11.5	6.5	76.0
1978	11.6	6.3	73.9
1979	10.7	6.7	74.1
1980	9.1	5.5	75.6
1981	8.4	5.3	74.7
1982	6.4	4.5	76.2
1983	7.3	4.6	75.0

Source: see text

Figure 2.5: Shares of national income: United States, 1946–83

In the interests of comparability, we have not followed the practice of some students of Australian income distribution in excluding certain groups of industries in which either self-employment or government influences are particularly strong. (Riach 1986).

Broadly comparable data are available for Australia from 1948/9 (the Australian statistical year begins on 1 July), and reveal a distinct downward trend in the share of wages, salaries and supplements during the 1950s (Neville, 1967: 3–4; Riach 1986, Fig. 1: 76). Unfortunately, in the limited time available to us we were able to obtain information only for the period beginning in 1962/3. We hope to extend the series backwards in subsequent research. Over the two decades covered by our data, the expected counter-cyclical fluctuations in the labour share are evident. There are also clear signs of a long-term, upward trend in the share of wages, salaries and supplements, which rose slowly in the

Table 2.3: Shares of national income: Australia, 1962/3 to 1982/3 (%)

	Gross operating surplus of companies	Gross operating surplus of unincorporated enterprises	Wages, salaries and supplements
1962–3	16.6	22.1	61.3
1963–4	16.9	23.0	60.1
1964–5	17.0	21.8	61.2
1965–6	16.6	19.9	63.5
1966–7	16.6	20.8	62.7
1967–8	17.9	17.8	64.4
1968–9	18.0	18.7	63.3
1969–70	18.8	17.1	64.1
1970–1	17.9	15.5	66.6
1971–2	17.4	15.9	66.7
1972–3	17.6	17.1	65.2
1973–4	16.0	17.8	66.2
1974–5	14.4	15.2	70.5
1975–6	14.5	14.7	70.7
1976–7	14.9	14.8	70.4
1977–8	14.5	14.1	71.4
1978–9	14.9	16.4	68.7
1979–80	15.5	16.1	68.4
1980–1	15.7	14.7	69.6
1981–2	14.7	14.0	71.3
1982–3	14.0	12.1	73.9

Source: see text.

later 1960s and then jumped sharply between 1973/4 and 1974/5. This celebrated shift resulted from a sudden acceleration of money wage awards in a 'hard' market environment which made it impossible for firms to raise product prices sufficiently to compensate (Riach 1986: 56).

The resulting 'real wage overhang' became a subject of intense controversy in Australia in the later 1970s. Neoclassical economists and conservative politicians blamed the sustained depression of output and employment upon the failure of the labour share to decline to its pre-1974 levels (see, for example, Corden 1979). Our series suggest that a similar upward displacement may have occurred in

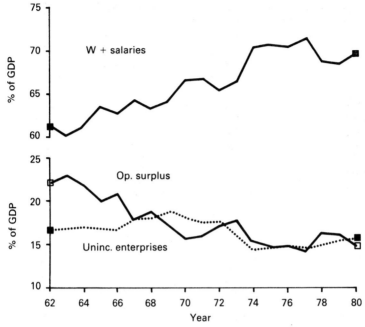

Figure 2.6: Shares of GDP: Australia, 1962–82

Australia between 1980/1 and 1982/3, when the labour share again rose sharply. These, however, were years of recession, and until we have access to data from the more recent recovery years, it is impossible to deny with any confidence that this was simply an abnormally powerful cyclical increase.

Japan
The evidence for Japan is presented in Table 2.4 and Figure 2.7, using the Japanese Economic Planning Agency Annual Reports on National Accounts. The data express shares as a percentage of national income, and reveal a marked upward trend in the employee compensation share from 1960 to the present. Although the share of employee compensation rose from 50 per cent to 70 per cent between 1960 and 1984, most of the increase is accounted for by a decline in self-employment income. Before 1960 corporate

Table 2.4: Shares of national income: Japan, 1952–82 (%)

	Corporate profits	Income of unincorporated enterprises	Employee compensation
1952	9.3	39.8	47.6
1953	9.1	36.8	50.3
1954	9.8	36.1	49.4
1955	7.9	37.1	49.6
1956	8.7	34.4	51.0
1957	12.1	31.2	49.8
1958	10.5	29.5	52.2
1959	10.6	28.3	52.3
1960	14.4	24.5	50.2
1961	14.4	25.8	50.3
1962	13.3	24.7	52.4
1963	12.0	24.6	53.7
1964	12.3	23.7	54.2
1965	10.6	23.4	56.0
1966	11.2	22.6	55.8
1967	12.8	22.9	54.2
1968	14.3	22.6	53.3
1969	14.7	21.6	53.6
1970	15.5	19.6	54.5
1971	13.9	18.3	57.1
1972	12.5	18.9	57.7
1973	10.2	18.7	60.1
1974	7.0	18.4	63.1
1975	8.6	16.2	63.4
1976	8.2	17.6	66.6
1977	8.4	16.4	68.0
1978	10.4	16.7	66.6
1979	9.9	17.0	67.0
1980	9.6	14.5	67.2
1981	8.9	13.4	68.9
1982	8.8	12.7	70.1

Source: see text

profits rose rapidly, with a fairly steady employee compensation share and a sharply falling share of self-employment
income. The post-war evidence contrasts sharply with that
of the pre-war periods, when the employee compensation
share was falling (see Okhawa, 1968). The cyclical evidence

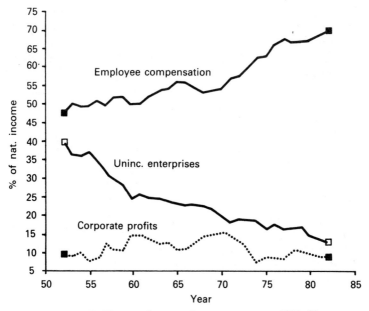

Figure 2.7: Shares of national income: Japan, 1952–82

is as expected but, in this case, given the steady fall in the share of the self-employed, employee compensation fluctuates around a strongly rising trend.

The labour market in Japan appears to exhibit a much greater degree of real wage flexibility than is the case in many other nations (see Coe, 1985), and unemployment has remained low by international standards. Nevertheless, since the 1973 oil price shock the corporate profit share has fluctuated around a considerably lower level than in the 1960s. The experience is similar to that of Australia, but in very different labour market conditions.

2.3 AN ASSESSMENT OF THE THEORIES

In section 2.1 we argued that there was a sharp difference in the implications of neoclassical and Post-Keynesian theories of relative shares. Neoclassical analysis predicts long-run stability in shares under equilibrium conditions of full employment, together with disequilibrium short-run fluctuations. Post-Keynesian theory implies that shares will be relatively stable in periods of demand-deficient unemployment, changing rapidly when supply constraints become important; changes in the investment–income ratio are of crucial importance. Marxian analysis offers no such clear-cut predictions (none, at least, which is testable without quarterly data), but suggests that the balance of forces in the class struggle is of great significance in explaining fluctuations in relative shares.

We carried out two sets of statistical tests of these hypotheses. First we investigated whether shares varied more or less under full employment than in periods of less than full employment. We then looked at the relationship between the ratio of investment to income and the corporate profit share. Our results are presented for each country, with some general conclusions being drawn at the end of this section.

United Kingdom

In Table 2.5 coefficients of variation are given for the shares of corporate profits and employee compensation for the periods 1946–69, when full employment prevailed, and

Table 2.5: United Kingdom coefficients of variation

Period	Corporate profits	Employee compensation
(1) Unsmoothed data		
1946–69	0.087	0.0132
1946–84	0.183	0.0218
1970–84	0.216	0.0303
1921–38	0.145	0.0303
(2) Smoothed data		
1948–69	0.074	0.00765
1948–82	0.164	0.0123
1970–82	0.123	0.013
1923–36	0.075	0.00783

Table 2.6: United Kingdom
A: Simple correlation coefficient (r²) of private gross fixed capital
formation as a share of GDP and relative income shares

	Corporate profits	Employee compensation
(1) Unsmoothed data		
1946–1984	−0.576	+0.233
1921–1938	+0.151	−0.489
(2) Smoothed data		
1948–1982	−0.787	+0.642
1923–1936	−0.311	−0.071

B: Simple correlation coefficient (r²) of gross domestic fixed capital
formation as a share of GDP and relative income shares

	Corporate profits	Employee compensation
(1) Unsmoothed data		
1946–84	−0.635	+0.435
1921–38	+0.320	−0.552
(2) Smoothed data		
1948–82	−0.778	+0.732
1923–36	−0.049	−0.462

1970–84, a period of demand-deficient unemployment. Data for the post-war period as a whole, and for the inter-war years, are also given. To allow for the possibility that the amplitude of the cycle may have been different between periods, we constructed five-year moving averages of income shares, and present data for both unsmoothed and smoothed shares in Table 2.5. It will be seen that shares fluctuated much more in the high unemployment period (1970–84) than in the era of full employment (1946–1969); this is true of both the smoothed and unsmoothed data. Fluctuations have also been greater since 1946 than between the wars, though the smoothed data reveal a coefficient of variation in 1948–69 almost identical to that for 1923–36.

The relationship between the investment–income ratio and relative income shares is shown in Table 2.6 and Figures 2.8 and 2.9. Both smoothed and unsmoothed data were

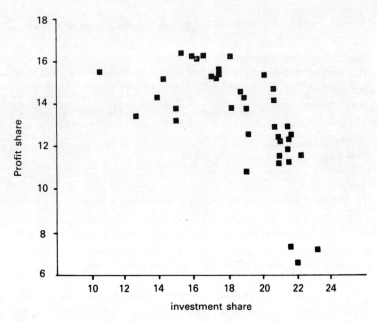

Figure 2.8: United Kingdom: scatter plot of investment share and profit share

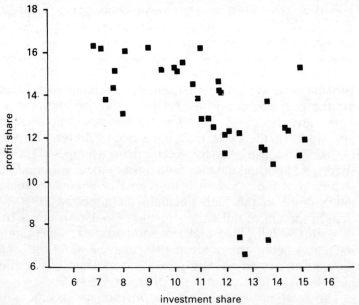

Figure 2.9: United Kingdom: scatter plot of private investment share and profit share

used, together with two measures of capital formation. In the main there is a negative relationship between the investment–income ratio and the profit share. This is true throughout the post-war period, though it is not always apparent in the inter-war period. The relationship of the investment ratio with the share of employee compensation is ambiguous.

United States

In the United States unemployment was significantly higher than the post-war average only after 1975, and the period of high unemployment was therefore too short to allow meaningful estimates of coefficients of variation in relative shares. Our analysis was therefore restricted to an assessment of the relationships between the investment–income ratio and relative shares for the period 1946–83. Unfortunately, data restrictions ruled out any comparison with the inter-war years. The results are shown in Table 2.7 and Figure 2.10. As in the case of the United Kingdom, there is evidence of a negative relationship between the investment ratio and the profit share (much more strongly for the smoothed data). This, however, conceals a significant break within the period, since the relationship appears positive up to 1970 and negative thereafter. There is also an unambiguously positive relationship between the investment ratio and the labour share.

Table 2.7: United States: simple correlation coefficient (r^2) between share of gross private domestic fixed investment in GDP and relative income shares

	Corporate profits	Employee compensation
(1) Unsmoothed data (1946–83)	−0.122	+0.336
(2) Smoothed data (1948–81)	−0.519	+0.486

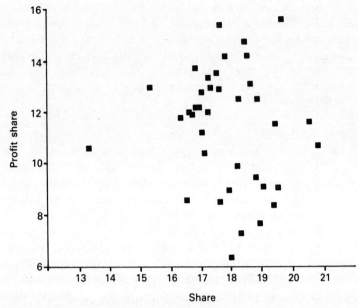

Figure 2.10: United States: scatter plot of investment share and profit share

Australia

Again the high unemployment period is too short for a meaningful test of the variability of shares to be carried out, and inter-war data were not available. Table 2.8 and Figure 2.11 show the results of tests similar to those conducted for the United States. They reveal, however, a very strong positive relationship between the investment–

Table 2.8: Australia: simple correlation coefficient (r^2) between share of gross investment in GDP and relative income shares

	Corporate profits	Employee compensation
(1) Unsmoothed data (1962/3 to 1980/1)	+0.743	−0.707
(2) Smoothed data (1964/5 to 1978/9)	+0.852	−0.824

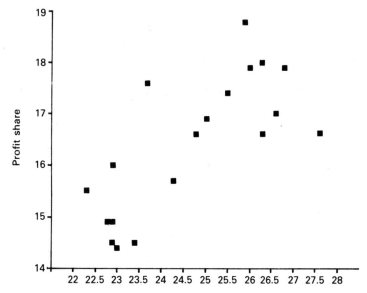

Figure 2.11: Australia: scatter plot of investment share and profit share

income ratio and the profit share, and a powerful inverse relationship with the share of employee compensation.

Japan

There is no part of the post-war period in which a significant amount of demand-deficient unemployment was experienced in Japan. Our investigation was therefore confined (as with the United States) to the relationship between the investment ratio and relative shares; again no data were available for the inter-war years. The results are shown in Table 2.9 and Figures 2.12 and 2.13, which reveal a strong positive relation between the investment-income ratio and the shares of *both* corporate profits and employee compensation. In the latter case this simply reflects the strongly upward trend in the share of employed labour as the self-employed joined the ranks of wage and salary earners (see Figure 2.7) The positive relationship with the profit share, which has no such upward tendency, cannot be dismissed as a statistical artefact.

80   *The Theory of Distribution*

Table 2.9: Japan: simple correlation coefficient (r^2) between the share of investment in national income and relative income shares

	Corporate profits	Employee compensation
(1) Unsmoothed data (1952–82)		
Gross investment	+0.475	+0.427
Net investment	+0.243	+0.243
(2) Smoothed data (1954–80)		
Gross investment	+0.456	+0.444
Net investment	+0.526	+0.332

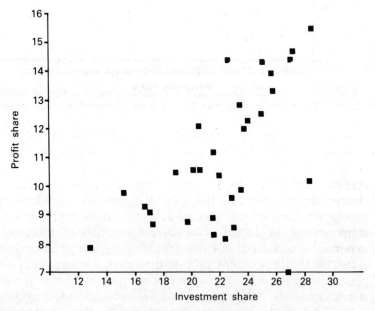

Figure 2.12: Japan: scatter plot of net investment share and profit share

Conclusions
Our results do not provide firm support for any of the theories of relative shares considered in section 2.1 of this paper. There is little evidence of the long-run stability in

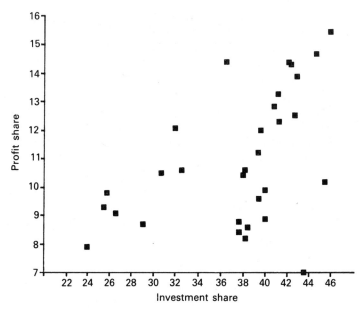

Figure 2.13: Japan: scatter plot of gross investment shares and profit share

shares predicted by the neoclassical model, while pro-cyclical fluctuations in the profit share and counter-cyclical changes in the labour share can be accounted for in non-neoclassical terms (see Appendix II of this chapter). Some support for neoclassical analysis does come from the British experience reported in Table 2.5, where it appears that since 1945 shares varied most abruptly in (disequilibrium) periods of high unemployment. But the inter-war experience is not especially favourable to the neoclassical argument.

Post-Keynesian theory has mixed fortunes. The United Kingdom evidence cited above is inconsistent with the implications drawn from Post-Keynesian analysis in section 2.1. The relationship between the investment–income ratio and relative shares is both inconclusive and puzzling. It is inconclusive, in that the United Kingdom and the United States yield results which are inconsistent with the Post-Keynesian model, and are completely opposed to those for

Australia and Japan. It is puzzling, because we would have expected the United Kingdom and Australia to have been ranged against the United States and Japan, since they have much stronger labour movements with a presumably greater ability to resist the real wage reductions implied by increased investment expenditures at full employment. That is to say, a Marxian variant of Post-Keynesian theory would suggest the incorporation in the model of a 'worker resistance' factor tending to offset the negative impact of an increased investment ratio on the labour share. It is difficult to believe that Australian workers are less able to resist than their American counterparts; yet this is what our results imply. The conclusion is inescapable: none of the theories considered offers a satisfactory explanation of recent developments in relative income shares.

APPENDIX I: DISTRIBUTIVE SHARES OVER THE CYCLE

There exists considerable evidence for several economies over many decades that the share of wages and (to a lesser extent) salaries, fluctuates counter-cyclically, increasing in periods of depression and declining during upswings. Conversely, the profit component of property income is subject to powerful pro-cyclical influences (King and Regan 1976: 17–18). A plausible explanation is illustrated in Figure 2.14, which is loosely derived from the work of the late P.W.S. Andrews and also has affinities with more recent Post-Keynesian analysis (Andrews 1949; King 1986).

In Figure 2.14 the suffixes D, N and B refer respectively to depression, normal and boom conditions, as reflected in the strength of product demand (D_D, D_N and D_B). The typical manufacturing firm faces constant average variable costs over the entire relevant range of output; it will not produce more than Q_B, but instead add to its order book and prolong delivery times. Average fixed costs are represented, as in conventional theory, by a rectangular hyperbola, and average total costs therefore decline right

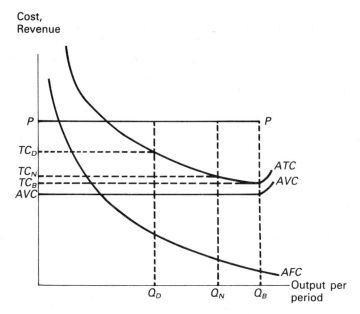

Figure 2.14: The 'representative firm' in depression and boom

up to Q_B. The firm sets its price by adding a constant unit mark-up (constituting its gross profit margin) to average variable cost, and will supply any quantity of output which is demanded (up to Q_B) at that price. The price line *PP* is in effect the firm's short-run supply curve (and *not*, as some of Andrews's critics mistakenly thought, its demand curve). Net profits per unit of output are given by the vertical distance between *PP* and the average total cost curve. If, for example, demand should be given by D_N, so that the firm is able to sell the 'normal' level of output Q_N, its unit profits will equal PTC_N, and total profits will be PTC_N multiplied by Q_N; they are equal to the 'normal' profits which it believes to be the maximum it can earn without provoking entry by potential competitors.

In depressions, average total cost will increase as output falls, and the net profit margin declines to PTC_D, while in boom conditions the reverse occurs and net profits per unit of output rise to PTC_B. At the level of the entire economy (and ignoring imports), raw material costs can be dissolved into the incomes of their respective producers. All variable costs can thus be represented as wage and salary incomes, to which must be added (in calculating total labour income) a proportion of fixed costs, paid as salaries to 'overhead labour'. Similarly, aggregate gross property incomes are given by the net profit margin, plus the relevant proportion of fixed costs (representing depreciation of capital). Assuming that the ratio of overhead labour to depreciation is constant over the cycle, it is clear from Figure 2.14 that there will be pronounced pro-cyclical fluctuations in property income, while labour income will fluctuate counter-cyclically.

The model is anti-neoclassical not only in its rejection of the traditional maximizing (marginal revenue equals marginal cost) model of price and output determination, but also—and more pertinently—in its assumptions concerning the behaviour of productivity over the cycle. It is implicit in the shape of the cost curves in Figure 2.14 that the productivity of variable labour is constant, while that of overhead labour moves pro-cyclically. This is almost certainly inconsistent with the shape of orthodox marginal product curves, but it does appear to accord with the experience of the 1930s. In the United Kingdom, Sweden and Germany (though not in the United States) real wages rose sharply between 1929 and 1933 because money wages declined much less rapidly than the price level. The resulting large rise in real wage costs to employers gave rise to a major increase in unit labour costs which was only reversed when, in the course of the recovery, productivity grew very fast indeed (Bonnell 1981; see also Ch.3 in this book).

This can be expressed in simple algebra. Let w^* represent real wage costs; L, the number of workers employed or the number of hours worked; Y, gross domestic product; and APL $(=Y/L)$, average labour productivity. Then real unit labour costs are given by $w^*/APL = w^*L/Y$, which is closely related to the labour share in gross income. The evidence suggests that the labour share rose in the depression years of the early 1930s partly because of a rise in w^* but chiefly due to a collapse in APL as output fell. Labour's share fell in the recovery after 1933 predominantly owing to a rapid increase in APL.

APPENDIX II

We start from equation (5) in the text of the paper:

$$I = s_p P + s_w W \tag{5}$$

I = investment
P = total profits
W = total wages
s_p = average propensity to save of capitalists
s_c = average propensity to save of workers

If $s_p = 1$, $s_w = 0$, and $I = P$; and
if $I = f(C)$, $f'(C) > O$, C = consumption and $W = C$

Then

$$P = I = f(W) \text{ with } \frac{dP}{dW} > 0 \tag{6}$$

Moreover

$$Y = W + P = W + f(W) \tag{7}$$

So that

$$\frac{W}{Y} = \frac{W}{W + f(W)} = \frac{1}{1 + \dfrac{f(W)}{W}} \tag{8}$$

and

$$\frac{d\frac{W}{Y}}{dW} = \frac{-1}{\left[1 + \frac{f(W)}{W}\right]^2}\left[\frac{f'(W)}{W} - \frac{f(W)}{W^2}\right] \qquad (9)$$

Three cases must be considered:

(a) if $f'(W)$ is large (investment is very sensitive to consumption)

$$\frac{d\frac{W}{Y}}{dW} < 0$$

(b) if $f'(W)$ is small:

$$\frac{d\frac{W}{Y}}{dW} > 0$$

(c) if $f'(W) < 0$ (investment is discouraged by wage rises):

$$\frac{d\frac{W}{Y}}{d\dot{W}} > 0 \text{ but larger than in case (b).}$$

Part II

Distribution, Employment and Economic Policy

3 Trends and Cyclical Changes in Real Wages, Productivity and Distribution of Income during the 1930s

S.M. Bonnell and R.J. Rimmer

The question of the influence on real wages of periods of boom and depression has a long history. But we need not go further back than the period of the 'eighties and 'nineties of the last century. (Keynes 1939: 35)

Keynes went on to canvass some factors worthy of further analysis in the light of his own reconsideration of the simple neoclassical proposition of an inverse relationship between wages and employment. Among these were that cyclical linkages between output prices, nominal and real wages, foreign and domestic prices, and changes in output, costs and in the profit share warranted 'statistical' investigation (Keynes 1939: 50–1).

During the mid-1970s, when nominal wage growth was very rapid in many developed economies, the OECD raised these same issues and conducted some statistical analysis in support of the view that much of the weakness in employment at that time was attributable to shifts in the distribution of real income away from profits (OECD 1977). Perhaps because Australia exhibited, over the period 1972 to 1975, the largest gap between the growth rates of real wages and productivity of the countries studied by the OECD, an intense debate developed there on the measure of real wage 'gaps'. (For accounts of the debate see CAER 1978; Bonnell 1979; Snape 1981). These measurements were central to the policy debate on whether demand stimulus or real wage reduction was the appropriate policy to deal with the unemployment of the time.

In a policy-oriented paper, Tobin (1984) observed that the coexistence of unemployment with high real wages does not permit discrimination between Keynesian and classical unemployment and that wage 'gaps', in the presence of unemployment, do not deny the efficacy of demand stimulation for the 1980s.

Our aim in this paper is to examine the course of real wages, employment and unemployment and shifts in factor shares of output in a number of countries during the 1930s. We aim to assess whether in that period the recovery was dependent on a prior reduction in real wage costs or the closure of the wage gap. In the next section we trace the recent development of the measurement of real wage cost. A series of tables containing indexes of selected measures of real wages, employment and unemployment for eleven countries are presented and analysed in section 3.3. Our concluding remarks are contained in section 3.4.

3.1 METHODOLOGY: THE DEVELOPMENT OF SOME MEASURES OF LABOUR COST

The theoretical proposition that the demand for labour is inversely related to the real wage is presented as a fundamental principle in basic texts. Given perfect competition in product and factor markets, profit maximizing behaviour induces firms to choose output levels and employ factors until marginal products are equated with the real value of factor rewards. For the neoclassical short run, labour demand functions may be written as

$$L_d = f(w/p) \qquad (1)$$

where L_d denotes the demand for labour, w is the average money wage and p is the price deflator.

In the tradition of the doubts raised by Keynes and his contemporaries at the end of the 1930s, Otani set out to test the conventional neoclassical view. He chose a wholesale price index as his deflator of nominal wages to reflect the concept of the real wage measured as a cost rather than as an income. Otani's data were for fourteen countries. In nine of these countries he obtained statistically significant coefficients. Six were supportive of the conventional view. His results for Germany, the Netherlands and the United States, while not statistically significant, produced positive correlation between proportional changes in real wages and employment (Otani 1978).

That a simple measure of real wage cost as in equation (1) above may not be the appropriate one, gained currency during the mid-1970s. The underlying notion was that despite nominal wage and price growth, constant real wages could be observed in the context of a deterioration in the labour market. With constant real wages, a fall in labour productivity would raise real labour cost per unit of output. In such circumstances, the constant real wage would be uncorrelated with changing employment despite a possible underlying neoclassical relationship between labour cost and employment. In this sense the growth in the real wage, measured as a cost, came to be compared with the growth in labour productivity. What was being sought was a measure of the gap between the growth rates of wages per worker and output per worker. In its *Economic Outlook* of July 1977, the OECD produced data on developments in real wages, measured as an income, and productivity for the period 1960–76 for sixteen countries (OECD 1977: 62–3). The graphical analysis of the data showed that for all but three of the countries 'the gap widened with increases varying between six per cent in Sweden and the Netherlands, 12–13 per cent in Austria, Finland, Denmark and Japan and 20 per cent in Australia' (OECD 1977: 64).

In the debate of the late 1970s it seems that at least some participants had in mind an employment relationship of the form:

$$L_d = f(w/p, q/L), \qquad (2)$$

in which the simplest neoclassical labour demand function was amended for the growth in labour productivity. Here q is real output and L is total employment. The OECD charts seemed to imply that equation (2) could be written as:

$$L_d = f(w/p - q/L),   (3)$$

where the difference between the terms w/p and q/L represented the wage 'gap'. The work at OECD stimulated an intense measurement debate in Australia. [1] At this stage the theoretical basis for the 'gap' measurement was largely ignored. Both in the annual OECD review of the Australian economy and at the forum of the National Wage Case hearings in Australia, the measurements of the 'gap' became an evaluation of the quotient:

$$(w/p) / (q/L).   (4)$$

Rearranging this expression reveals that the debate had slipped into a discussion of shifts in the share of wages in national output.[2]

In the theoretical context of equation (1) a wage gap should be a comparison of the measured real wage cost and the marginal product of labour. Objections to the use of the average product (q/L) as a proxy for the marginal product were raised by Gruen (1978) and Snape (1981). Explicit attention was given by Sachs (1983) to some circumstances in which the marginal product would be satisfactorily proxied by the average product, and also to the theoretical linkage between labour demand and the wage gap. Under the three assumptions that the production function is Cobb-Douglas, firms are not demand constrained and they remain on their production frontier, he was able to write labour demand as a function of a wage gap measure. Sachs took as his wage-gap measure the departure of a normalized labour share from the level it would have had at full employment (Sachs 1983: 261–2).

The preceding discussion includes reference to a number of indicators of changes in labour cost. In this paper we endeavour to relate changes in employment to three of these measures for eleven countries over the period 1929–38. Our primary aim is review the course of real wages over the 1930s depression and the subsequent recovery years. In particular, we attempt to discover whether the employment recovery was preceded or accompanied by falling real wage cost, whether or not real unit labour cost—the wage share—was falling, and what the role of productivity over the period was. Such an analysis is in the spirit of the statistical investigations suggested by Keynes in 1939. The present work extends the research of Bonnell (1981). In the four countries included in that earlier study of the 1930s recovery occurred in the labour market without a prior removal of a real wage gap. In addition, in all four countries there was a marked acceleration in productivity as recovery began.

We first investigáte the relationship between employment and the simple measure of the real wage as in equation (1). We take as our measure of p an implicit deflator for national product to reflect the idea of the real wage as a cost rather than the real wage as an income (although both the cost and income measures are included in our tables). Subsequently, we test the linkage between employment and real unit labour cost defined in expression (4). As already noted, this amounts to correlating the wage share with employment. Although we obtain correlations between employment and labour cost, we do not estimate labour demand equations.

With our third indicator of changes in labour cost we explore the consequences of fluctuations in the terms of trade for productivity. This was done in the OECD studies (OECD 1977, 1978). Sharp changes in the relationship between the prices of imports and exports impinge on the growth of distributable real output by causing variations in the quantity of imports that can be purchased with a given volume of domestic output. The form of our adjustment is to add to real output q an amount A given by

$$A = X/P_m - X/P_x, \qquad (5)$$

where X is the current value of exports and P_m and P_x are respectively implicit price deflators for imports and exports.[3] Here we limit our analysis of the terms of trade adjustment to a comparison of indexes of real unit labour cost with and without the terms of trade adjustment. Clearly, in economies where trade shares of national output are very low, such an adjustment would be negligible. For the 1930s this was the case for the United States, and for that economy we have not made an adjustment for changes in the income terms of trade.

3.2 RESULTS: LABOUR COST AND EMPLOYMENT IN ELEVEN COUNTRIES DURING THE DEPRESSION AND RECOVERY OF THE 1930s

In this section we begin our analysis of labour cost and employment relationships in eleven countries during the period 1929–38. The first four countries discussed—the United States, the United Kingdom, Germany and Sweden—were those analysed in the earlier research of Bonnell (1981). Here, we extend the list of countries to include another four small open European economies —Norway, Finland, the Netherlands and Switzerland—and three of the 'dominions' of the United Kingdom—Canada, Australia and New Zealand. For our data indexes, the base period adopted, with the exceptions of Norway and Sweden, was the single year 1929. Our preferred base would have been a weighted average of say, the five years 1925–9. However, for most data series, the first available year was 1929. The onset of the Second World War and the involvement of most of our countries in the war, precludes extending the analysis beyond 1938. We attempted to minimize the number of separate sources of data. The price deflator used to convert nominal wages to real wage cost was in each case the implicit price index corresponding to the measure of output at constant prices used in the productivity calculation. This preserved the correspondence between real unit labour cost and the wage share of output.

An underlying reason for shifts in the wage share over time could be a tendency for changes to occur in the ratio of wage and salary earners to total employment. In our work we measure labour cost per employee whereas productivity is generally calculated on an employed person basis. Further, our work suffers from using per capita rather than per hour measures in both the average cost and productivity calculations.

For all but three countries, we estimated the effect of changes in the income terms of trade on productivity. That is, we implemented equation (5). As we noted in the previous section, the low trade share in the United States did not warrant such an adjustment. In fact, over our whole survey period the largest adjustment would have been only 1 per cent of real GDP in 1934. In the cases of Switzerland and the Netherlands we were unable to obtain sufficient trade data to calculate the adjustment.

The remainder of this section is devoted to an analysis of our data for the eleven countries included in our survey. For most of the countries the layout of the tables is as follows. The first two indexes are the real wage measured as an income and a cost. Under the 'real unit labour cost' (wage share) heading, the unadjusted index is based on equation (4) whereas the trade-adjusted index incorporates the amount A obtained from expression (5). In each table there is an index of employment. Unless otherwise noted, all indexes are based on 1929. The final column is, except for Finland, the unemployment rate.

An observation can be made concerning the pattern of the real wage measured as an income. This is shown as the first index in each of the eleven tables. For most of the countries, in the early 1930s average real wage incomes remained at or above their base period levels. A notable exception is for Germany, where in 1930 real wage income was 6.4 percentage points below its level of the previous year. However, average real income recovered quickly and hovered above the base period level throughout the rest of the period. In New Zealand real wage income was below its 1929 level between 1934 and 1936.

The Large Economies
UNITED STATES In the largest economy real wage cost and employment both fell by over 15 per cent between 1929 and 1933. Nominal wages fell by around 30 per cent while

prices fell by about 16 per cent. Real unit labour cost grew by 1.5 per cent per annum on average. Productivity fell sharply to 78 per cent of its base value by 1933. Unemployment peaked in 1933. The trough in employment occurred in that year. While unemployment began to fall in 1934, real wage cost began an upward trend. Concurrently with the reduction in unemployment, employment growth occurred. Productivity was increasing in each year from 1934 to 1936. Real unit labour cost continued its upward trend in the recovery phase (Table 3.1). The coincidence of falling employment and real wages in the early 1930s and their simultaneous upward paths in the recovery do not support a simple neoclassical explanation of the labour market. Using slightly different data, the same broad result was found in Bonnell (1981).

Simple correlations were calculated between employment and (i) real wage cost and (ii) real unit labour cost. These results for all eleven countries are set out in Appendix Tables 1 and 2 respectively. The striking pattern of the 'tracking' of real wage cost and employment for the United States is confirmed in Appendix Table 1 at the end of this chapter. There we see that the positive correlation between the variables is high and statistically significant. We computed the correlation coefficient for the values of the employment and real wage cost variables using the data in Bonnell (1981). The degree of correlation was lower but was statistically significant.[4]

UNITED KINGDOM The pattern in the United Kindom was different. Real wages rose during the downturn. Indeed, as can be seen in Table 3.2, all four measures of the real cost of labour remained above the base period value throughout the period. The real wage measured as a cost rose by 14 per cent between 1929 and 1934. Underlying this increase the average nominal wage fell by 4 per cent but prices fell by 18 per cent. That is, the implicit price deflator for GNP fell more than four times as far as nominal wages. The real unit labour cost index reached its peak of 119.6 in 1933, but rapid productivity growth in the first year of the upswing allowed real unit labour cost to fall, in spite of continued growth in the real wage. Favourable

Table 3.1: Labour cost and employment: United States, 1929–38

Year	Real wage Income[a]	Real wage Cost[b]	Real unit labour cost Unadjusted[c]	Employment[d]	Unemployment[d] (%)
1929	100.0	100.0	100.0	100.0	3.2
1930	100.0	97.4	101.9	95.6	8.9
1931	102.4	97.6	103.0	89.4	16.3
1932	100.1	90.1	102.6	82.3	24.1
1933	99.0	82.4	105.5	82.4	25.2
1934	99.6	96.1	104.6	87.2	22.0
1935	101.2	102.5	106.7	90.2	20.3
1936	104.3	107.8	106.2	95.2	17.0
1937	106.9	111.9	110.5	99.7	14.3
1938	106.4	109.8	107.0	95.5	19.1

Sources and notes:
(a) Average money wage earnings including supplements from Phelps Brown (1968: 450) deflated by the Consumer Price Index (1914=100) from *Historical Statistics of the United States* (1975)
(b) Money Wages as in (a) above deflated by the GNP deflator in Phelps Brown (1968: 450).
(c) Real wage cost in (b) above divided by an index of labour productivity derived from GNP at 1958 prices and total employment (with unemployment accounted for) from *Historical Statistics of the United States* (1975).
(d) From *Historical Statistics of the United States* (1975).

changes in the UK's terms of trade are reflected in the trade adjusted measure of real unit labour cost at the start of our period.

Unemployment in the United Kingdom rose until 1932. Employment fell until 1931. The upturn in the labour market occurred while real wage cost went on rising and while real unit labour cost was approaching its peak. On a simple neoclassical view, the employment recovery should not have preceded a reduction in labour cost. Despite evidence of the co-existence of high real wages with unemployment, it would, as Tobin suggests, be difficult to rule out the presence of demand deficient unemployment in the early depression years. However, the positive relationship between real wage cost growth and employment

Table 3.2: Labour cost and employment: United Kingdom, 1929–38

Year	Real wage		Real unit labour cost		Employment[d]	Unemployment[c]
	Income[a]	Cost[a]	Unadjusted[b]	Trade Adjusted[c]		(%)
1929	100.0	100.0	100.0	100.0	100.0	10.4
1930	103.6	105.9	104.7	93.6	97.7	16.1
1931	117.1	112.7	110.0	111.9	95.0	21.3
1932	121.1	110.8	114.5	111.9	95.4	22.1
1933	127.1	112.8	119.6	116.6	97.8	19.9
1934	126.9	114.1	114.6	111.9	101.1	16.7
1935	125.0	111.2	114.1	111.4	103.3	15.5
1936	120.6	111.0	112.8	110.7	107.1	13.1
1937	111.8	104.2	105.7	104.4	111.2	10.5
1938	112.4	108.9	102.6	100.5	111.4	12.6

Sources and notes:
(a) Average annual money wage earnings deflated by the Cost of Living Index and the GNP deflator respectively from Phelps Brown (1968: 446).
(b) Real wage cost index in (a) above divided by a productivity index based on GNP at 1938 prices from Mitchell (1975) and total employment from Table 1 of Chapman (1953).
(c) Based on (b) and exports at current prices and import and export price deflators (1937=100) from Mitchell (1975).
(d) From Table 1 Chapman (1953).
(e) From the *ILO Year Book of Labour Statistics* (1940).

was very short-lived. The appendix tables show that the correlations between the real labour cost variables and employment were not significant.

GERMANY The severity of the downturn in the labour market in Germany was even more pronounced than it was in the United States. Despite having roughly half of the population of the United States, there were 1.9 million unemployed in Germany in 1930 compared with 1.6 million in the United States (Kindleberger 1973: 139). For the latter country, we detected a strong positive correlation between employment and real wage cost. For Germany the correlation is also very strong. But on both the simple measure of real wage cost as well as real unit labour cost, correlations are negative. That is, they provide support for the neoclassical case.

An indication of the effect of the severe deflation pursued by the German government is the fall in prices of 32 per cent between 1929 and 1932. Coupled with falling nominal wages, the real wage cost index in Table 3.3 shows a peak of 128.7 in 1932. Between 1929 and 1932, the real wage and real unit labour cost indexes moved together. The unemployment rate reached its peak in 1932. Employment began to recover in 1933. During the upturn, productivity growth was substantial and the real unit labour cost index fell rapidly. By contrast, real wage cost changed little. The strength of the relationship between real unit labour cost (the wage share) and employment is shown in Appendix Table 2. In Germany between 1929 and 1938, 86 per cent of the variation in employment is explained by changes in real unit labour cost. The real wage cost variable explains 53 per cent of the variation in employment (see Appendix Table 1).

The importance of Germany's trading relations in the early 1930s may be summarized as follows. '(Germany's) . . . prosperity in 1926–29 was largely financed by foreign short-term borrowing. Indeed, when in 1930–31, these loans were called in the country plunged into a recession aggravated by the loss of its export markets due to the trade war.' (Saint-Etienne 1984: 34). Germany faced

Table 3.3: Labour cost and employment: Germany, 1929–38

	Real Wage		Real unit labour cost		Employment[e]	Unemployment[f]
	Income[a]	Cost[b]	Unadjusted[c]	Trade adjusted[d]		(%)
1929	100.0	100.0	100.0	100.0	100.0	9.3
1930	93.6	103.9	103.9	102.2	91.7	15.3
1931	106.5	107.0	110.1	105.3	86.5	23.3
1932	102.8	128.7	128.7	121.7	82.4	30.1
1933	100.9	111.9	107.9	102.9	85.7	26.3
1934	100.0	103.8	100.0	96.9	95.0	14.9
1935	100.9	100.2	89.3	87.2	99.2	11.6
1936	102.8	104.2	89.9	88.1	102.3	8.3
1937	100.0	100.3	83.0	81.6	106.2	4.6
1938	104.6	103.4	83.6	81.5	109.3	2.1

Sources and notes:
(a) Average annual money wage earnings deflated by the Cost of Living Index, Phelps Brown (1968: 438).
(b) Earnings as in (a) above deflated by the GNP deflator in Phelps Brown (1968: 438).
(c) Real wage cost as in (b) above divided by an index of productivity in industry (real output per occupied person) Phelps Brown (1968).
(d) As in (c) above with exports at current prices from *UN Year Book of International Trade Statistics* (1950) and import and export price deflators from the *United Nations Statistical Year Book* (1948).
(e) Phelps Brown (1968: 382).
(f) Registered unemployed as in *ILO Year Book of Labour Statistics* (1940).

extreme difficulties with world trade conditions—the devalu-
ation of sterling, the gold bloc reaction to that, the intense
tariff war of the United Kingdom and its dominions, the
foreclosure of loans (Kindleberger 1973). In view of this it
might be expected that an adjustment for changes in the
income terms of trade would raise German real unit labour
cost growth. On the contrary, the trade adjustment (see
equation 5), lowers the index of real unit labour cost,
especially in 1931. The effect of falling trade volumes is
outweighed by the terms of trade price effect of a much
more rapid fall of import than export prices.

Five Small Open European Economies
Our results for the smaller European countries are set out
in Tables 3.4 to 3.8. The correlation coefficients for the
relationship between employment and labour cost are
significant for two countries—Norway (real unit labour
cost) and Switzerland (real wage cost and real unit labour
cost). However, for Norway the results favour a non-
neoclassical explanation. For Switzerland, there is support
for the neoclassical case when the real wage cost measure
is used. But there is, on the other hand, a positive
correlation between falling real unit labour cost and
decreasing employment.

In all five countries output prices fell with the largest
falls in the Netherlands (18 per cent) and Switzerland (20
per cent). Nominal wages fell in all five countries. The
index of real wage cost stayed above its base period value
everywhere except Finland. Employment fell until 1933 in
the Scandinavian countries. In Switzerland the employment
pattern was different. Employment was more than 20 per
centage points below its 1929 level between 1932 and
1936. In the Netherlands employment remained about 15
percentage points below its base level over that same
period. Switzerland and the Netherlands did not show any
sign of labour market recovery before the late 1930s.

SWEDEN In the Swedish case there is the example of
roughly constant real wage cost after 1931 (the base period
for this table is 1930). Real wage cost rose rapidly in the

downturn from 1929. Employment recovered strongly after 1933 in spite of real wage cost being about 3 per cent above the base period level. Of more interest is the course of real unit labour cost. After 1931 productivity grew at the rate of 3 per cent per annum and this resulted in real unit labour cost—the wage share—falling while employment recovered (Table 3.4) Despite the openness of the economy and the trade linkages to the largest economies in this study, the terms-of-trade adjustment was negligible in its influence on productivity.

NORWAY AND FINLAND The unemployment rate was comparatively high in Norway throughout the period of review. The employment recovery began between 1931 and 1932 and continued until 1937. Real wage cost rose, as employment grew, until 1934. Real unit labour cost grew continuously from 1931 with its most rapid increases being in 1932 and 1933, the start of the labour market recovery (Table 3.5). In Finland real wage cost changed little. As in Norway, the downturn was marked by real unit labour cost and employment falling together. In the recovery phase in Finland the changes in the labour market are abrupt. In the year to 1934 employment grew by 12 percentage points and the number unemployed fell by 7,000 (out of 17,000) in a single year (Table 3.6).

THE NETHERLANDS It was observed above that recovery began very late in the Netherlands labour market. In Table 3.7 the unemployment rate is shown to stay at around 30 per cent of the workforce for six years. Employment fell steadily in the downturn and changed little in the years from 1932 to 1936 despite a sharp reduction in real unit labour cost after 1931. Although real wage cost fell after 1932, it remained above its base throughout the survey period. The underlying rapid productivity growth was responsible for the fall in real unit labour cost—especially in 1932—however this was not accompanied by employment growth.

SWITZERLAND Some remarks were made at the start of this section on the weakness of employment in Switzerland.

Table 3.4: Labour cost and employment: Sweden, 1929–38

Year	Real wage		Real unit labour cost		Employment[c]	Unemployment[f] (%)
	Income[a]	Cost[b]	Unadjusted[c]	Trade Adjusted[d]		
1929	94.1	94.2	97.6	n.a	100.0	10.7
1930	100.0	100.0	100.0	100.0	99.8	12.2
1931	103.2	103.2	104.3	103.6	91.3	17.2
1932	102.3	103.1	100.8	102.5	86.0	22.8
1933	100.5	102.7	98.0	99.9	85.0	23.7
1934	100.5	102.0	95.6	96.6	91.6	18.9
1935	101.4	101.1	95.5	97.1	96.9	16.1
1936	101.2	100.8	93.6	94.9	102.1	13.6
1937	101.0	101.2	94.2	94.9	109.1	11.6
1938	104.6	105.2	95.1	93.7	110.0	11.8

Sources and notes:

n.a = underlying data were not available.

(a) Index of hourly money wages (1929=100) from *The International Labour Review* (1943), deflated by the Cost of Living Index, Phelps Brown (1968).

(b) Wage index as in (a) above deflated by IPI for GDP in Mitchell (1975).

(c) Real wage cost in (b) above divided by an index of labour productivity derived from GDP at constant (1913) prices in Mitchell (1975) and an index of employment (wage earners) from the *ILO Year Book of Labour Statistics* (1940).

(d) As in (c) above with exports at current prices and import and export price deflators from the *UN Year Book of International Trade Statistics* (1950).

(e) *ILO Yearbook of Labour Statistics* (1940).

(f) *ILO Yearbook of Labour Statistics* (1940), derived from trade-union returns.

Table 3.5: Labour cost and employment: Norway, 1930–38

| Year | Real wage | | Real unit labour cost | | Employment[c] | Unemployment[e] |
	Income[a]	Cost[b]	Unadjusted[c]	Trade Adjusted[d]		(%)
1930	100.0	100.0	100.0	100.0	100.0	22.3
1931	101.3	100.7	87.1	87.2	79.6	30.8
1932	105.6	99.9	94.3	94.2	91.4	33.4
1933	104.6	107.6	100.8	100.5	92.8	30.7
1934	105.7	107.1	102.3	102.0	98.0	25.3
1935	103.4	104.9	102.9	102.3	105.8	18.8
1936	104.3	103.8	104.0	103.5	115.2	20.0
1937	103.8	100.7	104.4	104.2	124.4	22.0
1938	111.1	108.8	107.2	107.3	121.0	18.3

Sources and notes:
(a) Daily wage rates for men from the *International Labour Review* (1943) deflated by the CPI—All Groups, Mitchell (1975).
(b) Wages as in (a) above, deflated by the IPI for GDP, Mitchell (1975).
(c) Real wage cost in (b) divided by an index of productivity. The productivity index was derived from GDP at constant (1910) prices Mitchell (1975) and an index of manufacturing employment from the *ILO Year Book of Labour Statistics* (1940).
(d) Based on (c) above and exports at current prices and import and export price deflators from the *UN Statistical Year Book* (1948).
(e) *ILO Year Book of Labour Statistics* (1940).

Table 3.6: *Labour cost and employment: Finland, 1929-38*

Year	Real wage		Real unit labour cost		Employment [d]	Unemployment [e]
	Income [a]	Cost [a]	Unadjusted [b]	Trade Adjusted [c]		
1929	100.0	100.0	100.0	100.0	100.0	3,877
1930	105.4	103.3	91.6	88.1	87.4	8,009
1931	100.0	97.7	82.7	80.5	78.4	11,495
1932	97.6	95.7	78.4	79.4	76.6	17,351
1933	102.5	99.3	83.0	83.2	84.7	17,139
1934	103.8	98.3	82.3	79.0	97.3	10,011
1935	103.7	97.1	77.2	76.9	95.4	7,163
1936	109.9	99.0	85.9	85.1	111.7	4,796
1937	114.1	98.0	86.6	84.8	125.2	3,695
1938	117.0	102.3	97.4	92.6	129.7	3,602

Sources and notes:
(a) Based on money wages in industry deflated by the CPI All Groups and the IPI derived from current and constant (1929) price estimates of GNP in Mitchell (1975: 784).
(b) Real wage cost divided by productivity derived from GNP at constant (1929) prices in Mitchell (1975) and an index of employment in 'All industries including agriculture', the *ILO Year Book of Labour Statistics* (1940).
(c) Based on (b) above and exports at current prices and import and export price deflators from the *UN Statistical Year Book* (1948).
(d) *ILO Year Book of Labour Statistics* (1940).
(e) Number of registered unemployed from Table VI in the *ILO Year Book of Labour Statistics* (1940).

Table 3.7: *Labour cost and employment: the Netherlands, 1929–38*

| Year | Real wage | | Real unit labour cost | Employment(c) | Unemployment(d) |
	Income(a)	Cost(b)	Unadjusted(c)		(%)
1929	100.0	100.0	100.0	100.0	7.1
1930	108.5	108.6	108.5	102.2	9.7
1931	112.4	113.8	113.6	96.0	18.1
1932	112.0	113.7	104.6	85.3	29.5
1933	107.2	108.8	102.8	85.0	31.0
1934	103.6	105.1	101.7	86.6	32.0
1935	103.8	105.3	96.9	84.2	36.3
1936	105.2	102.8	93.2	85.1	36.3
1937	102.5	100.2	91.7	91.5	29.2
1938	103.6	103.5	94.7	95.4	27.2

Sources and notes:
(a) Weekly wage rates for males (1929=100) from *International Labour Review* (1943) deflated by the Cost of Living Index (1929=100) from Mitchell (1975).
(b) Wage rate as in (a) above deflated by the IPI for GNP in Mitchell (1975).
(c) Real wage cost as in (b) above divided by productivity derived from GNP at constant (1969) prices from Mitchell (1975) and general level of employment, in *ILO Year Book of Labour Statistics* (1940).
(d) Non-farm unemployment from *ILO Year Book of Labour Statistics* (1940).

The usual data are set out in Table 3.8. What is notable is the extent of real wage cost growth after 1930. The peak occurred in 1934, but the index remained well above the 1929 value throughout the 1930s. Real wage cost explains 96 per cent of the variation in employment. This correlation is statistically significant, and negative (see Appendix Table 1). A supporter of the neoclassical position could hardly ask for better evidence for his case. the odd thing about the Swiss data is that an opponent of the neoclassical case could obtain, by using real unit labour cost as the measure, helpful evidence in the form of a statistically significant positive correlation (even although only 50 per cent of the variation is explained; see Appendix Table 2). How is it that the wage share is positively correlated with employment while the real wage is negatively correlated? Obviously the underlying productivity change is the key to the difference. Throughout the period the productivity index always exceeded the real wage cost index. Thus, where real wage cost was rising towards 1934, the productivity growth ensured that real unit labour cost was decreasing then.

The Dominions: Canada, Australia, New Zealand

'You take our manufactures and we'll take your foodstuffs' (Youngson 1963: 116). The dependence of this group of countries on primary production is exemplified in this remark. On some accounts the dominions felt the Depression rather earlier than the larger economies because of the collapse of agricultural prices in 1929 (Kindleberger 1973: 96 and Arndt 1963: 99). For example, in Canada's case, 'depression and subsequent recovery were governed almost entirely by exports' (Kindleberger 1973: 191). However, without denying the importance of the ties to the empire or to the role of agriculture, an Australian economist questions the timing of the impact of the fall in world agricultural prices: 'It should be stressed, however, that these trends in primary commodity prices had little impact on farming income prior to 1929. For example the falling wool prices had come at the very end of the season and had little chance to erode the value of the clip' (Schedvin 1970: 112).

Table 3.8: Labour cost and employment: Switzerland, 1929–38

| Year | Real wage | | Real unit labour cost | Employment[d] | Unemployment[e] |
	Income[a]	Cost[b]	Unadjusted[c]		(%)
1929	100.0	100.0	100.0	100.0	1.8
1930	102.0	101.5	96.2	95.8	3.4
1931	108.6	108.0	97.7	88.7	5.9
1932	116.3	117.0	96.8	78.8	9.1
1933	121.0	120.2	92.0	76.9	10.8
1934	122.5	122.2	94.4	78.1	9.8
1935	120.0	120.6	90.7	76.0	11.8
1936	114.8	117.4	88.6	76.4	13.2
1937	109.4	109.8	93.2	88.0	10.0
1938	110.6	111.0	91.5	86.3	8.6

Sources and notes:
(a) Weighted averages of male and female earnings from the *International Labour Review* (1943) deflated by the CPI from Mitchell (1975).
(b) Earnings as in (a) above deflated by the IPI derived from current and constant (1938) price estimates of Net National Product in Mitchell (1975).
(c) Real wage index in (b) above divided by a productivity index based on NNP at 1938 prices from Mitchell (1975) and total employment in 'Manufacturing', from the *ILO Year Book of Labour Statistics* (1940).
(d) *ILO Year Book of Labour Statistics* (1940), total employment in 'Manufacturing'.
(e) *ILO Year Book of Labour Statistics* (1940), 'Wholly Unemployed'.

In all three countries product price deflators fell sharply at the start of the Depression. However, only in Australia did nominal wages fall faster than prices. Unemployment was not as severe in New Zealand, where it peaked at 9.6 per cent of the labour force in 1934. The peaks came in Canada and Australia a year earlier and were about twice as great in percentage terms.

CANADA In Canada the real wage measured as a cost is shown in Table 3.9 as remaining well above the base value throughout the period. Employment deteriorated until 1933 while real wage cost rose. The steady growth in employment which occurred after 1933 was accompanied by both rises and falls in real wage cost. The increase in real unit labour cost was very great in Canada and happened during the period when employment was falling. All measures of labour cost stayed well above their 1929 values throughout the 1930s.

AUSTRALIA In this study, over the first year of the Depression, Australia (and also the Netherlands) experienced the highest increase in real wage cost. However, Table 3.10 shows that the real wage cost index fell thereafter until 1937 and was below the base value after 1934. Wages fell faster than prices. This may have been related to the 1931 policy of 'equal sacrifice' in which wage cuts were the government's policy intended to reduce domestic costs and improve competitiveness. However, a contemporary observer 'estimated that only about one-half of the wage-earners in the Commonwealth had been subject to the full 10 per cent cut in real wages' (Schedvin 1970: 345). Productivity growth in 1932 and 1934 in particular promoted the steady fall in the index of real unit labour cost. The adverse income terms of trade effect is evident on the trade adjusted real unit labour cost index.

In spite of the steady reduction in real wage cost in the early 1930s, employment continued to fall until 1932. From 1933 employment grew and real labour cost fell. That is, there was a negative correlation between both measures of labour cost and employment. These results, set out in the appended tables, are statistically significant.

Table 3.9: Labour cost and employment: Canada, 1929–38

Year	Real wage		Real unit labour cost		Employment[e]	Unemployment[f]
	Income[a]	Cost[b]	Unadjusted[c]	Trade adjusted[d]		%
1929	100.0	100.0	100.0	100.0	100.0	2.9
1930	101.3	103.2	103.3	103.9	95.9	9.1
1931	108.7	106.1	121.1	123.5	95.4	11.6
1932	111.0	108.6	130.5	133.9	90.2	17.6
1933	110.6	105.2	134.5	136.3	89.6	19.3
1934	110.2	104.9	128.6	129.7	96.3	14.6
1935	112.6	107.3	124.3	125.8	98.2	14.2
1936	112.4	105.9	121.0	121.3	101.2	12.8
1937	117.2	110.8	121.8	122.3	106.9	9.1
1938	119.3	114.2	123.2	123.5	105.7	11.4

Sources and notes:
The data source for this table is Urquhart (1965).
(a) Based on a general index of 'Average Wage Rates' (1949=100) and the CPI—All Groups (1949=100).
(b) As in (a) above, deflated by the IPI for GNE (1949=100).
(c) Real wage cost as in (b) divided by an index of productivity derived from GNE at 1949 prices, and civilian employment.
(d) As in (c) above with exports at current prices and implicit price deflators for imports and exports (1948=100).
(e) Total civilian employment.
(f) Persons without jobs and seeking work as a percentage of the civilian labour force.

Table 3.10: Labour cost and employment: Australia, 1929–38

Year	Real wage		Real unit labour cost		Employment[e]	Unemployment
	Income[a]	Cost[b]	Unadjusted[c]	Trade adjusted[d]		%
1929	100.0	100.0	100.0	100.0	100.0	6.7
1930	105.4	108.2	105.4	109.1	96.3	9.8
1931	108.0	107.8	108.9	118.1	89.2	16.4
1932	102.4	106.6	102.4	113.3	87.3	19.7
1933	103.1	103.4	100.7	110.4	92.4	18.9
1934	99.1	101.9	97.0	99.6	96.8	16.0
1935	98.8	98.2	97.1	103.8	101.2	13.9
1936	99.2	96.6	93.8	96.4	104.8	11.0
1937	100.3	95.9	89.3	90.9	107.4	8.8
1938	104.1	97.9	92.8	96.3	111.1	7.5

Sources and notes:
Unless otherwise noted, the data source for this table is Butlin (1984).
(a) Average earnings deflated by the Cost of Living Index (1929=100) in the *International Labour Review* (1945).
(b) Average earnings deflated by the IPI for GDP (1966/7=100).
(c) Real wage cost in (b) above divided by an index of labour productivity derived from GDP at 1966/7 prices and civilian employment.
(d) As in (c) above with exports at current and constant (1966/7) prices and the import price deflator (1966/7=100).
(e) Total civilian employment.

NEW ZEALAND Real wage cost rose very little in New Zealand at the onset of the Depression. In Table 3.11 it can be seen that it remained below the 1929 value until 1937. The employment downturn ceased in 1931–2 and grew very strongly after that. Although productivity growth ensured that the real unit labour cost index was below the index of real wage cost in 1930 and 1931, the deterioration was such that productivity weakness caused the former index to be above its base value from 1933 onwards. As for Australia, external factors caused the trade-adjusted measure of labour cost to grow more quickly. Statistically significant correlations were found between the first two measures of labour cost and employment. In contrast to our finding for Australia, these correlations are positive.

3.3 CONCLUDING REMARKS

There was a great diversity in the economic experiences of the eleven countries in this study. The course and impact of the Depression varied widely. Governments' reactions to the problems of the slump were far from uniform. The size and patterns of displacements of real wage cost and in the wage shares (real unit labour costs) from their base values differed. Our results give no clear picture as to whether a moderation in labour cost—however measured—was a precondition for recovery in the labour market. In six of the countries (including the United Kingdom, Germany and Australia) the employment expansions occurred while both the index of real wage costs and the wage share remained above their 1929 values. In four countries—the United States, Sweden, Switzerland and New Zealand—one or other of the labour cost measures remained high. Of this group, only the Swiss labour market did not regain its 1929 employment level.

From our regressions we observed that there was (statistically significant) evidence of both positive and negative correlations between labour cost and employment. For Australia, Germany and Switzerland, negative correlations were found between real wage cost and employment;

Table 3.11: Labour cost and employment: New Zealand, 1929–38

Year	Real wage		Real unit labour cost		Employment[e]	Unemployment
	Income[a]	Cost[b]	Unadjusted[c]	Trade adjusted[d]		%
1929	100.0	100.0	100.0	100.0	100.0	5.1
1930	103.1	101.2	98.0	100.1	94.0	5.7
1931	105.6	97.3	93.0	98.9	83.1	7.6
1932	100.0	93.1	96.8	104.6	83.1	8.0
1933	102.5	97.1	103.7	109.7	88.0	9.3
1934	95.1	97.3	101.2	105.9	95.2	9.6
1935	92.8	95.8	103.6	108.0	104.8	7.7
1936	94.2	97.4	105.2	107.2	115.7	7.7
1937	103.3	110.5	106.7	107.2	122.9	6.3
1938	109.5	113.2	n.a.	n.a.	n.a.	5.0

Sources and notes

n.a. = underlying data were not available

(a) Based on a weighted average of the earnings of men and women,' *International Labour Review* (1943) and an index of Retail Prices of All Goods (1929=100).

(b) Wages as in (a) above, deflated by the IPI for GDP (1955 prices) Butlin (1984).

(c) Real wage cost in (b) above divided by an index of productivity based on GDP at 1955 prices from Butlin (1984) and an index of employment in manufacturing from the *ILO Year Book of Labour Statistics* (1940).

(d) As in (c) above with exports at current prices and import and export price deflators from the *UN Statistical Year Book* (1948).

(e) Employment in manufacturing from the *ILO Year Book of Labour Statistics* (1940).

for Australia and Germany the same result was obtained using the wage share measure of cost. Support for a non-neoclassical view on the functioning of the labour market was obtained for the United States, New Zealand, Norway and Switzerland. For the first two countries the result came from the real wage cost measure.[5]

In six of the eleven countries there was a boost in average labour productivity in the upturn. This occurred in all but one of the countries for which the correlations were significant. However, in that case, Swiss productivity growth was rather rapid in the downturn and changed little until towards the end of our survey period. In six of the countries, unemployment fell back to or below its base period level, while the employment index had recovered in eight countries.

Except for the United States, where real wage cost was falling, we observed the coincidence of high unemployment and high real wage costs at the start of the Depression. But none of our evidence would allow us to support or reject the proposition that the real wage was a more important barrier to recovery than was a weakness in demand.

NOTES

1. A survey of the measurement debate and the sensitivity of the 'gap' to data and definitions is contained in Bonnell (1979).
2. Let S_L denote the expression in (4).
   Then:
   $$S_L = (w/p)/(q/L)$$
   $$= (w/p) (L/q)$$
   $$= wL/pq$$
   = share of labour in national output.
3. For a survey of possible forms of the adjustment, see Hibbert (1975).
4. On the Bonnell (1981) data the estimate of b was 0.64 ($t = 2.62$) and r was 0.68.
5. Significant correlations between real unit labour cost and employment in Switzerland and Norway may reflect situations where most of the variation is being caused by changes in productivity.

Appendix Table 1: Simple regression results, employment and real wage cost, 1929–38

Country	a	b	r	$\bar{R}^2$
USA	34.3	0.58* (3.91)	0.81	0.66
UK	137.9	−0.33 (0.70)	−0.24	0.06
Germany	180.5	−0.80* (3.02)	−0.73	0.53
Sweden	135.8	−0.38 (0.37)	−0.13	0.02
Norway (1930–8)	−1.0	1.0 (0.65)	0.24	0.06
Finland	171.0	2.72 (0.36)	0.34	0.12
Netherlands	107.0	−0.15 (0.31)	−0.11	0.01
Switzerland	204.1	−1.06* (13.93)	−0.98	0.96
Canada	31.1	0.63 (1.35)	0.43	0.18
Australia	244.2	−1.43* (4.77)	−0.86	0.74
New Zealand	−87.7	1.88* (2.39)	0.67	0.45

Note: These regressions of the form $Y = a + bX$ were performed with employment as the dependent variable and the real wage measured as a cost as the independent variable. The data were the indexes in Table 3.1 to 3.11. t statistics for b are shown in parentheses and those significant at the 5 per cent level are marked with an asterisk.

Appendix Table 2: Simple regression results, employment and real unit labour cost, 1929–38

Country	a	b	r	$\bar{R}^2$
USA	61.3	0.29 (0.39)	0.14	0.02
UK	138.9	−0.34 (1.05)	−0.35	0.12
Germany	156.1	−0.60* (7.16)	−0.93	0.86
Sweden	243.0	−1.50 (2.01)	−0.58	0.34
Norway (1930–8)	−107.5	2.10* (4.99)	0.87	0.76
Finland	−6.1	1.21 (1.63)	0.50	0.25
Netherlands	57.5	0.33 (1.02)	0.34	0.12
Switzerland	−77.0	1.72* (2.85)	0.71	0.50
Canada	117.8	−0.16 (0.96)	−0.32	0.10
Australia	206.8	−1.10* (4.38)	−0.84	0.71
New Zealand	−159.7	2.56* (3.91)	0.81	0.66

Note: These regressions of the form $Y = a + bx$ were performed with employment as the dependent variable and the real wage measured as a cost as the independent variable. The data were the indexes in Table 3.1 to 3.11. t statistics for b are shown in parentheses and those significant at the 5 per cent level are marked with an asterisk.

4 A Case Study on Functional Income Shares and the Distribution of Income between Investment and Consumption in 1965–85*

A.H.G.M. Spithoven

There are several arguments in favour of wage restraint, reduced social benefits and less government expenditure. In the Netherlands all are reiterated in policy statements related to unemployment. As in most other Western countries, unemployment has become a serious and persistent problem in the Netherlands. Most employers attribute it to wages which exceed the market-clearing rate, and plea for an overall lowering of wages. They claim that, by the marginal productivity relationship, employment will rise when labour becomes cheaper. The argument of diminishing marginal returns is not borne out by the empirical data in the Netherlands in the period 1965–85. This is the first argument for lowering wages. In fact, almost every year there was a rise in labour productivity which means a rise in marginal productivity. However, the *rate* of growth of labour productivity diminished. A second argument is that when wages and transfer payments are reduced, more money remains for employers to invest. More investment will cause unemployment to decline. In other words, unemployment is regarded as a result of a shortage of investment funds.

The argument for lowering wages is supported by the Central Planning Office (Centraal Planbureau, or CPB). This Office advises the Dutch government and is highly respected in the Netherlands. Even opposition parties and

---

* I presented an earlier version of this paper in Utrecht and at the Fourth World Congress on Social Economics in Toronto.

the trade unions make extensive use of its models. Its calculations are employed by all interested groups whenever they wish to convince the government or voters either in favour or against a given policy. In 1974 Den Hartog and Tjan extended an earlier Central Planning Office model. In their new model (which was given the name VINTAF) they assumed that: (1) production capacity is determined by installed equipment (capital coefficients were assumed equal for all vintages of equipment and remained fixed for as long as it remained in operation); (2) the rate of fall in the requirement for labour is constant as technical progress proceeds.

From this follows that a rise in real labour costs would cause unemployment, because high wages would reduce the economic life of machines to less than their technical lifespan. Older labour-intensive machines would be scrapped earlier than necessary and substituted by less labour-intensive equipment. In other words, a trade-off is assumed between capital and labour. Graphically, this analysis is presented in Figure 4.1.

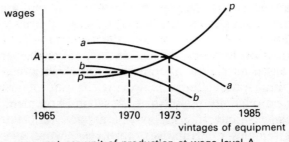

aa   = wage cost per unit of production at wage level A
bb   = wage cost per unit of production at wage level B
pp   = proceeds of production

Figure 4.1: Vintage analysis

Figure 4.1 reveals that at wage level A the last vintage of equipment employed would be 1973 and that at wage level B this would be 1970.

Taken together the earlier-mentioned arguments in support of a policy of wage restraint and of reductions in social benefits and government expenditure, amount to the claim that *profits are too low.* In the next paragraphs I present some empirical data which should prove the validity of this claim. Following this, I review the data and present some alternative ones, namely empirical data on realized consumption and investment. In other words, my concern in this paper is with the functional distribution of the national product in the Netherlands between providers of labour and the suppliers of land and capital. I limit my analysis to the 'primary' distribution of income.

4.1 RELATIVE INCOME SHARES

Pleading for wage restraint and other measures to cut government expenditure, employers and some civil servants frequently speak of a profit squeeze as the cause of the current difficulties. To prove their point they refer to the conception AIQ (*Arbeidsinkomensquote*). This is the share of labour income as a percentage of the net income of enterprises (i.e. the sum of wages of wage earners plus the imputed labour income of the self-employed which is measured as the average income from employment in the corporate sector) (Salverda 1978: 70). On the face of it the AIQ seems to fit in the classical concept of real income distribution between labour and capital. But in fact, as I will elaborate below, the AIQ has no expenditure meaning for the persons concerned; that is, the AIQ does not indicate what labour or capital has to spend. The AIQ has no class character: it does not compare the income of the class of workers with that of property owners. Taking into account that the AIQ concentrates on wage costs, it is more in line with the neoclassical concept of income distribution.

Before the AIQ, the income share of workers was calculated directly (*werknemersaandeel*). The Central Planning Office calculated it for the first time in 1956 (CPB 1956: 53). It then was meant to measure whether the wage earners' share in the national income was high enough. As a matter of fact, it measured the (un)equal distribution of income: it showed the average wage as percentage of the average national income at factor costs (excluding depreciation on investments) per head of the occupied population (wage earners, employers and civil servants) (Salverda 1978: 72). The concept had more or less a class character: it compared the income of the class of workers with that of the total occupied population. It did *not* measure the functional distribution of income.

In 1966 the Socio-Economic Council proposed to change the concept 'workers'-share' by the concept of AIQ. Although the new concept was carefully interpreted, the Central Planning Office soon considered the AIQ as a mirror of profitability: the higher the AIQ, the lower the profitability. For the sake of simplicity, profit was regarded as the residue of the net product of enterprises (at factor costs) after the subtraction of labour income, that is of wages and of the imputed labour income of the self employed (CPB 1975: 140; Salverda 1978: 67,73,75).

According to the Central Planning Office, the macro AIQ is distorted by the proceeds from natural gas. The latter contributes significantly to the national income, but makes hardly any direct contribution to the corporate sector (CPB 1975: 106; 1982: 64; Salverda 1978: 85). That is why in 1975 the Central Planning Office began with calculating a so-called corrected AIQ. The corrected AIQ excluded natural gas, public utilities (water, gas and electricity) and the exploitation of dwelling houses (by doing this some sectors are excluded in which the AIQ is low, or almost zero, or is not calculated at all). In the early 1980s both AIQ calculations were again revised together with many other statistics. This had become necessary, among other things, because some new statistics, particularly concerning the service sector, became available. Some estimates had to be revised (CBS 1981a: 13–14 +86–104).

Although the Central Planning Office admits that the AIQ is not a clear indicator of profits (CPB 1982: 103), the concept continues to be used. Table 4.1 presents the different AIQ modulations calculated by the Central Planning Office (CPB 1984: 366–7; 1985: 264–5).

Table 4.1: Share of labour income in percentages of total net income of enterprises (AIQ)

Year	Normal AIQ	Revised normal AIQ	Corrected AIQ
1965	75.6		
1966	78.5		
1967	77.7		
1968	72.1		
1969	77.4	73.4	
1970	79.3	75.5	
1971	81.0	77.5	
1972	79.9	76.4	
1973	79.6	76.5	
1974	81.4	78.0	
1975	84.3	80.6	
1976	80.2	77.1	
1977	80.7	77.4	87.8
1978		77.6	87.2
1979		78.4	88.6
1980		78.6	90.7
1981		76.5	91.0
1982		75.3	89.9
1983		74.8	90.5
1984		70.0	86.0
1985		69.0	84.5

4.2 CRITICISM ON THE CONCEPT OF AIQ

In the public debate and even among scientists it is often forgotten that the AIQ is calculated in terms of *net* incomes. Sometimes studies are published in which it is erroneously stated that the AIQ is calculated in terms of the gross income of enterprises. For example, this was recently done in the thesis of Appels (1986: 182). Often this leads to a too pessimistic view about the development of profits and enterprises' investment prospects. The exclusion of capital depreciation from the concept AIQ mismatches the relative income share of workers and of property-owners: property owners are capable of reproducing their assets even when the AIQ is 100 per cent. Another mismatch of the relative income shares arises from the way the 'wage income' of self-employed is imputed. The Central Planning Office imputes the wage income of self-employed in a manner which is far from self-evident. For example, why should property income be treated as a residual and not related to the average rate of profit on capital in the corporate sector? The AIQ would be lower if it were calculated on the basis of average wages paid to employees in the self-employed sector. Moreover, it is not satisfactory to impute the wage income of self-employed because the AIQ is measured with gross wage costs, which means that social premiums are included which the self-employed do not have to pay. In other words, the wage income of the self-employed is quite different from gross wage costs for labour. Furthermore, the AIQ is distorted by the exclusion of the difference of interests between lending and borrowing by banks, because services of banks are intermediate products and the difference of interests between lending and borrowing are not final product of banks. And last but not least, the AIQ has no real expenditure meaning for the persons concerned: (1) I have already mentioned that capital reproduction expenditures are excluded from the AIQ; (2) since wage taxes (and social premiums) rose sharply, the difference between gross and net income became larger and therefore it is not clear what the expenditure meaning of wage cost is; (3) consumption expenditures include Value Added Tax and in many cases at investment expenditures this indirect tax is restituted so that the expenditure power of wages and property earnings are not comparable (Salverda 1978: 70–80).

The Central Office for Statistics (Central Bureau voor de Statistiek, or CBS) and the Central Planning Office recognize some of the above mentioned criticisms: the Central Office for Statistics admits in the *National Accounts* that most of the time it is statistically impossible to distinguish between interest, profit and the share of wages of self-employed. That is why these incomes are taken together as income of households in the primary income statistics (CBS 1986a: 39); and the Central Planning Office admits in its discussion of the AIQ that it is theoretically correct to include the difference of bank interests between lending and borrowing. It only is income in the concept of distribution of primary income (CPB 1977: 186). It is mainly these two reasons that I deal here with the primary distribution of enterprises' income.

4.3 PRIMARY DISTRIBUTION OF ENTERPRISES' INCOME

In this section the primary distribution of income is divided into several sectors.

(1) The primary distribution of income of enterprises including government enterprises. Government enterprises are, for example, the Post, the Telephone and Telegraph corporation, airports, old people's homes and hospitals. However, schools, (local) governments and such like are not considered enterprises.
(2) Wages exclusive an imputed labour income of self-employed and managers' salaries (CBS 1986a: 37).

The division of property incomes into sectors shows that the income earned by the state and Other Public Corporations (OPC) has grown from 1.8 per cent of total primary income in 1965 to 8.2 per cent in 1984. Furthermore, it shows that more and more profits, interest and dividends are paid to enterprises abroad: 2.7 per cent of total primary income in 1965 and 9.7 in 1984. The property incomes of family households together with another heterogeneous category of income encompassing direct taxes and undistributed dividends, are not explicitly noted in Table 4.2 (CBS 1985a t/m 1973a: T1). Indirect taxes, including Value Added Tax, seem to be very constant.

Among other things, the rising primary income share of government can be explained by the growing income from oil and gas exploitation. Particularly in the early 1980s, the rising income share of profits, interest and dividends paid to enterprises abroad may perhaps be explained by higher interest rates. Profits, interest and dividends earned from abroad are partly disguised in incomes of institutional funds and property incomes of households.

Table 4.2 does not reveal a dramatic rise in labour income. In 1965 labour income was 52.4 per cent of total primary income; in 1970, 55.6 per cent; in 1980, 56.5 per cent; and in 1984, 50.7 per cent. But there has been a shift in property income. As a consequence of the oil crises (in 1973 and in 1979), the income of the state rose considerably. Another consequence was that costs in private enterprises rose.

With this it became a matter of income redistribution between one group of property owners, for example the banks, and others. It is, of course, true that the higher income of the state from oil and gas was not directly redistributed to private enterprises, but the oil crisis of 1973 raised energy costs in industry, in both the Netherlands and abroad. From the point of view of international competition there was no direct need to support Dutch industry. To stimulate investments the Act on Investment Accounts (*Wet op de Investeringsrekening*) was promulgated in the mid 1970s. It guaranteed a basic state subsidy for all enterprises and a special addition for those which met the requirements of the 'selectivity' programme, that is for enterprises which are particularly 'friendly' towards the natural environment. Often these state subsidies amounted to between 20 and 25 per cent of the planned cost of investment. So, in an indirect way, some of the government's gas and oil earnings were also directed towards private enterprises. Nevertheless, some political parties claimed that the oil and gas benefits were 'wasted' to pay for social transfers—the 'Dutch Disease'. All this comes to show that it was not the primary distribution of income between labour and property which was the main source of the assumed profit squeeze. For several enterprises wages are only a minor part of their production costs. All other costs which influence profits, like energy costs, are neither included in the primary distribution of income nor in the AIQ. That is, the reason why, when the share of property income is declining, the decline cannot be explained by a rising share of labour income.

I dealt with the question of the primary distribution of income and the AIQ because these statistics are often

Table 4.2: *Wages and property income in percentages of total primary income*

	Wages & social benefits	Income from property and profits			Indirect taxes	Total of listed incomes
		State and OPC	Institutional funds	Abroad		
1965	52.4	1.8	1.7	2.7	12.5	71.1
1966	54.4	1.8	1.8	2.7	13.0	73.7
1967	53.7	1.8	2.0	2.8	13.4	73.7
1968	53.3	2.0	2.1	3.0	14.0	74.4
1969	54.5	2.2	2.2	3.3	13.0	75.2
1970	55.6	2.3	2.3	4.1	14.0	78.3
1971	56.7	2.1	2.5	4.3	14.4	80.0
1972	55.7	2.3	2.6	3.6	14.9	79.1
1973	55.9	2.3	2.7	3.9	14.6	79.4
1974	57.7	2.8	3.0	5.2	14.0	82.7
1975	59.6	4.1	3.5	5.4	14.3	86.9
1976	56.9	4.9	3.6	4.8	14.5	84.7
1977	56.9	5.2	3.9	4.6	15.5	86.1
1977	55.5	4.9	3.7	4.3	14.6	83.0
1978	55.7	4.6	3.9	4.8	15.0	84.0
1979	56.5	5.1	4.2	6.1	14.8	86.7
1980	56.7	5.9	4.5	8.4	14.9	90.4
1981	55.3	7.4	4.9	10.9	14.5	93.0
1082	54.2	7.5	5.3	10.9	14.2	92.1
1983	53.1	7.5	5.6	9.3	14.6	90.1
1984	50.7	8.2	5.6	9.7	14.7	88.9

OPC = Other Public Corporations

quoted in support of claims that a shift in the functional distribution of income in favour of profits will stimulate savings and investments. But for the reasons mentioned, the AIQ cannot be interpreted to give a measure of share of income which is available for investment. This interpretation would assume that investment is dependent on realized profits. The fact is that a great share of the savings in the Netherlands comes from 'at source deductions': workers are obliged to pay every month a percentage of their income for their old-age pensions. These pensions are paid above the normal old-age pensions according to the General Old Age Pensions Act (*Algemene Ouderdoms Wet* or AOW). Furthermore, the assumption that investment is dependent on realized profits would deny the importance of future profit expectations. This, together with the criticisms of the AIQ, make the AIQ of less use for policy decisions. The same is true for the primary distribution of enterprises' income. It is true of course that this measure gives a more differential view on income distribution, but it still does not give information on which part of the national income can be spent by labour and which by property owners. It neither gives information on how much is saved or consumed. In view of all this it seems to be better to look at the realized savings instead of the AIQ or the primary income statistics.

4.4   SAVINGS AND INVESTMENT

Net national savings were larger than net national investment in the Netherlands. In 1970 savings were 1.2 billion guilders more than investment. Including the investment in stocks and contracted work (2.9 billion guilders) there was a shortage of savings of (1.7 billion guilders). In 1971 there was still a shortage, but in 1973 there was already a surplus of 4.3 billion guilders. Table 4.3 presents the surplus of savings together with the investments in stocks and contracted work (CBS 1976–86a).

The question arises, what happened with the surplus of savings? It seems that, while policy of wage restraint and

Table 4.3: Surplus of savings defined as the net national savings diminished with the net national investments

Year	Amount in million guilders	Of which in stocks and contracted work
1965	1,379	1,308
1966	243	254
1967	454	707
1968	825	555
1969	2,703	2,440
1970	1,214	2,916
1971	1,360	1,790
1972	5,420	1,090
1973	9,550	3,020
1974	11,510	5,500
1975	4,730	−440
1976	10,730	3,150
1977	3,850	1,790
1977*	3,600	1,540
1978*	−550	1,820
1979*	−2,370	1,500
1980*	−3,180	1,720
1981*	4,670	−3,090
1982*	10,620	−1,020
1983*	12,420	560
1984*	19,900	3,690
1985*	22,810	5,110

*Revised data by CBS

social benefit reductions was implemented, more and more money was invested abroad. According to the president of the Dutch National Bank, the amount of direct investments abroad was about 85 billion guilders greater than foreign investments in the Netherlands in 1985 [De Volkskrant, 27 November 1985; 4 December 1985]. I give the figures in Table 4.4 (van Nieuwkerk and Sparling 1985: 116–37; van Nieuwkerk 1986: 1089).

It seems that there were savings enough to invest in the Netherlands, but more and more savings were invested abroad. Particularly the huge enterprises invested abroad: almost 75 per cent of the volume of Dutch investment abroad came from the ten biggest multinationals (van

128   *Distribution, Employment and Economic Policy*

Table 4.4: The cumulative amount of Dutch investment abroad and of foreign investment in the Netherlands (in million guilders)

	Cumulative Dutch investments abroad	Cumulative foreign investments in the Netherlands
1973	44,173	20,659
1974	49,622	23,687
1975	53,561	26,382
1976	51,517	28,426
1977	57,805	30,179
1978	60,572	31,565
1979	71,974	36,147
1980	89,685	40,817
1981	99,508	45,432
1982	104,291	47,176
1983	119,886	51,865
1985	145,000	60,000

Nieuwkerk and Sparling 1985: 10). The question therefore arises of what happened with domestic investment.

4.5   DISTRIBUTION BETWEEN INVESTMENT AND CONSUMPTION

In the public debate it is often claimed that the share of government in the GNP is too large. Most of the time statistics concerning the burden of taxation and social benefits premiums are quoted to substantiate this claim. From this point of view the claim seems to be valid. The tax and premium burden exceeds 50 per cent of net national income (CPB 1985: 264–5). But the greatest share of taxes and premiums is reallocated back to the private sector. In spite of the rise in taxation and premiums, the share of government investment and consumption (including wages and salaries) in the GNP declined from 25 per cent in the period 1965–9 to 21 per cent in the period 1980–4 (CPB 1984: 360–1; 1985: 258–9). Figure 4.2 shows the development
     Figure 4.2 reveals that since the early 1970s the share of government in GNP declined—investment in particular.

of the shares of consumption and investment of the private
sector and the government sector.

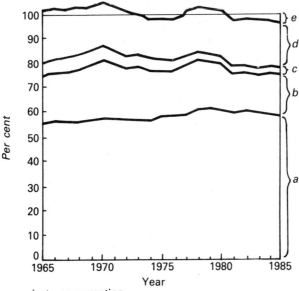

a   = private consumption
b   = gross private investment
c   = gross government investment
d   = consumption of government
e   = balance of imports and exports

*Figure 4.2: Share of investment and consumption of the private sector
and in the government sector in percentage of GNP*

Since the early 1970s much attention has been paid to the
problem of inflation. The relationship between inflation
and unemployment was widely discussed. There were
rumours that a report of the Organization for Economic
Cooperation and Development (OECD) had stated that
some unemployment had to be accepted to cope with the
problem of inflation (van der Klundert 1970: 1119). Whether
or not such a report really existed is not clear, but it is fact
that since the early 1970s one government after another
pursued deflationary policies. These met with little success.
For several years inflation remained high—on average 8
per cent per year between 1970 and 1979 and 4.4 per cent

between 1980 and 1985 (CPB 1985: 266–7). In addition to this it must be noted that in 1985 inflation was only 2 per cent, and that due to the falling oil prices and the lower rate of exchange of the US dollar, deflation is expected for 1986. Instead of abandoning the policy of wage cuts and of reducing government expenditure, which were designed to cure inflation or were at least presented as such, this policy was by the end of the 1970s presented as *the* instrument to combat unemployment. Even when the balance of trade showed a surplus of 4 per cent (see Fig 4.2) the government continued it. It was then that the first signs of real damage to the welfare state became evident.

From the above it seems that domestic investment declined because government investment diminished and because the growth of domestic consumption slackened and hence reduced the rate of domestic investment.

4.6 RELATION GNP, INVESTMENT AND CONSUMPTION

The growth of the GNP in the Netherlands slackened in the early 1970s and became negative in the early 1980s. In addition, government expenditures, particularly investment, declined. Furthermore, a policy of wage restraint and reductions in social benefits was implemented, but prices did not fall sufficiently sharply to maintain the growth of consumption at the level it had grown during the late 1960s (no Pigou effect). Since 1980 private consumption declined. Consumption per capita in prices of 1980 was in 1965. 8,930.—guilders, in 1970 11,350.—guilders, in 1980. 14,540—guilders, and in 1984 13,690.—guilders (CBS 1981a–1984a). The diminished growth of consumption dampened private investment. Changes in net private investment reflected changes in the consumption of durable goods. In the period 1955–85 the relationship between consumption and investment was as follows: $R^2 = 0.426577$; F–Test = 21.5735; Durbin-Watson = 2.15185. The slackening growth in investment diminished the growth of the GNP. The changes in GNP reflected private investment in the period 1955–85 as follows: $R^2 = 0.378151$; F–Test

= 17.6351; Durbin-Watson = 1.73686 (CPB 1965–85; CBS 1966a–86a).

With the decline in the rate of investment, the character of investment also changed. It is true that in the recession of 1974–83 the share of investment in equipment (machines) was higher in all branches of industry than in the growth period 1964–73. But at the same time the rate of labour productivity declined in almost all branches of industry. The overall rate of labour productivity in industry declined from 8.0 to 3.0 per cent (CPB 1983: 402–403). (This is calculated by dividing the change in volume of production by the change in volume of labour.) So it seems that the emphasis of investors in the period of recession was not on labour substitution. The explanation for the growing rate of the share of investment in equipment now seems to have been particularly in energy cost-reducing investments. As mentioned before, the oil crises of 1973 and 1979 meant a dramatic rise in energy prices, and in the framework of the already mentioned Act on Investment Accounts, an additional state subsidy was given to enterprises for energy conserving investments.

4.7 CONCLUSIONS

Employers and some civil servants in the Netherlands pleaded for a shift in the functional distribution of income. They claim that the last fifteen years have witnessed a dramatic shift in income in favour of labour. However, neither the often quoted statistics for labour income (*Arbeidsinkomensquote*) nor the primary income distribution of enterprises, justifies this claim. Nevertheless, investment in the Netherlands has diminished over the last fifteen years, particularly for employment-creating investments. Investments have been mainly cost-reducing and in substitution. This does not mean that there was a lack of savings. Huge amounts of money were invested abroad, mostly by huge corporations. Thus a policy to increase the share of property income by wage restraint and by reductions in social benefits seems to be no guarantee for more domestic investments.

5 Economic Stability and Political Expediency

J.P.G. Reijnders.

Since the beginning of the 1970s the world economy has faced a contraction in the level of activity of which the consequences, especially in terms of employment, are serious to the extent that one is justified to speak of another 'great depression'.

The Western governments are trying to cope with this problem by pursuing deflationary policies which mainly consist of cutting government expenditure, social security payments and wages. These policies receive a great deal of support from professional economists, but the support is not unanimous. There is a growing number of economists who oppose the view that depressions can be cured by means of 'economizing'. The latter's main arguments are:

(1) 'Economizing' diminishes effective demand and thus strengthens contractive forces and increases unemployment.
(2) Cuts in the social security system undermine the welfare state and thus threaten the survival of one of the main social achievements of twentieth-century economic development.

In the controversy between these groups, the arguments are often drawn from the experience and economic policies of the 1930s. But as with economic theory, opinions differ about the interpretation of historical data. The protagonists of 'economizing' stress the typical differences between the 1930s and the 1970s. The antagonists stress the similarities and maintain that a policy that was fundamentally wrong in the 1930s can also not be right under the present circumstances. However, historical comparisons are incomplete if the intervening periods are ignored. So the two crises might not be properly understood unless the important phase of growth and prosperity that links them is properly taken into account.

One of the schools of thought which tries to deal with the problem of long-term economic development within a unified framework is the school of the theory of the long waves (Freeman *et al.* 1982; van Duijn 1983; Kleinknecht 1984). Ignoring some important forerunners, this theory originated from the empirical and theoretical work of the Russian economist N.D. Kondratieff (1926, 1928, 1935, 1979, 1984).[1] According to Kondratieff, long-term economic development can be seen as a succession of long waves with a duration of forty to sixty years. The great depressions, like those of the 1870s, the 1930s and the present one, take a prominent place in this theory: they are interpreted as downswing phases of the long waves.

Although the empirical and theoretical basis of the theory has been contested (Eklund 1980; van der Zwan 1980; van Ewijk 1981; Maddison 1982; Reijnders 1984), I will for the present grant it the benefit of the doubt. It may well provide valuable insights which throw new light on the aforementioned controversy. In this paper I shall interpret European economic history within the framework of a long-wave concept. I shall make an effort to explain the mechanism of the long wave by means of a modified version of Hicks's model of constrained business cycles (Hicks 1950). From this some tentative conclusions are drawn with respect to the main strands of economic policy in the welfare state. They lead to a particular problem which is relevant in the context of the present conference, namely the share distribution of control over national income between the state and the private sector. This in turn leads to a particular intertemporal distribution of the costs and benefits of economic development between successive generations.

5.1 BROAD OUTLINES OF THE MODEL

The origins of the long-wave upswing can be traced to the conditions that prevailed after the Second World War. The largely devastated infrastructure and a productive capacity that fell short of even the bare requirements for providing the primary needs of the population together with ample reserves of labour power, formed the basis upon which the impressive new economic structure was erected. The reconstruction of the European economy produced a strong impetus for employment and, concomitant with this, strong income and expenditure impulses. From the point of view of real factors, the European economy had to lift itself by its own bootstraps. [2] It is precisely this process which gave such a strong boost to economic growth.

Although probably not inspired by the conditions in post-war Europe, Forrester rightly calls the mechanism that is responsible for a long-lasting and vigorous expansion of production, a *bootstrap structure* (Forrester 1977). This is one of the cornerstones of his explanation for the fact that his system dynamic model displays movements which closely conform with a long-wave pattern. The bootstrap structure may be explained as follows: an increase of the output in the consumer goods sector requires an increase in its productive capacity, therefore the output of the basic capital sector must be increased. But the basic capital sector uses its own output as a factor of production. If it is to expand production in a balanced manner to meet the increased demand, it needs both labour and capital equipment. Yet the only way for the basic capital sector to extend its productive capacity is to divert the capital equipment from the consumer goods sector, that is from the source of the increased demand. So the basic capital sector does in fact compete with its own customers and generates a tendency to supply less capital equipment in response to a demand for more of it. At the same time, however, it increases the demand for consumer goods by creating extra employment and hence it again stimulates the derived demand for capital equipment.

Such a structure can create tremendous tensions,

especially when the initial productive capacity is considerably lower than the desired capacity. Because of the gestation period of capital equipment, time elapses before delivery actually takes place and the time lag is multiplied by the recirculation of capital equipment. As this lag is generated in every successive stage of the interdependent industrial structure (i.e. the input–output matrix), the total time lag between the original demand impulse and the final increase in output of the commodity in question becomes considerable. During this lapse of time, production continues; that is, employment is generated and income and final demand increase. The effort to create additional productive capacity stimulates a mechanism which generates extra demand and consequently extra derived demand for capital equipment.

Properly speaking the 'bootstrap structure' is no more than a special case of Samuelson's mechanism of interaction between the multiplier and the accelerator (Samuelson 1939). However, unlike Samuelson's accelerator, Forrester's 'bootstrap accelerator' is not a single macro-economic parameter. It takes account of a part of the input–output structure in the capital sector. In this way it introduces non-linearities which result in a lengthening of the adaptation process.

I think that this principle can be improved by generalizing its basic idea by taking account of the fact that several basic sectors, tied by input–output relations, are participating in the building-up of productive capacity. In this case the 'bootstrap accelerator' becomes a vector that contains several sectoral capital–output ratios which are embedded in a more complicated lag structure. The magnitude of the 'bootstrap accelerator' depends upon the magnitudes of the sectoral capital-output ratios, the relative weights of the sectors and the number of sectors involved (i.e. the dimensions of the vector).

In my view this extension of the 'bootstrap accelerator' is important because it creates the possibility for explaining the influence of basic innovations on the process of expansion. Contrary to the views expressed by other authors on this subject (Mensch 1979; van Duijn 1983; Kleinknecht 1984), I think that innovations *do not* trigger off expansion.

It is rather the process of expansion that creates the climate which stimulates innovation. Expansion drags along innovations while the latter, when they are actually taking place, give an extra dimension to the expansion process.

As far as innovations create the necessity to construct specific installations, they give a specific impetus to economic growth. The power of this specific impetus is, however, not to be found in the new industries themselves but in the effect new industries have on the dimension of the industrial structure of the economy (i.e. the rank of the input–output matrix). By increasing the 'roundabout of production', basic innovations increase the magnitude of the 'bootstrap accelerator' to such an extent that the interaction mechanism produces an explosive upward movement. It produces a clear-cut explosive upward sweep, or an explosive cycle whose amplitude increases with time.

At first sight the definition of the long wave as an unstable movement may look rather odd. This is because it entails the possibility that one single shock may produce oscillations that will get larger and larger, until they result in total chaos. In reality, however, the economy possesses definite physical constraints that prevent its fluctuations from overshooting certain limits. Given these limits, there is nothing wrong with the assumption of an explosive movement; the system may then continue, periodically breaking against these limits without running away altogether.

Given these constraints, the hypothesis of explosive movements can explain the post-war long wave in a way that reasonably fits the evidence of economic history. In addition to this, it may also explain why long waves have recurred during such a long period without ever dampening out. [3] This type of explanation of cycles within external bounds may be traced back to Harrod (1948). It was, however, Hicks (1950) who developed this idea into a complete model of the business cycle. The core of Hicks's model is an accelerator/multiplier interaction mechanism where the accelerator is assumed to have a sufficiently high magnitude to produce an explosive movement. This movement cannot develop freely, because it is restricted by the external limits.

(1) There is a direct restraint upon the upward expansion: scarcity of employable resources. Thus it is impossible to expand output without limit. The 'Full Employment Ceiling' is defined in the Keynesian sense as the point at which output becomes inelastic to an increase of effective demand. In a progressive economy, that ceiling will shift in the course of time i.e. will display an upward trend.

(2) There is no direct limit on contraction. However, the working of the accelerator on the downswing is different from its working on the upswing. This difference in mechanism provides an indirect check upon contraction which is certain to become effective sooner or later.

On Hicks's assumption that autonomous investment increases at a regular rate, the system can grow within the limits set by the growth of the labour force and the minimum output level as determined by the minimum rate of autonomous spending. In principle, the system could remain in progressive equilibrium as long as it is not diverted from its equilibrium path. However, if there is a disturbance, which takes the form of an upward displacement, the explosive mechanism is triggered off. Output will diverge from its equilibrium path. The divergence will take the form of either oscillations which increase in amplitude, or of relentless expansion. Once started, the diverging movement can take several shapes depending on whether it has hit the ceiling or whether the cycle just oscillates above the rising floor.

Having sketched the broad outlines of the model, in the next section I will try to show that this framework fits reasonably well with the post-war development of the European economy.

5.2 POST-WAR DEVELOPMENT

Reconstruction and Upswing, 1945–65
The initial conditions that characterized the European

economy in 1945 are well known. The infrastructural system was devastated and so was a considerable part of the industrial installations and equipment. An important part of the working population was unemployed, or more precisely, redundant relative to the level of productive capacity.

Although the principal elements of the conditions which stimulate expansion were present, the original push to revival was given by the governments. Backed up by international financial aid, they embarked upon the reconstruction of the infrastructural system. In terms of the model this means that public spending produced, in the words of Hicks, the 'hump' in autonomous spending that lifted the economy from its slump equilibrium. Following this initial impulse, the recovery started. Employment slowly increased and the resulting increase in purchasing power fed the 'bootstrap' interaction mechanism. Things accelerated very quickly. By 1952, the major part of reconstruction was completed and the economy was in full swing.[4]

As the upswing gathered momentum, the basic industries expanded rapidly and in their wake innovations developed. The extension of the industrial network was mainly clustered around the petrochemical industry, the basic metallurgical industry and the electro-technical industry. This is well illustrated by the fact that in the Dutch economy in the period 1953 to 1963 the average growth rate of the earlier-mentioned industries was nearly twice as high as the average growth rate of all manufacturing industries (de Wolff and Driehuis 1980: 21).

It is important to note that the notion of 'extension of the industrial structure'—or in the vocabulary of the preceding section, increase of the magnitude of the 'bootstrap accelerator'—has two important implications.

(1) It implicitly assumes that in the process of economic expansion the economy builds up a dual structure. New sectors are added while old sectors remain. Substitution does not take place until the restructuring process of the downswing sets in.

(2) Because innovation is incorporated in the mechanism of the upswing, it can no longer be regarded as an external impulse (a cause of 'humps' in the level of autonomous investment). Innovation is transformed into an endogenous force. Consequently, the category autonomous investment is reduced to public investment and long-range investment, which is only expected to pay for itself over a long period.[5]

While the expansion process kept on feeding on itself, public investment added a permanent external impulse. The increase of government expenditure was in fact a continuous process that started in the early phases of the reconstruction period and continued until the early 1970s. In the 1950s and early 1960s the growth of public investment was mainly due to the massive construction of roads which became necessary because of the increasing number of motorcars.[6] In the 1960s the emphasis shifted towards investments to accommodate the growth of the public health system, to higher education and finally to the stimulation of residential construction. In this manner, the government not only accommodated the expansion of the economy by creating the necessary extension of the infrastructure, but also provided the economy with a train of impulses that kept the mechanism going. As a consequence of this and, of course, because of the explosive tendencies embodied in the mechanism, the economy expanded at an unprecedented rate.

The Period of Transition, 1965–70/71
However vigorous the expansion may have been, it was bound to come to an end. Ultimately, it was bound to hit the ceiling and be forced into reverse. Although there are slight differences between countries, the full employment ceiling was on the whole reached in the middle of the 1960s.

If the working of the model is interpreted in a purely mechanical fashion, one would expect the upswing to collapse immediately, or at least within a reasonably short time. In practice, however, things were different. The fact that the reversal was postponed for several years may partly be explained by the time lags involved. Yet this influence should not be overestimated. First, because in the case of negative impulses the stretching-out effect of the bootstrap mechanism does not operate. The 'halt instruction' is quickly communicated throughout the system. Second, because the appearance of a bottleneck in the labour supply will affect all sectors of the economy at the same time, which puts an immediate break upon the expansion.

The main reason why the reversal was postponed is the relatively high degree of flexibility of the ceiling. The shock was partly absorbed by the ceiling and a transition period was created in which expansion continued, though at a lesser rate.

To solve the problem of the tight labour market one can either try to increase the labour supply or to decrease the rate of growth of demand for labour. During the transition period both strategies were applied:

(1) In order to increase the labour supply workers were attracted from abroad. Beginning in the early 1960s an ever-increasing number of so-called guest-workers were invited to become members of the north-west European labour force. Originally, the hunting grounds were located in the southern periphery of Europe (Italy, Spain, Portugal), but soon it was extended to the south-east (Turkey and later Greece and Yugoslavia) and to the northern part of Africa (Morocco, Tunisia). The temporary character of this 'hospitality' became obvious in the early 1970s when unemployment figures started to rise. Immigration was more strictly regulated and it declined sharply.

(2) An obvious way of avoiding the tensions of the labour market is to switch to less labour-intensive techniques, by the introduction of labour-saving technologies. In this manner the physical restraint on the expansion is relaxed and the full-employment ceiling is given build-in flexibility.[7]

Besides the strategies employed in an effort to cope with this problem in a general way, there was also the immediate and individual reaction to the scarcity of labour: the 'natural' their individual demand for workers, employers started competing with each other in the labour market by bidding-up wages. Besides being a symptom of the workings of the market mechanism, the rise in the wage level was, at least initially, one of the factors that kept the economy growing during the transition phase.

As stated earlier in this paper, the principle of the growth process is the interaction of output growth and the growth of employment. But as, under the influence of a tight labour market, the growth of employment is slowing down, the growth of wage income and consequently the growth of consumer demand—the final stimulus to the growth of output—also slows down, unless the wage rate is increased. This is what actually happened. As far as the technical solutions failed to fill the gap in the labour market, wage rates increased. The latter, in its turn, filled the potential gap in the growth of demand. It must, however, be pointed out that this mechanism, although it proved to work out positively for a time, is a very weak basis for the process of growth. The part played by the rising wage level especially, makes it very vulnerable. I shall elaborate this point in the next subsection.

As for the intervention of the government during the transition period, a different story must be told. Except for its active role in the early phase of the reconstruction period, the government was very reluctant to interfere with the private sector. During the post war period, largely due to tariff reductions, the tax-rate in the Netherlands declined from 30.5 per cent in 1948, to a minimum of 24.0 per cent in 1957. Between 1957 and 1963 the rate rose slowly to 24.8 per cent. From there on it began to rise more steeply. From 26.9 per cent in 1970 and 29.2 per cent in 1979, it rose to a maximum of 31.0 per cent in 1980. Finally, it declined again to 27.9 per cent in 1982 (CPB 1985: 264).

The expansion of the government's share in national income is in fact nothing else but the 'passive' result of the prosperous development of the private sector which led to the automatic increase of tax receipts because of the build-in mechanism of tax progression. Later on, this process was amplified by the effects of inflation on tax returns.

Not only tax receipts increased. Government expenditure

continuously growing requirements put to the public sector in the 'Golden Age' of the construction of the welfare state. The upshot of this was that right in the middle of a period of tensions in the labour market, the government initiated a stimulating policy. Initially, this policy may have had a positive effect but as time went by, its impact became increasingly negative—especially when the government, in order to be able to run the institutions of the welfare state, started to increase employment in the public sector. It thus created extra competition within the already overheated labour market and contributed to the bidding up of wages. The rate of increase of production costs accelerated even further. Especially towards the end of the transition period, this influence was highly destabilizing.

The reversal and the ensuing downswing
The delicate mechanism that kept expansion going thoughout the transition period was extremely vulnerable:

(1) In spite of the fact that the growth process continued, the mechanism could not keep the growth rate from slowing down. A diminution of the average growth rate means that the stimulus of the bootstrap accelerator fades and causes a reversal.

(2) Rising wages as a solution to the problem of a possibly deficient growth of demand can only have a temporary effect because of its self-contradictory nature. Rising wages help as long as the labour-saving strategy is kept in line with the rise of the wage rate. If this requirement is not met, it will either lose its effect or its working will be reversed. If wages rise faster than labour pro-ductivity, the rising costs will act as a profit squeeze (in which case the effect is reversed), unless the producers succeed in passing the rising costs on to the consumers of the product (in which case the positive effects are neutralized).

What actually happened is well known. The increase of labour productivity did not keep in line with the rising wage level. The consequent rise in costs was passed on to the consumers by a rising price level. Within a few years, the inflationary movement resulted in double-digit figures. From the point of view of the real factors, this circumstance resulted in a neutralization of the temporary positive effects of high wages on purchasing power (or even in a reversal of the effects in the case of the older and weaker industries). In this situation the reversal became only a matter of time.

Although opinions differ as to the exact dating of the turning point, one may safely assume that it took place around 1970/1. At this point employment in most countries reached its peak level. In general the fall of investment in non-residential building and in capital equipment took place in 1971/2. After this, unemployment increased.

During the downswing, the interaction of the multiplier and the bootstrap accelerator does not produce the spectacular results known from the upswing. Unemployment and the concomitant decline in consumers demand results in the laying-off of workers in the consumer goods industries, while the resulting overcapacity leads to a sharp decline in investment. The decline in investment leads to overcapacity and unemployment in the investment goods industry, and so on. The problem of overcapacity spreads throughout the entire economy, reducing output and increasing unemployment in all industries. The process of economic decline keeps on feeding on itself because any increase in unemployment leads to a decline in capacity utilization. In spite of this, the downswing is not as vigorous as the upswing. There is a marked lack of symmetry. This is so because disinvestment can only take place by a cessation of gross investment. The adjustment of productive capacity to a decline in the level of output can only take place by a time-consuming process of physical decay. (Hicks 1950: 101). In addition to this, the downward movement is dampened because the decrease of income does not lead to a concomitant decrease in expenditure (the average propensity to spend increases with falling income). Therefore the contracting economy approaches the *slump equilibrium* (Hicks's expression for the floor of the downward movement) very slowly in an asymptotic way.

The downward movement has a high degree of inertia; it will hardly respond to a policy of stimulation because of the existing overcapacity. Only time can cure the 'patient'. I'm however afraid that time is running against him. Because of the conditions that have come to prevail during the downswing, the time necessary for the 'patient' to regain strength is also the time that is necessary to revive the ideology of depression.

As to the conditions prevailing during the downswing, one must turn to the vicissitudes of the welfare state. The immediate result of the growth of unemployment is that the 'safety net'—the social security system—comes into operation. The safety net has a dual function: on the one hand, it must protect the unemployed against serious losses of income, and on the other hand, in doing so, it must protect the economy from a strong downward spiral.

From the point of view of the economy as a whole, the social security system is just a buffer to prevent effective demand from falling to an extremely low level. If this buffer is put into operation—that is, if an increasing number of people are forced to make use of this facility—the volume of transfer incomes increases. If, then, the growth rate of national income is slowing down whilst the growth rate of income transfers is going up, it is only natural that the share of transfer incomes in the net national income increases. In the Netherlands, for instance, the social security premiums as a percentage of the net national income increased from 15.0 per cent in 1970 to 22.2 per cent in 1980, thus continuing the time-path of growth of the 1960s. It reached a maximum of 24.8 per cent in 1983 (CPB 1985: 264). The increase of the share of social security transfers moved in step with this. After fluctuating about 10 per cent during the 1960s, it rose via 16.5 per cent in 1970 to 25.5 per cent in 1982. Later, largely due to cuts in the system, it stabilized about a slightly lower level (Miljoenennota 1972–84).

Unfortunately, it is exactly this effect, the rising unemployment becoming visible in the financial records, that must have twisted the minds of economists. It is not the concern for the unemployed but the concern for the rising costs of unemployment that made the economists rediscover the principles of ordinary bookkeeping. Obviously, they were so much impressed by this 'discovery' that they made its principles the foundation of their version of modern 'enlightened' economics. It is this generalization, the declaration of the universal law of sound finance, that contains the gist of the ideology of depression. Everybody who becomes unemployed because of the declining growth of the national income contributes to the relative rise in transfer incomes from the social security system, and so provides proof for the gloomy predictions of the science of assets and liabilities. The longer the duration of the downswing, the stronger the pressure to cut the costs of the social security system.

In order to see the likely consequences of such a course of action one must elaborate upon the nature of the slump equilibrium. Hicks holds that there is a minimum level of autonomous investment which rises over time. The minimum level of investment determines the minimum level of income and a corresponding minimum of desired productive capacity. During the downswing, actual capacity declines and ultimately falls below this minimum capacity. The ensuing shortage of capacity will induce investment and initiate recovery.

This definition of slump equilibrium may apply in the short run, but it is doubtful whether the hypothesis of the upward-sloping minimum level of autonomous investment also holds in the long run. [8] If public investment—which constitutes an important part of autonomous investment[9]—is indicative of the 'floor level', then the latter is sloping downward. For instance, the volume index of Dutch gross public investment steadily decreased from a level of 138 in 1971 to a level of 86 in 1985 (CPB 1985: 263). Consequently, the gap between actual income and slump equilibrium income has grown. A downward-sloping 'floor level' may imply that the slump could last for years and that the ultimate recovery would begin from a level of income which may well be compared to the levels of the 1950s. In view of the downward slope, there is also a possibility that the 'floor level' is never reached. In this event there is, however, an alternative definition of slump equilibrium and the beginning of recovery. A 'technical recovery' obtains if real capacity falls below the level of desired capacity corresponding with actual income. Such a 'technical recovery' is possible whenever the rate of capacity decay is larger than the rate of income decrease. In this event the length of the depression depends upon the degree of initial overcapacity and on the ratio of the rate of capacity decay to the rate of income decrease.

If we now return to the question of the effects of cutting social security, the obvious conclusion in the light of the last-given definition of slump equilibrium is that the immediate effect of the cuts must be a prolongation of the depression. Because cuts in the social security system increase the rate of income decrease, they also increase the ratio of the rate of capacity decay to the rate of income decrease. Given the initial degree of overcapacity, this postpones recovery. In this case the principles of sound finance become self-contradictory. In order to cut the cost of social security a situation develops in which the period over which the system must operate is extended. Thus in the end the cumulative costs will be higher. As the financial problems of unemployment are not solved, the pressure to accomplish further reductions in the social security system will go on. Giving in to the common sense of 'sound finance', therefore, entails the danger of a downward spiral or purchasing power, of income and employment at a rate that postpones structural recovery[10] for a considerable number of years.

Unfortunately, it is precisely the ideology of 'sound finance' that became the leading principle of economic policy in the late 1970s. At first only small 'technical' changes were made in the social security system, but soon the impact of 'necessary' adjustments grew. By now the stage has been set for more drastic cuts. In the United Kingdom the Conservative government got their voters' support for a third round of monetarist crisis policy. In Germany the Liberals caused a government crisis and found the Christian Democrats waiting to join them in trying to put the squeeze on the economy. Even the former Socialist government of France was cajoled into adjusting its compass to a more 'realistic' course. In spite of all arguments to the contrary, the Dutch Christian-Democratic/Liberal coalition forced a reform of the legal basis of the social security system and seems determined to obtain a considerable reduction in government spending. Excluding, for instance, Sweden, where the government explicitly stimulates its economy, the only positive exception in the alliance of 'reason' seems to be the US government, which in spite of all 'Reaganomic' conservative rhetoric, conducts a stimulating policy which is based upon deficit spending.[11]

5.3 GOVERNMENT POLICY IN THE LONG RUN

An evaluation of the general characteristics of government policy during the post-war era shows that its development may be subdivided into four separate phases.

In the *first phase* government policy had a positive effect on the reconstruction and the growth of the economy. It gave a strong impulse to recovery and put the economy back on the right track. While on the whole it was reluctant to interfere with the development of the private sector, it precipitated conditions for the growth of the private sector and stimulated the upswing.

The strongest expansion of the public sector was associated with the *second phase*. Using the side-effects of the strong nominal expansion of the economy, the relative influence of government activity was increased, and the institutions and infrastructure of the welfare state were constructed. From the point of view of long-run economic stability and from the point of view of economic and social security, this expansion of government activity was desirable. However, there was one fundamental negative aspect connected with this development, namely its *timing*. By rapidly expanding, the government gave a long-lasting sequence of impulses to the economy at a time when the economy did not need them. This policy even had negative results. Due to the overheated labour market, it created a crowding-out effect. The public sector became an important rival to the private sector in the tight labour market. Both the private sector, to keep its expansion going, and the public sector, to support its growing level of activities, needed labour. The opposing forces belonged to the factors which ultimately disrupted the delicate mechanism of the transition period and resulted in the downturn.

At the outset of the downswing the public sector entered into the *third phase*. The mechanism of the social security system was put into operation. The downswing, the decrease in the growth of income, was accompanied by an increase in the growth of transfers out of the social security system. Consequently, the share in national income of social security transfers and related government transfers began to grow. In its early stages, when the social security system cannot prevent an initial fall of effective demand, the downswing operates in a purely mechanical fashion, as an autonomous movement. Under these circumstances, efforts to revive the contracting economy are destined to fail. This can be seen from the lack of success of the stimulating policies of the Labour government in the United Kingdom during the early 1970s (the 'Barber boom') and from the Social Democratic/Christian Democratic coalition's efforts in the Netherlands during the years immediately following the 'Oil crisis' of 1973. Because the social security system is a defensive mechanism which does not come into its own until the later stages of the downswing, when it forces income to converge to the slump equilibrium, its effects do not become visible. However, the financial effects of its working are as clear as sunshine.

The seemingly insurmountable financial problems involved in the maintenance of the social security system cause the public sector to enter into the *fourth phase*. In order to cope with the financial problems, efforts are made to cut government expenditure and to curtail the social security system. This policy exerts a deflationary influence at a time when the economy may be in need of stimulus, and it reduces the impact of the social security system at a time when the latter's powers are growing. In this manner the duration of the depression is extended, the financial problems are intensified and the risk of a downward spiral, that might ultimately lead to a complete dismantling of the social security system, is increased.

In retrospect, the four phases of the development of government economic policy do in a general manner correspond to the different phases of the post-war long wave in economic development. Except for the phase of recovery and upswing, and partly for the early stages of the downswing, the influence of government economic policy was in the wrong direction. It gave positive impulses in a period when there was absolutely no need for them. Presently, it tends to give negative impulses which, in the light of historical experience, must be considered dangerous. From the point of view of the long wave, one could say that the development of government economic policy was *pro-cyclical*. In this way, economic policy in the long run is at variance with full employment, balanced growth and economic stability, the principal goals of economic policy in general. The criticism of state intervention which is implicit in this conclusion plays right into the hands of the ones who consider the increased influence of government in economic life to be a factor which destabilizes economic development anyway and who therefore urge that governments restrict their interference in economic matters. I want to point out that this is only relatively true. It is only valid in the period when government expanded above the level which economic conditions allowed, namely during the transition period, the 'Golden Age' of the welfare state. On this basis the opponents of state intervention conclude that this overexpansion must be counteracted for the sake of economic stability. They are wrong, however, when they try to initiate this counteracting policy in the present situation, when economic conditions do not permit it. Under the present circumstances the application of a restrictive policy can only result in the opposite mistake, which is also pro-cyclical.

The pro-cyclicity of public policy is in fact the consequence of incorrect phasing. From this point of view the contradiction between 'Keynesian' and 'Anti-Keynesian' policy prescriptions is resolved in the question of timing. If it were necessary to diminish government deficits in order to reduce national debt, then the phase of long-term expansion would be the proper time to do so. In this phase the tempering of state activity creates room for the private sector to unfold its growth potential in full. The increase in tax revenue which accompanies the growth of the private sector creates the financial basis for the sanitation of public debt. The possibilities in this direction are further improved by the fact that, unlike during the downswing, the upswing is characterized by the absence of automatic mechanisms which provoke an autonomous increase of government spending. Such a policy implemented during the expansion. phase is not only directly anti-cyclical but also preparatory for the next phase. It makes sure that the government can start with a clean slate at the beginning of a new downturn. When the downward phase begins, the safety net of the social security system comes into operation. This is the signal for changing the policy paradigm. Government reticence must be replaced by an active expansionary policy by which the government fills the vacuum resulting from the sluggish development of the private sector. When the tensions on the labour market subside, the time is ripe for expanding the potential of the institutions of the welfare state by creating employment in the public sector. If in spite of this the growth of effective demand stagnates public spending must be increased, especially in the sphere of public investment. The expansionary policy is not only an anti-cyclical strategy. It also creates the possibility of increasing the level of government activity to the structurally desired level, that is to the level that corresponds to the growth of national income that was attained during the preceding expansion phase. In this way the share distribution of command over national income between the state and the private sector varies over the cycle. In the upward phase, government reticence creates room for the private sector, which is then in a position to enlarge its relative command over national income. In the downward phase, the government recovers its share by expanding into the domain where the private sector leaves resources unemployed. The goal of the expansionary policy is to reduce both the length and the intensity of the depression to minimize its cumulative costs and to facilitate recovery at the highest possible level of national income. The necessary degree of government restraint in the next phase must then depend upon the relation between these cumulative costs and the resulting level of national income. The balance between both these opposite policy options determines the intertemporal distribution of the advantages and disadvantages of the economic tide. The expansionary policy relieves the generation which has to bear the weight of the depression and shifts part of its cost upon the next generation. The second generation has the advantage that its initial position in terms of income and economic stability is relatively better than if there had been no expansionary policy. They may reap the fruits of prosperity, but their relative disadvantage is that part of their potential prosperity is diverted to the redemption of debts which resulted from the expansionary policy of the past. After the completion of a whole policy cycle, the slate is clean again and the next generation is free to react in the necessary manner when the hard times return.

The outlined stabilization scheme does not yet exist. Lacking continuity, the initiation of such a policy will probably be a painful process. Presently, the implementation of such a long-term anti-cyclical policy is complicated by a disadvantageous starting position. It will have to carry the weight of errors from the past. From this point of view one is justified in criticizing the political opportunism of previous governments, which resulted in a disproportional increase in government spending during the prosperous 1960s. One is, however, also justified in criticizing the inverse form of political opportunism, which results in a disproportional decrease of government spending during the adverse conditions of the 1980s. The former belongs to the past and it is a lesson for the future. The second belongs to the present and must be the first to disappear from the stage of history. *One cannot repair a mistake from the past by a policy that will prove to be a mistake in the future.*

NOTES

1. The publications of the years 1935, 1979 and 1984 refer to English translations of Kondratieff's work. Kondratieff (1935) is an abbreviated version of the German publication of 1926. Kondratieff

(1979) is the complete translation of the same article. Kondratieff (1984) is the translation of Kondratieff's contribution to a book edited by Oparin which was published in 1928. It must be considered the most complete source to Kondratieff's ideas.

2. This process was of course strongly assisted by international financial aid like the Marshall Plan.

3. Thus fulfilling at least one of Kuznets's requirements for establishing the existence of a wave of a given type (Kuznets 1940: 267).

4. This applies to the Dutch economy. Other nations, like for instance Germany, took considerably more time to recover from the war.

5. This reduction of Hicks's definition of autonomous investment (Hicks 1950: 59) is part of the explanation of the cyclical movement of autonomous investment (see page 145).

6. In the Netherlands these investments were supplemented after the floods of 1953 by the construction of a completely new sea-defence system (Delta works).

7. In practice this process was supplemented by the effects caused by the so-called 'run-away industries'. Weak sectors moved to 'low-wage countries' and thus provided some relief for the domestic labour market.

8. In the Preface to the third impression, Hicks remarks, 'In a long depression long range investment may disclose itself as induced, not autonomous' (Hicks 1950: viii).

9. Compare page 138 and note 5.

10. By structural recovery I understand a definite return to the path of sustained growth. In my view the recent weak revival in the world economy is only a temporary phenomenon.

11. The American policy appears a strategic factor in the recent 'revival' of the world economy. I am afraid, however, that this spark will soon be put out under the pressure of the 'beggar thy neighbour' policy which became the vogue in Europe.

Part III

Trade-Off: The Policy-Makers', the Poor
Men's and the Rich Men's Choice

6 Trade-off between Economic Growth and Income Equality: A re-evaluation*

Jae Won Lee and Suk Mo Koo

Numerous studies have been done in the area of economic growth and size distribution of income. Such a surge of interest in the relation betwen economic growth and income distribution is primarily due to dissatisfaction with using economic growth as an almost exclusive measure of economic development, disregarding its impact on income distribution. There has been a growing concern that a rapid economic growth may be achieved at the expense of equality in income distribution. This suggests a possible trade-off relation between economic growth and income equality.

The trade-off relation, if it exists, may be of two types: the long-run relation between income equality and the *level* of income, and the short-run relation between income equality and the *rate of growth* of income. A clear distinction between the two types of the relation is necessary, because they carry different implications, and furthermore, the existence of one type of trade-off relation is neither the necessary nor the sufficient condition for the existence of the other. Nevertheless, most researchers in the field have not clearly distinguished the two types of trade-off relations from each other.[1]

* The authors are indebted to Irving Stone, Peter M. Gutmann and other colleagues at Barch College for their valuable comments and suggestions. Tsing-Tzai Wu and Y.Y. Cheng provided competent assistance at various stages of the research.

6.1   LONG-RUN AND SHORT-RUN TRADE-OFF RELATIONS

Long-run Trade-off Relation
Kuznets suggests that inequality may increase at the early phase of economic development, which is the long-run trade-off relation discussed in the previous section, and that the trend is reversed at the later stage of development (Kuznets 1955: 18–20). Graphically, this hypothesis implies an inverted-U relation between income equality and real income as a measure of economic development. Such a graph is known as the Kuznets curve.

If this relation does exist, a rise in the degree of inequality during the early stages of a country's development will be inevitable, although it will be a transitory phenomenon, lasting only until the economy reaches an advanced stage of development. Consequently, this type of trade-off relation is beyond the scope of government's optimal policy decision.

The Kuznets Curve has been empirically verified by a number of researchers and accepted by many as a matter of fact (Kuznets 1963: 1–94; Paukert 1973: 97–125; Adelman and Morris 1973; Oshima 1962: 439–45; Chenery and Syrguin 1975; Ahluwalia 1976: 307–42; Ahluwalia 1978; Lydall 1977; Cline 1975: 359–400; Fei, Ranis and Kuo 1979).

Short-Run Trade–Off Relation
As a country attempts to speed up its economic growth, the equality in income distribution might suffer, regardless of its current level of income, because the factors responsible for an accelerated economic growth may also lead to a deterioration of the equality.

If such a short-run trade-off relation exists, the policy makers should pay a close attention to the distributive consequences of their growth-intensive policies. Unlike the case of the long-run trade-off relation, which is in a sense a sealed fate, the short-run trade-off calls for a policy decision to choose the optimum combination of growth rate and equality by using the estimated short-run trade-off relation as the constraint and the society's welfare function

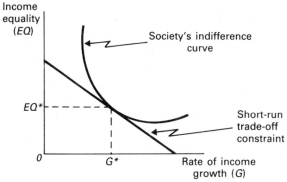

EQ* and G* = optimum combination of income equality and growth rate

Figure 6.1: Optimum policy decision on growth and equality

as the objective function. Such an optimization process can be illustrated in Figure 6.1, where EQ^* and G^* represent the optimum combination of equality and growth rate. The policy-makers will also face a longer-term task of raising the position of the trade-off curve itself by adopting efficient income distribution policies and choosing the speed of growth which will accompany less growth-induced inequality.

On the other hand, if the short-run trade-off relation does not exist, the government can pursue the policy of an accelerated growth without a serious concern about its distributive consequences.

Despite its importance, the short-run trade-off relation has not received adequate attention by the researchers in the field. Those few who have dealt with it have not found any strong evidence of its existence (Chenery *et al.* 1978; Fields 1980).This is rather surprising.

Welfare function and trade-off relations
The society's welfare function may vary from one society to another. The determinants of the welfare include the level of income, economic growth rate and the degree of income equality in addition to other economic as well as non-economic variables.

$W = f(Y, EQ, G;u)$
where: W = society's welfare
Y = level of income
u = the term representing
all the remaining variables
EQ = income equality
G = economic growth rate

$$\partial W/\partial EQ > 0, \ \partial W/\partial G > 0, \ \partial W/\partial Y > 0$$

The welfare function postulates that a society's welfare is, *ceteris paribus*, directly related to its level of income, economic growth rate, and equality. The independent variables in the welfare function may be related to each other. In fact, Kuznets's Inverted-U Hypothesis and the long-run trade-off relation suggests that Y and EQ have a negative correlation in the early stage of development, followed by a positive correlation at the later stage. On the other hand, the short-run trade-off relation focuses on the possibility of a negative correlation between G and EQ. Therefore the presence or the absence of the trade-off relations can be expressed in the following way:

Long-run trade-off	*Short-run trade-off*
$\partial EQ/\partial Y \ < \ 0$: present	$\partial EQ/\partial G \ < \ 0$: present
$\partial EQ/\partial Y \ \geq \ 0$: absent	$\partial EQ/\partial G \ \geq \ 0$: absent

6.2   PLAN FOR THE RESEARCH

Objective
In this paper an attempt will be made to empirically test the existence of the long-run and the short-run trade-off relations by using the international cross-section data for thirty countries, which include both the developed countries (DC) and the less-developed countries (LDC).[2]

Although a time-series estimation of the trade-off relation within each country is more desirable than the estimation based on the inter-country cross-section data, the lack of satisfactory time-series data on income distribution does not render any choice but to rely on the latter type of estimation. This makes the current study vulnerable to the usual problems associated with the use of the cross-sectional estimations for the purpose of a time-series analysis. Nevertheless, the issue is important enough to warrant a further empirical research.

Data
As the aggregate measure of the income equality, a variant of the Gini index (*EQ*) is chosen for the following two reasons: first, the Gini index satisfies the Pigou–Dalton condition.[3] Second , the measure of equality *EQ*, which is needed in our trade-off analysis, can be derived in a straightforward manner, simply by subtracting the Gini index from unity.

In addition to the aggregate measure, such disaggregate measures of equality as the income shares of the highest 5 per cent, the highest 20 per cent and the lowest 40 per cent income groups are also introduced, because the disaggregate measures can deal with some structural changes in income distribution, which the Gini index cannot.

The data for the Gini index and the disaggregate measures of equality have been computed and published by Jain (1975). Unlike most of the previous studies which have used income distribution data based on household (HH) as the unit, in this study the income distribution data based on income recipient (IR) will be used along with HH data. The results are expected to be different, possibly even to the extent that the conclusion of the empirical tests of the trade-off hypotheses may depend on which type or data, IR of HH, have been used for the tests.

Jain has compiled the national and/or the regional income distribution data for eighty countries. However, many of the countries had to be excluded from this study either for the lack of national-level data for the comparable periods or for being socialist countries which may need different treatment from other countries. To compound the problem, the data on the measure of imbalance in economic growth, which are from Yotopoulos-Nugent, are also not available for a number of countries, thereby reducing the total number of countries with the appropriate set of data to thirty. Even among the thirty countries, some do not have the national data on their income distribution based on the unit, while some others lack the national level data based on IR's. Therefore, thirty countries have been classified into two groups based on the availability of the income distribution data, that is IR and HH groups. The result is that thirteen countries have IR data, nineteen countries HH data and two countries both IR and HH data.

It is true that Kuznets recommended the use of income distribution data based on family-expenditure units properly adjusted for the number of persons in each (Kuznets 1955: 18–20). However, most of the available HH data are not adjusted for the number of persons in each household,[4] and, therefore, inadequate for a cross-country regression analysis due to a strong probability that the household size as well as its structure varies widely from country to country, leading to the distortions warned by Kuznets and Kakwani (Kakwani 1980; Bartlett and Poulton-Galahan 1982). Therefore, until the type of data which meets Kuznets's specifications are made available in many countries, the IR data seem to be a better choice than HH data, especially for a cross-country analysis. The data on the measure of imbalance in economic growth are from Yotopoulos-Nugent's V^* series (Yotopoulos and Lau 1970: 376–83), which is a weighted coefficient of variation of the sectoral growth rates.

6.3   ESTIMATING EQUATIONS

For the estimation of both the long-run and the short-run trade-off relations, numerous forms of estimating equations with various combinations of the relevant variables have been tried. A partial list of the estimating equations will be presented below, which will be preceded by the definitions of the variables. Since, however, the most common time points of the cross-sectional observations are around 1960 and 1970, and some countries have data for both time periods, the number of observations can be increased by pooling the cross-section data at two different time periods.[5] When the data for the two periods are pooled, the IR group has total of nineteen observations, while the HH group has thirty-one.

Per capita GNP in 1970 SDR (Special Drawing Right) unit is used to obtain internationally comparable measures of each country's real per capita income, and its annual percentage change is used as the measure of economic growth rate. The source of the data is *International Financial Statistics* (Washington, DC, 1975).[6]

List of the variables

EQ	= measure of equality in income distribution, where
EQ	= $1 -$ Gini index
$SH5$	= share of the highest 5 per cent income group
$SH20$	= share of the highest 20 per cent income group
$SL40$	= share of the lowest 40 percent income group
Y	= real per capita income in 1,000 SDR
G	= annual percentage growth rate of Y (e.g. G for 1970 = percentage change in Y from 1969 to 1970)
YI	= $1/Y$
YSQ	= Y squared
GI	= $1/G$
$G1$	= G lagged by 1 year (e.g. $G1$ for 1970 = percentage change in Y from 1968 to 1969)
$G2$	= G lagged by two years (e.g. $G2$ for 1970 = percentage change in Y from 1967 to 1968)
$G3$	= G lagged by three years
AVG	= average growth rate for four years. $AVG = (G + G1 + G2 + G3)/4$
$AVG1$	= average growth rate for three preceding years. $AVG1 = (G1 + G2 + G3)/3$
$AVG2$	= average growth rate for two and three lagged years. $AVG1 = (G2 + G3)/2$
$AVGSQ$	= AVG squared
$AVG1SQ$	= $AVG1$ squared

$\triangle$ = prefix to the variables denoting changes in the variables

UBG   = degreee of unbalanced growth

*D*1   = decade dummy variable, where:
                              $D1 = 0$ for 1960 observation
                              $D1 = 1$ for 1970 observation

*D*2   = development stage dummy variable, where:
                              $D2 = 0$ for LDC
                              $D2 = 1$ for DC

*D*3   = Asian dummy variable, where:
                              $D3 = 0$ for non-Asian countries
                              $D3 = 1$ for Asian countries

*D*4   = European dummy variable, where:
                              $D4 = 0$ for non-European countries
                              $D4 = 1$ for European countries

*D*5   = African dummy variable, where:
                              $D5 = 0$ for non-African countries
                              $D5 = 1$ for African countries

*D*6   = Latin American dummy variable, where:
                              $D6 = 0$ for non-Latin American countries
                              $D6 = 1$ for Latin American countries

*D*7   = $D4 = D5 = D6 = 0$ for Canada and the United States

Estimating Equations

For the estimation of the trade-off relations, equations (1) to (31) have been used with and without various combinations of dummy variables *D*1 through *D*6, totalling forty-eight estimating equations for each of IR and HH groups. Equations (1) to (6) are for the long-run trade-off relation with or without standardizing variable(s), whereas equations (7) to (31) are for the short-run trade-off relation.

To allow for the possiblity of non-linear relations, various forms of non-linear equations have also been used. To simplify the presentation of the basic equations, the additive stochastic error terms are not shown below, and all the equations are linear in parameter.[7]

$EQ = f(Y)$	(1)	$EQ = f(YI)$	(2)
$EQ = f(Y,YSQ)$	(3)	$EQ = f(Y,UBG)$	(4)
$EQ = f(Y,YSQ,UBG)$	(5)	$EQ = f(Y)$	(6)
$EQ = f(G)$	(7)	$EQ = f(G,G1)$	(8)

$$EQ = f(G1,G2) \qquad (9)$$
$$EQ = f(AVG) \qquad (11)$$
$$EQ = f(G,G1,G2,Y) \qquad (13)$$
$$EQ = f(G,G1,Y) \qquad (15)$$
$$EQ = f(AVG,Y,UBG) \qquad (17)$$
$$EQ = f(AVG, Y, UBG) \qquad (19)$$
$$EQ = f(G,Y,UBG) \qquad (21)$$
$$EQ = f(AVG,AVGSQ) \qquad (23)$$

$$EQ = f(G1,G2,G3) \qquad (10)$$
$$EQ = f(G1,G2,G3) \qquad (12)$$
$$EQ = f(G,G1,Y) \qquad (14)$$
$$EQ = f(G,G1,G2,G3,Y) \qquad (16)$$
$$EQ = F(G,AVG1, Y) \qquad (18)$$
$$EQ = f(G,AVG1,Y,UBG) \qquad (20)$$
$$EQ = f(G,UBG) \qquad (22)$$
$$EQ = f(AVG,AVGSQ,Y) \qquad (24)$$

$$EQ = f(AVG,AVGSQ,Y,UBG) \quad (25)$$
$$EQ = f(AVG1,AVG1SQ) \qquad (26)$$
$$EQ = f(AVG1,AVG1SQ,Y) \qquad (27)$$
$$EQ = f(AVG1,AVG1SQ,Y,UBG)$$
$$(28)$$

$$EQ = f(G) \qquad (29)$$
$$EQ = f(G1,G2,AVG2) \qquad (30)$$
$$EQ = f(G1,G2,AVG2,Y) \qquad (31)$$

The degree of unbalanced growth (*UBG*) is introduced to see if the pattern of growth has any effect on the income equality. To reflect a possible lag effect on income equality, some lagged values of the growth rate and/or the average growth rates have been introduced in some of the equations.

Various combinations of the six dummy variables have been added to the basic equations to see if any of those dummy variables can be effective standardizing variables in the estimating the trade-off relations. Dummy variable *D*1 is introduced to detect any significant difference between the two periods, the observations for both periods can be pooled, thereby increasing the number of observations in the estimating equations. Dummy variable *D*2 is for the detection of possible difference between DC and LDC groups. Dummy variables *D*3, *D*4, *D*5 and *D*6 have been introduced to standardize the trade-off relations for the possible socio-cultural differences among the countries in different geographical locations and also for the dualistic aspect.

Estimating equations (1) to (31) have been repeated with each of the disaggregate measures of equality, that is *SH*5, *SH*20, and *SL*40, as the alternative dependent variables.

6.4 ANALYSIS OF THE ESTIMATION RESULTS

A careful examination of the estimation results has revealed very interesting points which will be discussed in this section. For an orderly presentation of the massive estimation results, only the selected results will be presented in Tables 6.2

Table 6.1: List of countries under study

	Type of data and observation year	
Country	Income Recipient (IR)	Household (HH)
Australia	(n.d. = no data)	1968
Brazil	1960 & 1970	(n.d.)
Canada	(n.d.)	1961 & 1965
Chile	(n.d.)	1968
Columbia	1962 & 1970	(n.d.)
Costa Rica	(n.d.)	1961 & 1971
Denmark	1963 & 1966	(n.d.)
Finland	1962	(n.d.)
France	(n.d.)	1962
West Germany	1960	1960 & 1970
India	(n.d.)	1960 & 1968
Japan	(n.d.)	1962 & 1971
Kenya	1969	(n.d.)
Korea, Republic of	(n.d.)	1966 & 1971
Malaysia	(n.d.)	1960 & 1970
Mexico	(n.d.)	1963 & 1969
Netherlands	1962 & 1967	(n.d.)
New Zealand	1971	(n.d.)
Norway	1957 & 1963	(n.d.)
Pakistan	(n.d.)	1964 & 1970
Panama	1960 & 1972	(n.d.)
Peru	1962	(n.d.)
Philippines	(n.d.)	1961 & 1971
Sri Lanka	(n.d.)	1963 & 1973
Sweden	1963 & 1970	(n.d.)
Taiwan	(n.d.)	1960 & 1972
Tanzania	(n.d.)	1969
Thailand	(n.d.)	1962
Turkey	(n.d.)	1968
United Kingdom	1967	1960 & 1968
United States	(n.d.)	1965 & 1971
Venezuela	(n.d.)	1962

through to 6.6, and the summary of findings is presented in Table 6.7. The selection criteria include $\bar{R}^2$ and t-statistics. In addition, the results of the estimating equations which are expected to be of particular interest on *a priori* ground are also included in the select group regardless of their statistical significance.

Long-run trade-off relation

AGGREGATE MEASURE OF EQUALITY (*EQ*)   In this section, the empirical results for the test of the existence of the long-run trade-off relation as well as the Kuznets curve will be presented. The results are based on *EQ* as the aggregate measure of the equality, whereas those based on the disaggregate measures such as *SH5*, *SH20*, and *SL40* will be presented in a later section (p. 170). *Income recipient (IR) group*: The long-run trade-off relation and the early phase of the Kuznets curve anticipate a decline in income equality as the level of income increases. On the contrary, the results presented in Table 6.2 show a positive and statistically significant relation between *EQ* and *Y*. Among the estimating equations, equation (3) shows the highest $\bar{R}^2$, 0.67. The coefficient of *YSQ* is negative and statistically significant at 5 per cent level, which means that income equality rises at a decelerating rate during the early stage of growth as income increases and, then, reverses its movement downward during the later stage. This is the opposite of the Kuznets curve. Consequently, the evidence does not support the belief that it is inevitable for countries to sacrifice income equality during the early stage of growth or development.

One possible explanation for this may be that the countries in the sample might have already passed the critical turning point and moved into the later phase of the curve where inequality decreases as income level rises. Paukert estimated the turning point to be around 200 to 300 dollars in GDP per capita as of around 1965. However, at least nine countries in the sample used in the present study had income levels below Paukert's critical turning point (Paukert, 1973).

Another possible explanation for this positive relation between *EQ* and *Y* may be that the countries with higher income are likely to place progressively more emphasis on income distribution and also have more efficient system of income redistribution than the countries with lower income. Consequently, even if there were the long-run trade-off relation, it might have been overshadowed by the differences in the emphasis on income distribution as well as the

Table 6.2: Selection estimation results for the long-run trade-off relation, 1960 and 1970 (Dependent variable: EQ)

Type of data	Estimating equation	Constant	Y	YSQ	YI	UBG	D1	D2	$\bar{R}^2$
					Explanatory variables				
IR	(1)	0.421 (14.48)	0.078 (4.44)						0.50
IR	(2)	0.603 (26.34)			-0.042 (5.08)				0.57
IR	(3)	0.355 (11.35)	0.202 (4.34)	-0.35 (3.23)					0.67
IR	(1)*	0.424 (13.17)	0.079 (4.17)				-0.007 (0.18)		0.47
IR	(5)	0.394 (5.67)	0.187 (3.95)	-0.032 (2.77)		-0.059 (0.64)			0.66
IR	(5)*	0.397 (5.54)	0.184 (3.76)	-0.032 (2.70)		-0.072 (0.72)	0.014 (0.43)		0.64

							$\bar{R}^2$
HH	(1)	0.530 (25.98)	0.300 (2.24)					0.12
HH	(2)	0.573 (25.06)	−0.004 (0.94)					0.01
HH	(3)	0.518 (21.52)	0.062 (1.67)	−0.009 (0.92)				0.11
HH	(1)*	0.525 (2.07)	0.029 (0.37)		0.012 (0.37)			0.09
HH	(1)*	0.531 (25.70)	0.018 (0.81)			0.038 (0.66)		0.10
HH	(5)	0.530 (14.18)	0.058 (1.46)	−0.008 (0.80)			−0.015 (0.40)	0.086

The numbers of observations for IR and HH groups are 20 and 35, respectively. The numbers in the parentheses are the absolute values of t-statistics. The equation with the highest $\bar{R}^2$ in either IR or HH group.

* This denotes that the equation is a variant of the basic equation. For example, equation (5)* is a variant of equation (5).

Table 6.3: *Selected estimation results for the short-run trade-off relation, 1960 and 1970* (Dependent variable: *EQ*)

Type of data	Estimating equation	Constant	G	Y	UBG	AVG1	D1	$\bar{R}^2$
						Explanatory variables		
IR	(7)	0.564 (13.27)	−0.008 (1.19)					0.02
IR	(12)	0.486 (7.20)	−0.007 (1.25)			0.015 (1.46)		0.08
IR	(13)	0.458 (12.12)	−0.006 (1.46)	0.77 (4.50)				0.53
IR	(21)	0.609 (8.30)	−0.010 (2.34)	0.55 (3.11)	−0.224 (2.32)			0.62
IR	(21)*	0.616 (8.09)	−0.010 (2.32)	0.050 (2.50)	−0.243 (2.31)		0.019 (0.54)	0.61
HH	(7)	0.538 (30.24)	0.007 (2.41)					0.14
HH	(12)	0.542 (26.44)	0.007 (2.38)			−0.001 (0.44)		0.11
HH	(13)	0:513 (25.11)	0.006 (2.33)	0.027 (2.16)				0.24
HH	(21)	0.500 (13.86)	0.007 (2.25)	0.029 (2.18)	0.017 (0.44)			0.21
HH	(21)*	0.495 (13.03)	0.007 (2.22)	0.027 (1.95)	0.015 (0.39)		0.015 (0.49)	0.19

See notes in Table 2.

Table 6.4: Analysis of covariance for 1960 and 1970 observation groups
(Dependent variable: EQ)

	Computed F-Statistics to test difference in:		
Model	Intercept	Slope	Intercept and slope
Long-run trade-off			
IR group: equation (3)	0.029	0.943	0.486
HH group: equation (1)	0.132	0.092	0.110
Short-run trade-off			
IR group: equation (21)	0.294	0.148	0.172
HH Group: equation (21)	0.237	0.394	0.351

effectiveness of the redistribution system. More research is needed in this area.

The decade dummy variable, $D1$, is statistically insignificant at the 5 per cent level in all the estimating equations, including (1–1) and (5–1), which allows us to proceed with the pooled regression.[8] Nevertheless, a complete analysis of covariance has been done to reassure the legitimacy of pooling the observations, and the results presented in Table 6.4 are affirmative. All the computed F statistics were well below the critical F values at the 1 per cent level, accepting the null hypotheses that no significant difference exists between 1960 and 1970 data groups in terms of both intercepts and slopes.

Dummy variable $D2$, which distinguishes LDC from DC, is not statistically significant at the 5 per cent level in nearly all the estimating equations, implying that there is no significant difference between LDC and DC in the relation between Y and EQ.

As for dummy variables $D3$, $D4$, $D5$, and $D6$, which were introduced to standardize the possible socio-cultural differences among the countries, their coefficients are also statistically insignificant at 5 per cent level in all the estimating equations, indicating that there is no significant difference in the relation between Y and EQ in different continents. The coefficient of *UBG* is also insignificant at 5 per cent level in all the estimating equations, indicating that the difference in the pattern of growth does not significantly affect the relation between Y and EQ. Above all, it is remarkable that more than 65 per cent of the variation of income equality could be explained by a single variable, Y, in a quadratic form in equation (3). In contrast to this result, the same estimating equation with the HH data has shown a drastically lower goodness of fit.

Household (HH) group: When the HH data on the income equality are used, both $\bar{R}^2$ and t-statistics for the coefficients in all the estimating equations are substantially reduced. As Table 6.2 shows, the highest $\bar{R}^2$ is only 0.12 in equation (1). Although $\bar{R}^2$ in equation (1) is very low, its result is basically consistent with those of the selected estimating equations in the IR group. The coefficient of Y in equation (1) is positive and statistically significant at 5 per cent level. Consequently, in both the IR and the HH groups, there is no evidence of either the Kuznets curve or the long-run trade-off curve. Even the coefficients of all the dummy variables are statistically insignificant at 5 per cent level, eliminating the possibility of improving the fits with the dummy variables The coefficient of *UBG* is also insignificant at 5 per cent level, indicating that the pattern of growth has no significant influence on income equality. It should be repeatedly pointed out that the estimating equations in this group show extremely low values of $\bar{R}^2$.

Disaggregate measures of equality (*SH*5, *SH*20, *SL*40)
Income recipient (IR) group: For this data group, the result of the estimating equation (3), as shown in Table 6.5, was the best in terms of $\bar{R}^2$ and t-statistics for all the disaggregate measures of income equality. The results for *SH*5 and *SH*20 indicate that the relations between the level of income and the shares of the highest 5 per cent and 20 per cent income groups are U-shaped, which means that as the level of income rises, the shares of the highest 5 and 20 per cent groups decrease in the early period and increase later. In other words, an increase in the level of income accompanies an initial improvement in the income equality, which is

reversed in the later period. This is opposite to the Kuznets curve. Furthermore, since all the actual observations fall on the declining segment of the estimated parabolic relation, an increase in the income level is associated with an increase in the equality. This rejects the idea of the long-run trade-off relation.

The result for $SL40$, on the other hand, shows a bell-shaped relation between the level of income and the share of the lowest 40 per cent income group. This implies an initial improvement in the income distribution followed by a deterioration at later period. This is also the opposite to the implication of the Kuznets curve. Furthermore, all the actual observations, except one, lie on the increasing segment of the parabola, which means that an increasing share of the lowest 40 per cent income group is associated with an increasing income level. This is inconsistent with the idea of the long-run trade-off relation.

Household (HH) group: As in the case of EQ, the switch from IR data to HH data results in a drastic decrease in the goodness of fit in all the estimating equations. The estimation results presented in Table 6.5 show negative relations between Y and $SH5$ as well as $SH20$. As the level of income rises, the shares of the highest 5 per cent and 20 per cent income groups decline, implying an increase in equality. This is inconsistent with the idea of the long-run trade-off curve and the Kuznets curve. The relationship between Y and $SL40$, on the other hand, is a positive one. However, the coefficient of Y is not statistically significant at the 5 per cent level. Consequently, the results show no evidence of either the long-run trade-off relation or the Kuznets curve.

Short-run trade-off relation

AGGREGATE MEASURE OF EQUALITY (EQ) *Income recipient (IR) group:* Table 6.3 shows that equation (21) has the highest R^2 of 0.623 and also that all the regression coefficients are statistically significant at the 5 per cent level. The negative coefficient of G indicates the existence of the short-run trade-off relation. This means that any increase in the speed of growth, holding Y and UBG

constant, is associated with a decrease in the aggregate income equality.

Based on the result of equation (21), we can estimate the short-run trade-off line for each country by substituting the country's specific values of Y and UBG. With the estimated short-run trade-off line obtained this way, each country can try to choose the optimum combination of growth rate and income equality in the way presented in Figure 6.1.

The positive sign of the coefficient of Y in equation (21) is another indication of the rejection of the long-run trade-off relation between the level of income and income equality. The negative sign of the coefficient of UBG signifies that the greater the degree of imbalance in growth, *ceteris paribus*, the greater the deterioration of the income equality. As in the case of the long-run trade-off relation, none of the dummy variables have any significant influence on the short-run trade-off relation. It should be reminded

Table 6.5: Selected estimation results for long-run trade-off relation based on disaggregate measures of income equality

Dependent Variable	Estimating equation	Constant	Y	YSQ	$\bar{R}2$
IR Group					
SH5	(3)	0.450 (12.46)	−0.215 (4.57)	0.037 (2.91)	0.635
SH20	(3)	0.673 (25.64)	−0.184 (5.37)	0.032 (3.55)	0.704
SL40	(3)	0.085 (8.61)	0.061 (4.71)	−0.010 (3.07)	0.648
HH Group					
SH5	(1)	0.269 (16.15)	−0.034 (3.08)		0.220
SH20	(1)	0.530 (29.05)	−0.031 (2.59)		0.160
SL40	(1)	0.139 (15.17)	0.009 (1.52)		−0.032

Note: The numbers in the parentheses are the absolute values of the *t*-statistics.

that the $\bar{R}^2$ value of 0.62 is remarkably high for this type of cross-country regression estimation.

Household (HH) Group: When the HH data are used instead of the IR data, the value of $\bar{R}^2$ decrease drastically. Furthermore, none of the dummy variables is capable of improving the estimation, because all of them are statistically insignificant at the 5 per cent level. *UBG* also loses statistical significance. These findings are also opposite to those of the IR data group.

DISAGGREGATE MEASURES OF EQUALITY (*SH5,SH20,SL40*)
Income recipient (IR) group: In this group equation (21) is the best one for *SH5* and *SH20*, as Table 6.6 shows, while equation (13) is the best for *SL40*. The results further indicate that the shares of the highest 5 per cent (*SH5*) and the highest 20 per cent (*SH20*) are directly related with the rate of growth (G); inversely related with the level of income (*Y*); and directly related with the degree of

Table 6.6: Selected estimation results for short-run trade-off relation based on disaggregate measures of income equality

Dependent variable	Estimating equation	Constant	G	Y	UBG	$\bar{R}2$
IR Group						
SH5	(21)	0.123	0.013	−0.053	0.308	0.701
		(1.72)	(3.21)	(3.04)	(3.26)	
SH20	(21)	0.448	0.008	−0.050	0.196	0.634
		(6.99)	(2.28)	(3.23)	(2.33)	
SL40	(13)	0.112	−0.002	0.023		0.473
		(9.15)	(0.81)	(4.24)		
HH Group						
SH5	(13)	0.282	−0.004	−0.032		0.292
		(16.51)	(1.99)	(3.01)		
SH20	(13)	0.545	−0.005	−0.029		0.259
		(29.60)	(2.21)	(2.52)		
SL40	(13)	0.132	0.003	0.008		0.144
		(14.17)	(2.11)	(1.39)		

Note: The numbers in the parentheses are the absolute values of the *t*-statistics.

Table 6.7: Summary of the estimation results 1960s and 1970s

	Evidence of trade-off relation	
	Long-run (Kuznets curve)	Short-run
IR data		
Aggregate measure (*EQ*)	No	Yes
Highest 5 per cent (*SH*5)	No	Yes
Highest 20 per cent (*SH*20)	No	Yes
Lowest 40 per cent (*SL*40)	No	No
HH data		
Aggregate measure (EQ)	No	Yes
Highest 5 per cent (*SH*5)	No	No
Highest 20 per cent (*SH*20)	No	No
Lowest 40 per cent (*SL*40)	No	No

imbalance in growth path (*UBG*). The positive relationship between *G* and *SH*5 as well as with *SH*20 is consistent with the short-run trade-off relation, while the inverse relation between *Y* and *SH*5 as well as *SH*20 is not consistent with the long-run trade-off relation. Statistical significance of the coefficient of *UBG* indicates that not only the rate of growth but also the pattern of growth exert significant influence on the income equality. *Ceteris paribus*, the more unbalanced a country's growth, the larger the shares of the highest 5 per cent and 20 per cent income groups, signalling the greater inequality in income distribution. As for the share of the lowest 40 per cent income group (*SL*40), Table 6.6 shows that *SL*40 has an inverse relation with the rate of growth (*G*) and a positive relation with the level of income (*Y*), which is consistent with the results of *SH*5 and *SH*20. The inverse relation between *SL*40 and *G* is consistent with the short-run trade-off relation, while the positive relation between *Y* and *SL*40 implies the existence of the long-run trade-off relation. Nevertheless, the coefficient of *G* is statistically insignificant at 5 per cent level, which makes the short-run trade-off relation insignificant in so far as *SL*40 is used as a measure of income equality.

Household (HH) group: For this group, estimating equation (13) resulted in the highest $\bar{R}^2$, as shown in Table 6.6, although their values are substantially lower than those obtained for the IR group.

As in the case of the IR group, *SH*5 and *SH*20 are inversely related to *Y*, and their coefficients are statistically significant at the 5 per cent level, which is inconsistent with the long-run trade-off relation. Unlike the case of the IR group, the coefficient of *G* is negative, which does not support the existence of the short-run trade-off relation either. As for *SL*40, the coefficients of both *G* and *Y* are statistically insignificant at 5 per cent level, and consequently, the results neither support nor reject the existence of either the short-run or the long-run trade-off relations.

6.5 SUMMARY OF FINDINGS AND POLICY IMPLICATIONS

Contrary to the popular belief and the findings of many other researchers, the estimation results of the current study indicate that there is no statistical evidence to support the existence of the Kuznets curve or the long-run trade-off relation between income equality and the level of income representing the stage of growth and development. The results are basically the same whether the aggregate measure of income equality or the disaggregate measures are used.

Both types of data on income equality, that is income distribution by the income recipient (IR) and by the household (HH), consistently negates the possible existence of the long-run trade-off relation as well as the Kuznets curve. Furthermore, the HH data show substantially poorer fits than the IR data. The results also indicate that the degree of imbalance in economic growth does not have any significant long-run influence on the equality.

As for the short-run trade-off relation, the results are highly sensitive to the type of data used for the estimation.

When the IR data are used, there is a strong evidence of the short-run trade-off relation between the income equality and the rate of economic growth. However, when the HH data are used, there is no statistical evidence of the trade-off relation. In addition, the significance of the influence of the growth pattern on the income equality also varies depending on the type of data used. The results of the estimation with the IR data indicate that the greater the degree of imbalance in economic growth, *ceteris paribus*, the greater the decrease in the income equality. However, the results with the HH data indicate that the degree of imbalance in the economic growth does not have any significant effect on the income equality.

As in the case of the long-run trade-off relation, it should be pointed out that the estimations with IR data resulted in impressive fits, while those with HH data resulted in poor fits. At the purely statistical level, this fact plus the shortcoming of the available household data discussed in section 6.3 gives the results with IR data more credence. At the theoretical level, however, since there is no reason why income distribution among individual recipients and among households should be the same; it is quite possible that the short-run trade-off exists between the equality among the income recipients and the growth rate, while no significant trade-off exists between the equality among the households and the growth rate.

Two important policy implications of our findings are as follows: first, since there is no evidence of the existence of the long-run trade-off relation between the level of income and the degree of income equality, the policy decision-makers should not resign themselves to the fatalism that a deterioration of the income equality is inevitable for the economy to advance to a higher stage of development. Instead, they should actively pursue various policy measures such as efficient transfer payment mechanism, tax reforms and broad concept of incomes policy, which will remedy the deterioration of the income equality. Second, since there is some significant evidence of the existence of the short-run trade-off relation between the income equality and the rate of economic growth, the policy planners should seriously consider the adverse effect of an accelerated growth policy on the income distribution, and should adopt the combination of the rate of economic growth and the income equality that is most acceptable to the society.

The studies of size distribution of income have always been plagued with the lack of reliable data on income distribution, and this study is no exception. It is extremely desirable for various governments to compile reliable time-series data on size distribution of income for more conclusive verification as well as estimation of the trade-off relations. Since the size distribution of income will ultimately have to be connected to the functional distribution of income for a more comprehensive and systematic analysis, reliable time-series data on the functional sources of income groups should be compiled along with the economic profiles of the income groups.

NOTES

1. Labels such as the long-run and the short-run trade-off relations may not be the ideal ones. However, in the absence of more appropriate labels, they will be used in this paper.
2. In recent decades, considerable interest has been generated in the area of economic development and absolute poverty. This study, however, will focus only on the relative equality in income distribution.
3. This condition is met if any measure of income inequality shows an improvement in income distribution when some positive amount of income has been transferred from a relatively rich person to a relatively poor person. For more details, read Dalton (1920) and Sen (1973).
4. Jain points out that households in his data may refer to either a single-person household or a multi-person household. For details, read Jain (1975: xii).
5. The exact years in which observations were made are not the same for all the countries. For instance, for some countries the observation years are 1960 and 1970, while for the others they may be in 1961 and 1971.
6. The list of the countries in the IR and the HH groups is presented in Table 6.1.
7. The observations in the estimations are arranged in alphabetical order, and therefore there is no *a priori* reason to suspect autocorrelation among the residuals.
8. Estimating equations (1–1) and (5–1) are the estimating equations (1) and (5) with the decade dummy variables.

7 IMF Policies: The dilemma of their effect on growth and income distribution in developing countries, 1980–5

J.K. Verkooijen

The debt crisis management policies of the IMF which were implemented by the developing countries may have had negative effects on the per capita growth of their GNP. If growth is slack, all incomes are affected but those of the poor most of all. This paper is concerned with the sharp decline in recent years in net capital inflows in developing countries. Between 1981 and 1985 these inflows fell by 52 per cent (World Bank 1986:37). The decline may have led to the fall in per capita GNP in both African and several Latin American countries. Many developing countries receive assistance from the IMF. It has been suggested that the conditions set by the Fund might have been harmful for the poor (NIO-Vereniging 1985; Khan and Knight 1985: 1).

7.1 SOME GENERAL OBSERVATIONS

For the world as a whole the income of the richest countries, the top decile, exceeds the bottom decile by a ratio of 63 to 1. On the whole there is much more equality in countries with high levels of income per capita than in poor countries. The Gini indices in the study of van Ginneken and Park give values for industrial countries which are invariably lower than 0.40 and falling to 0.30. For non-industrial countries the Gini indices range from 0.40 to 0.60 (with the exception of Bangladesh and Yugoslavia) (van Ginneken and Park 1984:5). It is, however, important to take note that this relationship is more complex than these figures suggest. If the various structural characteristics, the different policies with regard to distribution and the different stages of economic development are taken into account, it can be seen that the relationship between the level of income and the degree of inequality is not always negative. The level of per capita income can therefore serve only as a rough indicator for the inequality of income distribution.

A positive relationship between the level of income per head and the degree of equality in income distribution suggests that policies to improve growth will benefit the lower-income groups. However, Kuznets's so-called Inverted-U Curve Hypothesis presents the opposite picture for countries in a certain range of income. The 'relative income inequality rises during the early stages of development, reaches a peak and then declines in the later stages' (Fields 1980: 61). This feature of the development process does not necessarily affect the generally positive influence of growth on actual incomes. With regard to the poor's absolute levels of income, international cross-section analyses show that 'although the poor lose out relatively, they do not lose out absolutely' (Fields 1980:166). Therefore, given the very serious situation of the poor in both absolute and relative terms, growth must be welcome. But to increase the positive consequences of growth for the poor it becomes necessary to take additional measures to make distribution more equitable. In short, it is worthwhile to investigate which economic policies can simultaneously promote economic growth and greater distributive equality in developing countries. The conventional wisdom that to stimulate investment in the relatively capital–intensive export activities is the best means for promoting economic growth, tends to ignore its distributive consequences. This approach implies a lower share of labour income and therefore greater inequality. In contrast, an approach which accords greater importance to labour-intensive activities, agriculture in particular, may have certain relative merits. As 70 to 80 per cent of the labour force is engaged in agriculture in low-income countries, the stimulation of this sector would of course promote greater equality.

7.2 THE DEBT CRISIS AND PROSPECTS FOR ECONOMIC GROWTH

From 1980 to 1983 the economies of the major industrial countries expanded only very tardily—by about 1 per cent GNP annually. In the developing countries there was a lagged stagnation. It concentrated in the years 1982 and 1983. In 1982 there was even a fall in the volume of exports. The terms of trade also worsened. The ratio of debt to GNP increased from 21 per cent to 33 per cent. This increase occurred mainly before 1984. As the growth of exports did not keep pace with the growth of the external debt, the ratio of debts to exports also rose from 90 per cent to 136 per cent. The debt could no longer be serviced in the normal way. In short, the creditworthiness of the developing world deteriorated. A sharp decline in new commitments to public and publicly guaranteed loans followed. They fell from about $95 billion in 1980 to $70 billion in 1984 (World Bank 1986:32–3). This forced the developing countries to reduce their external imbalances by drastic measures—among others, by cuts in public spending and by the imposition of import restrictions. The measures met with some success. The combined deficit of the indebted developing countries (except the eight major oil exporters) fell from $113 billion in 1981 to about $38 billion in 1984 (IMF 1985:51). However, this result was obtained by a fall in imports rather than a rise in exports—the measures were restrictive instead of expansionary.

In the latest *World Development Report*, projections ('not forecasts') were made for the coming ten years. Two scenarios were elaborated: a 'high case' and a 'low case' scenario. In the 'high case' scenario, growth in the industrialized countries was expected to increase by an average of more than 4 per cent per year. In the low case scenario, annual growth rates were taken to reach no more than 2.5 per cent. But even the latter exceeded the actual average growth rate of the last five years. In the 'high case' scenario GNP per capita in developing countries was projected to grow by some 4 per cent and in the 'low case' scenario by only 1.5 per cent. For Africa the optimistic scenario projected a very slight per capita income growth (less than 0.5 per cent) and the pessimistic scenario projected a decline. The conclusion reached by the World Bank with regard to the pessimistic scenario is rather alarming. To maintain or restore creditworthiness, the developing countries would have to improve their trade balances. But with the slow growth in world trade it will be difficult to increase export earnings. In addition, the diminished net inflows of capital (basically non-concessional loans) will cause further shortages of foreign exchange and this must force these countries to restrict imports, which in turn will reduce investment. Hence economic growth is indispensable. Meanwhile, the adjustment processes must go on. For these reasons the World Bank advocated a strategy of 'adjustment with growth'. This combination also forms the core of the Baker Initiative. Multi-lateral organizations such as the World Bank and the IMF can contribute to the realization of this objective by supplying financial assistance and by mobilizing private capital flows. But even so it must be evident that the envisaged growth rates of the per capita GNP can hardly do much in the short run for the improvement of the position of the poor and underfed. Apart from this, it also remains uncertain how the adjustment process will affect the latter in many other ways. Under these circumstances it is necessary that the social aspects of the economic policy be given greater attention by both the domestic policy-makers and the foreign monitoring organizations.

7.3 INCOMES POLICY

Any development policy affects incomes. The most important elements for income distribution are the allocation of factors of production; unemployment and price policy play a central role. In developing countries, especially in the least developed, where the majority of the population is engaged in agriculture with low levels of productivity, the intersectoral disparity in average incomes is very large. As Lecaillon, Morrison and Germidis as well as Paukert, observed 'the difference in productivity and in average income between the agricultural sector and the non-agricultural sector accounts for about half of the general inequality of incomes' (Lecaillon *et al*. 1984: 111).

The distribution of land ownership, the different levels of technology and the various degrees of market integration, exert a great influence on the income differentials within the agricultural sector and between geographical locations. Population growth, too, has a considerable impact on inequality. Cross-country analysis shows that 'a positive difference of 1 per cent in the rate of population growth is correlated with a negative difference of 1.6 per cent in the income share of the poorest group', that is of 40 per cent of the population (Lecaillon *et al*. 1984: 11). Other variables of a socio economic nature also exert an important influence, among these the employment status (employee or self-employed), the amount of capital per worker, the level of education and the state of health. These characteristics permit the definition of socioeconomic groups. 'In developing countries the disparities in average incomes between these groups . . . account for 60 to 80 per cent of income inequality' (Lecaillon, *et al*. 1984: 95). An improvement of the income distribution in favour of the poor requires a combined modification of various interrelated socioeconomic structural factors which can only be realized in the long run. But there is no evidence that redistribution of incomes by way of structural changes cannot go hand in hand with economic growth. They may well be the two sides of the same coin.

Another, preferably supplementary, instrument for diminishing income inequality is the budget of the public sector. Taxation can be used to redistribute incomes and so can public expenditures, particularly on things like education, public health, housing, social assistance and food subsidies, and expenditure for the stimulation of agriculture and industry. When low incomes are raised by budgetary policy or by a stabilization of the cost of living, changes in the structure of demand have to be matched by a flexible supply of essential agricultural and industrial products. If national output is inelastic, imports may in the short run help to avoid inflation. In the long run, however, domestic, preferably labour-intensive production of foodstuffs and of other essential goods, may in many cases offer attractive opportunities for a stable supply and employment. In developing countries where agriculture has been depreciated for a long time, agrarian production requires government assistance (infrastructure, credit, extension services) in order to increase productivity and production. Investment of this kind requires considerable public funds. Yet, given the circumstances of the rural and urban poor, such investment is indispensable, and so a sound price policy is also essential.

In industrialized countries taxation and government expenditure can be powerful instruments for redistribution, but in developing countries their strength is relatively small. The reasons for this are, first, because the size of the public sector tends to be positively correlated with the level of per capita GNP. For example, in the poorest countries at the bottom decile, the public sector amounts on average to no more than between 15 per cent–20 per cent of the GNP. Second, because income policies are hardly effective. This can be seen from the case studies of the effectiveness of income policies by Lecaillon *et al*. Although the abundance of statistical problems and imputation difficulties made the findings, in the authors' words, no more than an approximation, they show that 'the greater the inequality of primary incomes, the smaller the redistribution' (Lecaillon *et al*. 1984: 152). The overall incidence of revenue-raising and expenditure of the public sector on the primary incomes, shows a redistributive effect which is less for developing countries than for developed countries.

Given the structural characteristics of the public sector (e.g. the share collective goods have in it), it is not realistic to expect that a more effective income policy can emerge in the developing countries without a substantial rise in the GNP.

7.4 THE IMPACT OF THE ADJUSTMENT PROCESS ON INCOMES

The debt problem and the rather moderate prospects for economic growth form a particular threat for the poor. Policies aimed at restoring external balance and increasing internal savings seem inadequate to regain sufficient creditworthiness to increase the net inflow of capital. These policies can hardly succeed without assistance from multilateral organizations. In recent years 70 per cent of the low-income countries have received financial assistance from the IMF. Capital aid by the World Bank is aimed at structural improvements; one of the Bank's objectives is to alleviate poverty. This has recently been reconfirmed in Seoul (October 1985) (World Bank 1985: 48). The Fund provides temporary financial support to solve balance-of-payments problems. Moreover, a great share of the IMF capital aid is conditional. The recipient has to adopt, or propose, a macroeconomic adjustment policy which appears to be capable of reducing the external imbalance. Because IMF assistance implies consent to such a policy, IMF involvement tends to encourage other capital suppliers. Support from the IMF seems increasingly a prerequisite for new flows of private capital.

Nevertheless, the data given in the recent *World Development Report* show that new commitments from private sources diminished sharply during the first half of the 1980s. They decreased by 40 per cent between 1981 and 1985. As mentioned before, total net flows of long-term capital to developing countries decreased by 52 per cent (from $75 billion in 1981 to $35 billion in 1985). This was principally due to the reduction of the disbursements from private creditors by 39 per cent. At the same time there was a slight increase in debt repayments (World Bank 1986: 37)

In the 1980s, the growth of GNP in developing countries reached approximately half the level of the annual growth rates in the previous decade. Given population growth, many of the poor were faced with diminished incomes and consumption. In the literature a great deal of attention is paid to the relevance of growth in order to restore creditworthiness.

Again I stress the importance of growth for the improvement of the incomes of the poor. The question which remains to be considered is how policies aimed at restoring the balance of indebtedness affect economic growth and income distribution. Fund policies and programmes have come under mounting criticism for failing to encourage economic growth. Killick and others found 'that programmes have not generally had strong deflationary effects but there are indications that negative growth effects were stronger in the most recent years' (Killick 1984: 265). Their analysis is mainly based on stand-by loans and the EFF programmes in the 1970s. Obviously, it is very difficult to find a systematically general and statistically significant relation between all the Fund-supported adjustment programmes and the economic growth in the countries concerned. As the IMF notes, there is a paucity of empirical studies that directly examine the relationship between Fund programmes and economic growth, and further research is needed. However, the IMF makes some inferences stating that 'there is no clear presumption that Fund-supported programs adversely affect growth' and concludes optimistically that 'it has to be recognized that a Fund program may lead to a lower growth in the first year, but can pave the way to a recovery in succeeding years' (Khan and Knight 1985:25).

All the same, on the basis of the World Bank's recent data it can be argued that in most of the low-income countries in Africa south of the Sahara and in the deeply indebted middle-income countries in Latin America and in the Caribbean area, the general process of adjustment to the reality of the world economy during the first half of the 1980s has been characterized by a negative growth of GNP. (The exceptional cases of Brazil and some indebted countries in Asia require an additional analysis.) Despite the variety of circumstances from country to country, many of them, often with the assistance of the IMF, embarked on stabilization programmes with certain common policy components. During the early 1980s this adjustment has been characterized by a drastic reduction of imports 'following at least partly from necessary exchange-rate adjustments, cuts in public spending, but also partly from a more worrisome increase in import restrictions and tighter rationing of private sector credit' (World Bank 1986:36). These conditions have been an obstacle to the import of indispensable capital goods for new investments. At the same time, it is difficult to imagine how the reduction of public expenditure could not have restrained government investments and assistance for the promotion of greater flexibility of output in the traditional sectors of agriculture.

Other things, too, have disturbed the flow of imports and investment. As mentioned before, the volume of export of the indebted countries has increased, but its effect has partly been cancelled by a deterioration in the terms of trade. The average annual percentage change was −0.6 between 1980 and 1985 (World Bank 1986:159). At the same time, the increasing debt service absorbed a growing part of export earnings and of domestic savings. The latter, given the fall in real wages, could hardly have grown. Thus little was left to finance new capital formation. This mix of conditions clearly shows the difficulties for investment and growth which the dramatically worsened economic situation in the first half of the 1980s brought about. Net borrowings were required, but in 1985 the developing countries paid out $422 billion more in long-term debt servicing than they received that year in long-term loans. Between 1981 and 1985, new private commitments and net inflows stagnated in the low-income African countries and in the indebted countries of Latin America. In some countries, like Mexico, there was the additional problem of capital flight. The fall in interest rates in the industrialized countries was the one positive financial development. But to date it has not changed the situation substantially. Adjustment and growth are necessary, but in the given conditions many developing countries will be forced to try to reschedule their debts because further reductions in investment and lower consumption are not only harmful but politically infeasible.

Globally, the adjustment strategy ought to be both supply and demand-oriented. More emphasis needs to be put on labour-intensive production of essential goods and services for national and regional markets. At the same time, traditional and non-traditional exports continue to be important. Inevitable adjustments should spare import restrictions and cuts in public expenditures which favour investment. General improvemements in the use of human and capital resources are necessary, and the flight of capital must be controlled. Additional short-term financing is also essential. Likewise, less protectionism and reduced public deficits and lower interest rates in industrial countries are required. In many developing countries, both debt rescheduling and a reduction in interest rates seem inevitable. A limitation on debt-servicing related to a share of export earnings (as Peru proposes) deserves consideration. The advantage of such a mechanism is that it may counteract the disadvantages from the deterioration in the terms of trade of the developing countries and the detrimental effects of protectionism which hamper the availability of foreign exchange for investment.

The question in what way adjustment policy will affect income distribution has been the subject of a study by the Fund's staff. The measures undertaken between 1980 and 1984 in ninety-four Fund-supported adjustment programmes were investigated. The measures comprised monetary and exchange rate policies, fiscal policies, restraint of wages and salaries, taxes, subsidies and transfers. Sisson concluded that, in general, fund-supported programmes have not been 'inimical to the goal of improving distribution of income' (Sisson 1986: 36). Killick and others found 'rather complex effects on income distribution without any systematic tendency either to increase or reduce income concentration' (Killick 1984: 265). NIO ascertained several cases of increasing inequality (NIO-Vereniging 1985: 122–3). An analysis of such a problem is of course very difficult. Nevertheless, there are cases in which a clear judgement can be made.

The most important elements analysed by Sisson were exchange rate and monetary and credit policies, which in general did not have a direct effect on income distribution and whose indirect impact was very difficult to assess. Most programmes included a restructuring or introduction of new taxes. Because in most developing countries income tax is not of great importance it was concluded that its effect is limited but still generally favourable for the reduction of income inequality. With regard to taxes on goods and services, the distributional effect depends mainly on the consumption habits of individuals and is therefore difficult to ascertain. Furthermore, 90 per cent of the programmes made only limited use of central government expenditure, but a very small number of these programmes referred to a specific functional expenditure. This suggests that the distributional effects could only have been limited. In other cases, however, such an impact was strongly prevalent. It was noted, for example, in the evaluation of Fund-supported food subsidy programmes, that domestic incomes in the agricultural sector often increased after food subsidies had been reduced. But when food subsidies were channelled directly to the lower-income groups (e.g. by food coupons and by distribution in schools) their distributional effect was positive. Generally, the benefit of subsidies for different income groups depends on the way such measures are actually designed. In several cases the larger share of the benefits accrued to a rather small part of the population, sometimes even to the richest groups. Hence the best way to reduce income inequalities remains to direct subsidies precisely to those who are most in need of them. It must be possible to pay more attention to the distributional effects of expenditure cuts and tax reforms. The items discussed in the Fund's study leave the impression that a less neutral attitude could improve distribution without impairing the effectiveness of the other policy proposals.

7.5 CONCLUSION

In this paper some insight has been given into the prospects facing the developing countries in the near future. Their need to reduce their external imbalances and to solve their debt problems does not leave them much room for economic growth. Some policy suggestions were made to promote growth and to improve income distribution. A modification of the adustment process is required to improve the long-term growth prospects. It is proposed that debt rescheduling and debt servicing should be linked and restricted to export earnings. It is further suggested that redistributional aspects be taken into account when Fund-supported adjustment programmes are elaborated. The recent study of the IMF shows that such recommendations can be made. There is no evidence for a trade-off between more attention to income distribution and the achievement of the Fund's main objectives. With this it cannot be denied that the inclusion of these elements in the Fund's policy implies political choice. The proposed adjustments require further research, discussion and substantial political support which cannot easily be obtained. The position of the poor makes it very necessary.

8 Equity and Efficiency in Holland: An overview

J. Hartog and J.G. Odink

Within the neoclassical framework, the role of the government in structural economic policies can be prescribed as 'implementing the trinity' (Hartog 1987). This is meant to say that there are the following tasks for the government:

(1) promote the conditions for competition,
(2) correct for market failure,
(3) strike a balance between equity and efficiency.

The first two tasks follow immediately from Paretian welfare theory. Perfect competition, in a static environment with no uncertainty, generates a Pareto-efficient market outcome, except for two notorious cases of market failure: pure public goods and external effects in consumption and production. Hence static Pareto-efficiency can be obtained if the government takes care of the public goods and provides a solution for external effects (defining property rights, internalizing social costs and benefits, activities to counter external costs, etc.). The government should also implement and maintain the institutions that go with a free-market system: maintain a legal system to enforce contracts, prohibit barriers to entry to profitable market sectors, and so on.

Pareto-efficiency is neither the only nor the ultimate goal of government activity in this view. Even an efficient outcome may be unacceptable, on account of the welfare distribution among members of society. Ethical beliefs about social inequality may lead to preference of one state of affairs over another, and the government can act as the intermediary to improve distributive justice. Within the standard neoclassical, Paretian, framework, the best way to accomplish justice is to affect the distribution of individual endowments. Lump-sum taxes and subsidies should create the proper initial-wealth distribution; the market will then transform this, efficiently, into a final welfare distribution. However, in practice it may not be feasible to impose a sufficient redistribution of initial wealth to obtain the desired goal. For example, it is hard to redistribute initial human capital, even though it can be affected by schooling and training policies. This implies that efficiency sacrifices may be made, to obtain particular distributive goals. If initial-wealth policies (lump-sum redistribution) are incapable of satisfying the objectives of distributive justice, the goal can only be reached at a cost: a loss of efficiency. This paper is concerned with the efficiency cost of egalitarian policies, but it is only a beginning. It documents such policies in the Netherlands, and calculates the relative redistributive effects. The possible efficiency losses are only considered in an illustrative setting. In particular, this latter part can only be a modest initial attempt of what is really needed.

The framework spelled out here is obviously not without shortcomings. One may fundamentally criticize the Paretian framework, and the two Fundamental Theorems on Welfare Economics used here (Atkinson and Stiglitz 1980: 343), because of the underlying notion that perfect foresight can never be a meaningful condition. While the Theorems are valid in the static conditions spelt out, the unavoidable uncertainty about the world, and in particular about the future, makes them irrelevant, so it is argued. In a less fundamental sense, one may argue that inevitably some sectors of the economy cannot satisfy the first-best Pareto-conditions, and as a consequence it is useless to use first-best conditions for other sectors as a guideline. And finally, the efficiency–equity borderline may be blurred beyond recognition if one accepts the Hochman and Rodgers view that individuals can have preferences about an equitable distribution. They may then willingly reduce their income through transfers to poorer people, and in fact, one may then search for efficient egalitarian policies. That is, caring for redistribution, for example through social security, becomes a Pareto-efficient activity. It would eliminate the conflict, or large parts thereof.

While the present paper indeed draws its inspiration from the equity–efficiency trade-off notion, it is not invalidated by the criticisms above. Documentation of redistributive policies is useful even without that notion, and the same goes for attention for the effects of redistribution on the behaviour of the economy and its individual members. What does change, however, is the evaluation of the result. It is no longer necessarily possible to denote the efficiency losses as the price-tag of egalitarian policies. So be it.

8.1. LONG RUN CHANGES IN INEQUALITY

Egalitarian policies can take many forms, and one may distinguish some broad categories. Distribution of welfare may be deliberately affected by institutional policies, wealth policies, factor pricing policies, commodity pricing policies and by compulsory consumption. Institutional policies affect the rules of the game. Legally enforced or otherwise, the government sets rules that aim to change the distribution of welfare. For example, the government may outlaw discrimination by sex and race or it may restrict entry to certain professions if it (fore-)sees overcrowding. Wealth policies affect the distribution of individual wealth and perhaps come closest to Pareto-efficient lump-sum transfers, in particular if they are unanticipated (like a sudden land reform). Factor-pricing policies affect the net rewards to production factors, by setting minimum, maximum or binding rates or by taxes and subsidies (like a minimum wage or a payroll tax). Commodity pricing policies affect net consumer prices of commodities, usually taking the form of subsidies, to bring the commodities within easier reach of low-income groups (housing subsidies, food stamps). Compulsory consumption involves a legally binding obligation to consume: minimum education attendance, compulsory health insurance, and so on.

It is at least a book-length endeavour to describe the existence and development of these policies over any extended period of time. The present scope is much less ambitious: to give an indication of changes in measured income inequality in the Netherlands during the greater part of the twentieth century. It draws heavily on Hartog and Veenbergen (1978), which is also the source for the details of results presented here. By looking at changes in the inequality of personal incomes, an indication is obtained of the effect of egalitarian policies, as far as they indeed affect personal incomes. The most important omission is then the effect of commodity pricing policies (the benefit incidence of government expenditures) and compulsory consumption. It is only a look at the resulting inequality, subsuming the effects of reactions to government policies (such as tax shifting, perhaps increasing pre-tax income inequality) and including the influence of other factors than government policies.

Turning now to the observed development of income inequality in the Netherlands in the period 1914–72, it should be stressed first that the data are based upon income tax files and relate to fiscal income. In the Netherlands, this excludes capital gains, includes transfers (such as poverty assistance, alimony, pensions, social security transfers) and labour income of the wife. The inclusion of transfers poses the greater problem, since working wives make up only a small percentage of the labour force. This means essentially that the income concept represents income after redistribution through social security arrangements (contributions are deductible). Note that, since the income concept is 'fiscal income', it includes the spouse's labour income, but is *not* equal to income per family or consumer (it is essentially per recipient), it is neither before nor after all transfers (since social security contributions are subtracted, but the income tax is not).

A full discussion of the data is given in Hartog and Veenbergen (1978). One feature is still worth stressing, however. Data on 'fiscal income' usually omit incomes below the exemption level. Before 1940 this level was very high, but fortunately, the number of incomes below that level could be estimated. All these low incomes were lumped together in one lowest interval, admittedly a very crude procedure, but in practice without reasonable alternative. After 1940 such a correction could not be made, and incomes below the exemption level (which is now quite low) were neglected. Due to improved coverage of this category over time, observed inequality in later years represents an overestimation relative to the earlier post-war years.

The data have been employed to calculate a number of commonly applied measures of dispersion: the variance of income σ^2_y; the variance of real income σ^2_y/p^2; the variance of the logarithm of income σ^2_{1ny}; and the coefficient of income variation $k = \sigma^2_y/\bar{Y}$ (see Table 8.1). The latter three series are also drawn in Figure 8.1 (the series on σ^2_y is omitted since it is heavily affected by purely nominal developments). The variance was chosen as a basic inequality indicator because of its ready analytical link to a linear earnings equation (see section 8.4).

The first thing that strikes the inspector of Figure 8.1 is the parallel of development in k and σ_y/p, and strongly deviant development in σ^2_{1ny}. The former indicates a gradual decline in inequality , the latter a gradual increase. However, this increase can be understood from the high relative sensitivity of σ^2_{1ny} to inequality at the bottom of the distribution (Champernowne 1974) and the fact that *observed* inequality at the bottom has increased: observational detail at the bottom is much larger after the war than before. The data on the coefficient of variation and the standard deviation of real income indicate a long-run downward trend in inequality and a cyclical pattern around this trend. In Hartog and Veenbergen (1978) an equation representing such a pattern indeed led to a very good fit (an R^2 of 0.98). But although the description of observed aggregate inequality by means of a smooth continuous trend apparently works well, it is nevertheless useful to draw attention to an alternative interpretation. One might distinguish three periods in Figure 8.1: 1914–20, 1921–39 and 1950–72. In the first period, only (part of) a cycle is observable; the period is too short for detecting a trend.

Considering the longer period 1921–39, one might defend the thesis that there is no trend. The post-war period again has no strong trend, and even hints at increasing inequality (inequality, whether measured by σ_y/p, σ_{1ny} or k, is higher in 1972 than in the early 1960s. The early 1960s might then represent a turning point in cyclical development. One might therefore state that the long-run development, which can be described by a significant downward trend, actually is dominated by two main steps: a permanent fall in inequality in the years 1920–22 and another permanent fall in the years between 1939 and 1950. Although the alternative interpretations (smooth continuous change versus radical shocks) have rather different implications, we will not pursue the matter any further here.

In Hartog and Veenbergen (1978), the data are also used for a regression analysis attempting to explain the observed developments. The attempt was not very successful, however. In the end, that paper led to the following conclusions:

(1) In the Netherlands, over the period 1914–72, the distribution of personal income measured in deciles, exhibits a smooth development. This development apparently entails a gain in almost all decile shares at the expense of the top decile, which lost considerably.

(2) Income inequality, as measured by the coefficient of variation, exhibits a downward trend and a clear cyclical pattern. Both trend and cycle are reduced considerably after 1939, and there is evidence of increased inequality after the early 1960s. The variance was chosen as a basic inequality indicator because of its easy link to a linear earnings equation (see section 8.4).

(3) The cyclical development of inequality, as measured by coefficient of variation or by the income share of the highest decile, reverses its sign with respect to unemployment during the war: they move opposite to the unemployment rate prior to 1939, roughly parallel afterwards.

(4) The development of the variance of the log of earnings deviates from the other inequality indicators. This may be largely due to problems of observation.

Table 8.1: Income dispersion, 1914–72 (taxable incomes)

Year	σ_y	$\sigma_{y/p}$	$\sigma_{\ln y}$	$k = \sigma_{y/\bar{y}}$
1914	5.37	22.35	6.44	3.15
1915	7.42	27.48	6.57	3.69
1916	8.51	28.38	6.63	4.01
1917	8.33	26.02	6.70	3.96
1918	7.50	19.74	6.85	3.36
1919	8.47	20.65	7.03	3.35
1920	7.24	15.73	7.15	2.85
1921	6.01	15.42	7.09	2.58
1922	5.15	14.30	7.05	2.31
1923	4.89	14.38	7.03	2.25
1924	5.34	15.70	7.02	2.44
1925	5.51	16.22	6.99	2.56
1926	5.54	16.78	6.97	2.60
1927	5.63	17.58	6.97	2.62
1928	5.88	17.81	6.98	2.70
1929	5.47	16.59	6.98	2.54
1930	5.79	18.69	7.47	2.80
1931	4.59	15.83	7.41	2.29
1932	3.77	13.97	7.28	1.97
1933	3.60	13.34	7.21	1.91
1934	3.49	12.94	7.16	1.89
1935	3.49	13.41	7.11	1.91
1936	4.48	17.22	7.16	2.44
1937	5.02	18.58	7.22	2.67
1938	4.80	17.16	7.22	2.58
1939	4.47	15.98	7.29	2.41
1950	4.89	7.89	7.00	1.61
1952	5.88	8.17	7.19	1.71
1953	5.51	7.76	7.24	1.55
1954	5.99	7.99	7.38	1.53
1955	6.18	7.93	7.52	1.44
1957	6.63	7.80	7.72	1.35
1958	8.03	9.23	7.77	1.55
1959	7.23	8.22	7.82	1.36
1960	7.57	8.32	7.94	1.31
1962	8.27	8.62	8.08	1.28
1963	9.33	9.33	8.05	1.35
1964	10.70	9.90	8.31	1.32
1965	13.25	11.62	8.29	1.58
1966	11.38	9.40	8.53	1.23
1967	14.77	11.82	8.64	1.48
1970	18.68	12.71	8.69	1.49
1972	24.43	14.04	8.97	1.56

Source: Hartog and Veenbergen (1978).

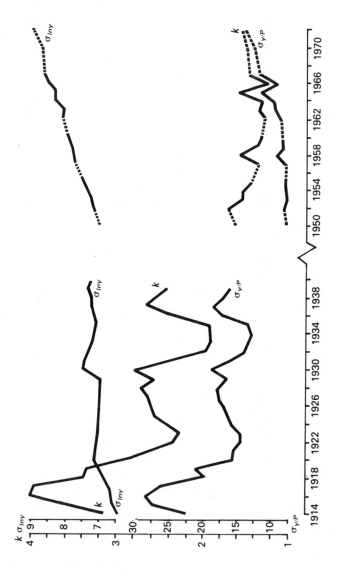

Figure 8.1: Income inequality measures, 1914–72

(5) It is very difficult to explain the variations in income inequality. For a number of variables commonly held to be of relevance to this process, significant contributions could barely be detected. There is some weak support, however, for the thesis that the variance of the age distribution has a positive effect on income inequality, that the share of wages in national income has a negative effect, and that unemployment has a positive effect. Social security consistently comes out with an unanticipated positive sign.

In Hartog (1983), the same data have been used to calculate the extent of income redistribution through income taxes. In the pre-war period, with a fairly low income tax rate, different measures come by and large to the same conclusion: the inequality reduction is somewhere between 1 per cent and 10 per cent. In the post-war period (1946–73), with much higher tax rates, redistribution measures are also wider apart. Since the analytical model of section 8.4 uses the standard deviation of income, the results will now be summarized for the coefficient of variation (the analytical model is static, with constant mean income). This summary follows Hartog (1981). In the first period of the income tax, 1914–17, the average tax rate was about 2 per cent, and the inequality reduction about 2.5 per cent. In the second period, 1918–39, the average tax rate is still about 2 per cent, but the inequality reduction increases to about 8 per cent. In the third period, after the Second World War, the average tax rate climbed from 14 per cent to 18 per cent (mainly in the last three years); inequality reduction was not very stable, but fluctuated between 30 per cent and 40 per cent of the coefficient of variation. These data will be used for later reference.

8.2 POST-WAR INCOME REDISTRIBUTION

The most important government intervention in the Netherlands income distribution concerns the transition of primary to secondary incomes. The influences of taxes and social security contributions as well as that of transfer payments should be taken into account. In addition to this there is the redistribution through benefit incidence that subjects enjoy from collective goods and from subsidies and transfer payments related to goods.

As we have seen above, the inequality by taxes was substantially greater after the Second World War than before. However, the amount of inequality reduction heavily depends on the measure of income inequality. Table 8.2 gives some results for the post-war period (1946–73) according to Hartog (1983).

As the average tax rate is substantial for the higher incomes only, the low reductions of Gini and the standard log incomes as compared with Theil, the standard deviation and the coefficient of variation are consistent with Champernowne (1974).

Taxes are only part of the total transfers to and from the government. The redistribution is also influenced by social security contributions, transfer payments and benefits in kind from the state. For further calculations, additional distributions of primary and secondary incomes are required. Only from 1975 (CBS 1980b) and later on, distributions of primary incomes have been published. Beginning in 1977, the Dutch income definitions have been changed in such a way that the differences between primary, gross, taxable and disposable income are equal to transfer payments, social security payments and taxes repectively. As figure 8.2 shows, the redistributive effects of taxes, transfer payments and social security contributions can now be

Table 8.2: Income inequality post-tax relative to pre-tax

Measure used	
Standard deviation	0.57
Coefficient of variation	0.67
Standard deviation log income	0.94
Gini	0.89
Theil	0.71

Source: Hartog (1983).

	1 primary	2 gross	3 taxable
2 gross	1 → 2 + transfer payments		
3 taxable	1 → 3 + transfer payments − social security contributions	2 → 3 − social security con- tributions	
4 disposable	1 → 4 + transfer payments − social security con- tributions − taxes	2 → 4 − social security con- tributions − taxes	3 → 4 − taxes

Source: Odink (1983).

Figure 8.2: Relations between income concepts

calculated not only separately but also in combination. Note that it is now possible to be much more careful about the income concepts used than in the time-series analysis, where the available data refer to a rather mixed type of concept.

In table 8.3 the mean incomes in 1977 are given for different socioeconomic groups in The Netherlands. The reduction of inequality between the incomes of those in the labour force and those not in the non labour force is very substantial: the ratio of their disposable incomes is only 1.4 against 13.2 for their primary incomes. Although the reduction between the different socioeconomic groups within the labour force is less substantial, the income ratios between for example company director and employees is reduced from 2.4 for primary incomes to 1.9 for disposable incomes, which is still not negligible.

Table 8.4 gives the results for different measures of income inequality for 1977 according to Figure 8.2 (see Odink 1983). Unfortunately, it was impossible to calculate the standard deviation of the log incomes, not only because of the occurrence of negative incomes (which could have been ignored) but because of the fact that about 18 per

Table 8.3: Income recipients and their mean incomes for socio-economic groups, 1977

	Number (in 1,000)	Income (guilders)			
		Primary	Gross	Taxable	Disposable
Labour force	3,927	35,053	37,880	33,189	26,349
Self-employed	410	47,402	50,049	45,233	32,833
Company directors	88	78,979	83,474	75,520	47,262
Employees (included unemployed)	3,428	32,449	35,256	30,663	25,037
Non labour force	1,802	2,653	21,955	21,104	18,241
Pensioners	1,669	2,640	22,482	21,682	18,699
Others	133	2,815	15,354	13,862	12,505
Total	5,729	24,861	32,871	29,387	23,798

Source: CBS (1982b, table 1).

cent of the primary incomes are zero. It is impossible to ignore those zero incomes because zero disposable incomes do not occur. It also appeared impossible to make the assumption of those incomes being positive, as the results for the standard deviation of the log incomes differ very substantially according to different assumptions made. Therefore, Theil, Gini, the coefficient of variation (k) and the income ratio between the tenth and the third decile are calculated; in addition, the Theil index for inequality between the socioeconomic groups is presented.

As Table 8.4 shows, received transfers cause a great decrease in income inequality, varying from 31 per cent for the coefficient of variation to 89 per cent for the 10/3 decile ratio; this is substantially more than the effect of taxes. As social security contributions are slightly degressive to income, due to their upper limits, they cause a slight increase in inequality. Nevertheless, the reduction by taxes and social security contribution together is hardly smaller than by taxes alone.

All together, the inequality reduction from primary to disposable incomes is very great for all the measures used, varying from 47 per cent for Gini to 92 per cent for the 10/3 decile ratio. The major part is caused by the reduction in the inequality between the socioeconomic groups. The between group Theil decreases from 0.277 to 0.022, this is about two thirds of the total reduction from 0.513 to 0.131.

The figures for 1981 show an increase in inequality of primary incomes. Nevertheless, the distribution of disposable incomes is less unequal than in 1977. So the inequality reduction has 'recently' become even somewhat greater than before. The CBS will publish in 1987 for the first time a distribution of primary houshold incomes. For those 1983 data Odink (1987) shows that redistribution by transfers in percentages almost exactly equal that in Table 8.4, being 47, 46, 94 and 74 for G, *k*, 10/3 and T respectively.

In fact, what should have been investigated is the redistribution from primary to secondary incomes, instead

Table 8.4: Income inequality measures for different income concepts, 1977

Income concept	Gini	*k*	10/3	Theil	Between group Theil
1 primary	0.508	1.085	29.82	0.513	0.277
2 gross	0.320	0.748	4.30	0.193	0.043
3 taxable	0.321	0.785	4.35	0.201	0.038
4 disposable	0.270	0.556	3.30	0.131	0.022
Changes (as percentages of the maximum possible reduction)					
1→2	−37	−31	−89	−62	−84
2→3	+ 0	+ 5	+ 2	+ 4	−13
3→4	−16	−29	−31	−35	−43
1→3	−37	−28	−88	−61	−86
2→4	−15	−26	−30	−32	−50
1→4	−47	−49	−92	−74	−92

Source: Odink (1983 and 1985).

of to disposable incomes. However, the necessary income data are lacking. In the Netherlands there is not a published distribution of disposable incomes plus benefits from transfers in kind from the state: the distribution of so-called tertiary incomes. However, there has been ample investigation of the individual benefit of government expenditures by the Social Cultural Planning Bureau (SCP). There has been no publication by the SCP of the distribution of the disposable incomes plus the individual benefits. One could more or less deduct a distribution of this kind from the deciles of the disposable SCP household incomes (SCP 1981).

Odink (1985) shows that, based on the SCP distribution of household incomes, there is a considerable reduction of the inequality by benefits in kind, more or less to the same degree as the inequality reduction by taxes. The definition of the concept of 'household' by the SCP shows a strong discrepancy with that of the CBS. The separation of the children over 18, who are still living at their parents' home, as independent households, might be of great influence on the results found. A correction for the family size is evidently needed. When correcting for the household composition, based on the fiscal method, as proposed by the SCP, the reduction is still larger.

Another method is the calculation of the distribution of income per capita. This method is a good approximation, according to van Ginneken (1982) of the distribution based on equivalence scales. When the incomes per capita are calculated, based on a simple method, the inequality reduction shows a tremendous rise. However, based on a more subtle method, using the decomposition formula for Theil, the simple method has to be rejected (see Odink 1985). Once more, the reduction, as a result of the benefits in kind from the state, turns out to be to the same degree as the reduction by taxes, found earlier.

Concluding, it can be stated that the effect of redistribution via taxes and social transfers is considerably reinforced by the benefits in kind from the state.

8.3 THE TRADE-OFF BETWEEN EQUITY AND EFFICIENCY: A SIMPLE ILLUSTRATION

In principle, each and any redistributive policy measure can be evaluated in terms of its cost to other goals of economic policy. Rather than discussing all these policies, a simple formal illustration will be given by focusing on one particular policy measure: a redistributive linear income tax.

To be specific, assume that individuals, given a choice between effort and consumption have Cobb-Douglas preferences:

$$U = L^{\alpha} C^{1-\alpha} \tag{1}$$

where C is consumption and L is hours of leisure (the analysis can be easily generalized to a broader measure of effort, provided output is related to it). If labour hours can be sold at a wage rate w, consumption has a price p and the individual has non-labour income Z, the full-income constraint M equals

$$M = wH + z \tag{2}$$

where H is total hours available. The utility-maximizing individual chooses the optimum positions

$$wL = \alpha M \tag{3}$$

$$pC = (1 - \alpha)M \tag{4}$$

Indirect utility V is given by

$$V = U(L^*, C^*) = \alpha^{\alpha}(1 - \alpha)^{1-\alpha} M w^{-\alpha} p^{\alpha-1} \tag{5}$$

Suppose, a this point a linear income tax is introduced:

$$t = \theta w(H - L) + \theta Z + \theta_{o} \tag{6}$$

The cost of this tax to the individual can be expressed as the monetary compensation needed to maintain utility at the pre-tax level. This requires

$$dV = -(\alpha V/w)dw + (V/M)(dM + m) = 0 \tag{7}$$

Now, the change in the wage rate relevant to the individual equals $-\theta w$ and the change in full income equals $-\theta M - \theta_{o}$. Substituting this into (7) and applying some simple manipulations yields

$$m = (1 - \alpha)\,\theta M + \theta_o\,, \qquad (8)$$

where m is the amount to be paid to compensate for the tax. Now, note that the budget constraint in the new situation allows to write

$$w(H - L) + Z = (pC + \theta_o)\,(1 - \theta)^{-1} \qquad (9)$$

while consumption in the new equilibrium is chosen as

$$pC = (1 - \alpha)\,\{(1 - \theta)M - \theta_o\} \qquad (10)$$

Substituting (9) and (10) into (6) yields, after rewriting

$$t = (1 - \alpha)\,\theta M + (1 - (1 - \alpha)\theta\}\theta_o(1 - \theta)^{-1} \qquad (11)$$

Next, add subscripts i to identify individuals, who differ in M_i and in α_i. As the tax is meant to be purely redistributive, $\Sigma t_i = 0$ and this can be solved for the intercept:

$$\theta_o = -\theta(1 - \theta)p\overline{C}\{1 - \theta(1 - \overline{\alpha})^{-1} \qquad (12)$$

where

$$p\overline{C} = \frac{1}{n}\sum_{i=1}^{n}(1 - \alpha_i)M_i\,, \quad \text{average consumption} \qquad (13a)$$

$$\overline{\alpha} = \frac{1}{n}\sum_{i=1}^{n}\alpha_i \qquad \text{average leisure preference} \qquad (13b)$$

The welfare cost of the tax, γ_i, can be calculated as the difference between the tax revenue raised and the amount fo money needed to compensate the individual for the introduction of the tax ('dead-weight loss'). Simple manipulation then yields

$$\gamma_i = m_i - t_i = -\alpha_i\theta(1 - \theta)^{-1}\theta_o \qquad (14)$$

Aggregating, substituting (12) and expressing the welfare cost relative to the value of total resources leads to

$$\omega = (\Sigma_i\gamma_i)/\Sigma_iM_i) = \overline{\alpha}\,\theta^2(1 - \alpha_M)\,\{1 - \theta(1 - \overline{\alpha})\}^{-1} \qquad (15)$$

where α_M is the weighted average of leisure preferences:

$$\overline{\alpha}_M = (\Sigma_i\alpha_iM_i)/(\Sigma_iM_i) \qquad (16)$$

Now, note that the linear income tax transfers individual full income M into after-tax resources $(1 - \theta)M - \theta_o$.

Hence, the pre-tax standard deviation of resources, σ_M is transformed into an after tax-deviation $(1 - \theta)\sigma_M$. The reduction in inequality of full-income, ρ, can thus be simply defined as

$$\rho = 1 - \{(1 - \theta)\sigma_M\}/\sigma_M = \theta \qquad (17)$$

This leads to a neat explicit formulation of the trade-off between equity and efficiency. The welfare cost, as a share of total pre-tax full income, of inequality reduction ρ equals:

$$\omega = \overline{\alpha}\rho^2(1 - \overline{\alpha}_M)\{1 - \rho(1 - \overline{\alpha})\}^{-1} \qquad (18)$$

The cost is seen to depend on leisure preference α_i and on the magnitude of inequality reduction. It is easily verified that $\partial\omega/\partial\rho > 0$ and $\partial^2\omega/\partial\rho^2 > 0$: inequality reduction has increasing cost.

To get some indication of the magnitudes involved, ω has been calculated for some combinations of α and $\rho(=\theta)$. To simplify, it has been assumed that $\overline{\alpha} = \overline{\alpha}_M$.

Thus Table 8.5 shows the welfare cost of a linear income tax, in a world where individuals can freely choose their hours of work (and where, e.g. unemployment or hours rationing are ignored). The welfare cost is measured as the difference between the amount of income tax paid and the amount of money that would be needed to compensate the individual for the introduction of the tax (i.e. to restore his utility level). It is expressed as a proportion of full income, that is the income obtained at zero leisure. It will depend on the marginal tax rate θ and on the leisure preference parameter α.

The table shows that the welfare cost is zero if θ equals zero (no tax), and if $\overline{\alpha}$ equals either 0 or 1; in the latter cases, the substitution effect is zero, and this eliminates deadweight losses. Note that when the marginal tax rate surpasses 25 per cent, the welfare loss (in terms of full income, not observed income!) can become quite substantial.

Now, suppose $\overline{\alpha}$ is about 0.60 (this is based on a rough calculation, noticing mainly that people work forty hours out of $7 \times 16 = 112$ available hours a week). Then, with the low inequality reduction rates before the Second World

War, the welfare cost would be easily below 1 per cent. However, the inequality reduction rates (and marginal tax rates) substantially increased after the war and the welfare cost may well have risen to more than a few per cent of total resource value (8 per cent?).

8.4 SUMMARY

Income inequality, as measured by the coefficient of variation, has exhibited a downward trend and a cyclical pattern in the Netherlands since 1914. The reduction of income inequality by taxes in the post-war period is substantially greater than before the war. However, the amount of inequality reduction depends heavily on the measure used.

The reduction in inequality comparing disposable incomes with primary incomes varies from almost a half as measured by the Gini coefficient and the coefficient of variation, to more than 90 per cent as measured by the ratio of the tenth and third deciles. In addition, this redistribution by taxes, social security contributions and transfer payments is considerably reinforced by the benefits in kind from the state.

An illustration is given of what the relative welfare cost of inequality reduction in the Netherlands might amount

Table 8.5: *Relative welfare cost* ω *($\times 100$) as a function of* $\bar{\alpha} = \bar{\alpha}_M$ *and* $\rho(=\theta)$

$\bar{\alpha}$	$\rho = \theta$							
	0.00	0.05	0.10	0.15	0.20	0.25	0.50	0.75
0.00	0.00	0.00	0.00	0.00	0.00	0.00	0.00	0.00
0.20	0.00	0.04	0.17	0.41	0.76	1.25	6.67	22.50
0.40	0.00	0.06	0.26	0.59	1.09	1.76	8.57	24.54
0.60	0.00	0.06	0.25	0.57	1.04	1.67	7.50	19.29
0.80	0.00	0.04	0.16	0.37	0.67	1.05	4.44	10.59
1.00	0.00	0.00	0.00	0.00	0.00	0.00	0.00	0.00

to. Before the Second World War the welfare cost would be easily below 1 per cent. However, after the war the welfare cost may well have risen to more than 5 or 8 per cent of total resource value. So the trade-off between equity and efficiency is now more than a theoretical problem. Yet it is only a back-of-the envelope calculation for the leisure-consumption choice, neglecting other choices. The enormous redistribution in the Netherlands warrants a much more elaborate investigation of the issues, in a discussion started so stimulating by Robert Haveman (1985).

Part IV

Power and Distribution

9 Production Technology and Distribution Theory

A. Manders

In this paper attention is focused on recent trends in production systems and their impact on the Theory of Income-Distribution. The theoretical framework is the Degree of Monopoly Theory of Distribution and the discussions around certain elements which form part of it. The empirical data presented in this paper support the theory that technological developments have a major impact on income distribution. New products as well as new production processes affect the distribution of income through industrial concentration. In the neoclassical approach technological developments are directly related to income distribution through marginal productivity. Income distribution is determined by the elasticity of substitution of production which itself is determined exogenously and is embedded in the prevailing technology (Cowling 1982: 30). When recent trends in production technology are concerned I do not think that this theory provides an adequate framework.

To begin with, I will summarize some relevant elements of the Degree of Monopoly Theory. Then I will present some information about recent trends in production processes. This information is based on research in one Dutch multinational electronics enterprise. Finally, I shall highlight the impact of these trends on the problem of income distribution.

9.1 SOME ELEMENTS OF THE DEGREE OF MONOPOLY THEORY OF DISTRIBUTION

The essential point of the paper is to draw attention to a new trend in production technology and to its impact on factor-income distribution. For this it is not necessary to discuss the entire theory nor do I wish to enter into the controversial discussion about the strong and weak points in the neoclassical theory of distribution. Only this: whatever else may be said about the neoclassical theory, it loses its coherency once the assumption of perfect competition is abandoned.

The elements I wish to stress here are precisely those which the neoclassical approach ignores, namely *the process of concentration, the influence of enterprises on prices and market shares, and of trade unions in distribution.*

One of the essential features of the *degree of monopoly* model is its assumption about the microeconomic behaviour of the firm, namely the shape of the cost curves. Another relates to the firms price policy, and yet another to the relevant ranges of output and capacity underutilization.

In Kalecki's opinion, supply is elastic and firms normally operate below capacity. Furthermore, he believed that the unit prime (variable) costs are independent of the degree of utilization of the plant and its equipment and that this excess capacity plays a major role with regard to a firm's price-setting possibilities. And finally he assumed that over the relevant range of output short-run prime costs per unit of output are more or less stable, that is that marginal costs (consisting of non-overhead wages and the cost of materials), are relatively constant. This is of importance in relation to Kalecki's other assumption that each industrial firm fixes the price for its product by 'marking-up' its average unit prime costs in order to cover overheads and obtain profits. The crucial proposition, then, is that the level of the *mark up* depends on the process of industrial concentration and market imperfections, in his own terminology that the 'mark up' depends on the *degree of monopoly*. Hence the *degree of monopoly* indicates the development and significance of concentration. In the discussion this concept has given rise to a great deal of misunderstanding. It is therefore important to stress that the *mark-up* is not defined as the degree of monopoly but as a symptom of the degree of monopoly. The degree of monopoly determines the relationship between the price of the product and unit prime costs which is reflected in the mark-up. If the relationship of the cost of materials and the wage bill is given, it is the degree of monopoly which 'determines' the distribution of the industrial product between wages and profits (plus overheads). The share of output to wages is a diminishing function of the degree of monopoly and the proportion of the prime costs spent on materials.

Although the degree of monopoly is not the *only* determinant of the shares of the factors of production in national income, its role in distribution theory is very important. A difficulty with this concept is that it is not easy to quantify the many influences that affect the degree of monopoly and this hinders the determination of a firm's degree of monopoly. However, in the context of this paper this is a minor problem. Here it is more important to detect the *influences* of concentration. The assumption is that the forces that lead to a high average degree of monopoly imply a lowering of the share of wages and a raising of the share of profits and overheads in the fruits of production. In terms of factors which lead to a change in the degree of monopoly (and thereby to the possibility for the firm to change the mark-up) the focus is on the process of concentration, sales promotion, the level of overheads and the power of trade unions.

In the first place the degree of monopoly is the result of the firm's ability to influence the elasticities of demand in the industry in question. Firms in a highly concentrated industry, with a high degree of product differentiation and high advertising costs, are expected to influence the elasticities of demand for their own product as well as for those of their competitors; that is, they are able to reduce their dependence of the prices of competitors. The absolute value of the industry's price elasticity is inversely related to the degree of monopoly. The aggregate share of profits and overheads in national income, and therefore the share of wages in national income are determined by the average degree of monopoly. A high average degree of monopoly implies a lower share of wages and thus a higher share of profits and overheads.

This contrasts with the neoclassical view that the behaviour of consumers, given that their tastes determine the elasticity of demand, determine the actions of the firms. Therefore the essential question is, to what extent consumers' wants are determinated exogenously and to what extent by the firms own actions. Next to this the degree of monopoly is the result of the concentration and collusion policy of giant corporations. The innovation policy of firms is expected to be biased in the direction of greater concentration. Innovations facilitating the control of large organizations are therefore likely to be dominant. The same aims which encourage concentration are also those which are pursued by collusion. (In recent times it becomes more difficult to discern between concentration and collusion. This problem is more widely discussed in the following chapter.) Finally, the power of trade unions is important for the degree of monopoly. A powerful trade union influences the distribution of the total revenue of the firm in favour of wages. According to the Degree of Monopoly Theory, trade union power is related to business cycles. With regard to research and development (R. & D.) of new production processes, it needs, however, to be stressed that in recent years with regard to research and development of new production processes this power has become less dependent on business cycles and more on the management strategies of giant corporations. The increasing possibilities for multinational companies to set aside trade unions is an aspect of industrial change the impact of which has not yet sufficiently been studied. It is in this sphere where this paper may contribute to the extension of the Degree of Monopoly Theory.

9.2 RECENT TRENDS IN PRODUCTION TECHNOLOGY

In this section the management strategy is reviewed of a Dutch multinational in electronics with regard to production technology. Before this, as background information, some general developments are outlined.

General developments

As a consequence of the decreased profits in the 1970s—firms' rentability of *internal capital* in industry did not exceed 5 per cent (van Empel 1986)—the top management of various giant corporations gave priority to efforts to reduce production costs. One of the measures to achieve this was to increase R. & D expenditure on the discovery of new production technologies. To begin with this was a defensive strategy, intended to stop profits from falling. The idea was to concentrate R. & D. on gathering *know-how* about production processes, about systems and about equipment, in order to become less dependent on the traditional suppliers of capital goods. These measures were accompanied by the reorganization of the production process. The developments in microelectronics itself were another important reason for investing in production technology in electronics corporations. The chip technology opened up new perspectives not only for the traditional products but also for extension into the unknown area of production systems.

Other general developments which are of interest in this context were:

(1) the change that had taken place in the process of concentration from 'horizontal mergers' to 'vertical integration'.
(2) the progress of cooperation between giant corporations in non-competitive areas.

As for the change in the process of concentration, it should be noted that in the 1960s many managers were convinced of the profitability of economies of scale. It then seemed logical to reduce risks by the diversification of the firms' products and by penetrating different markets. Smaller firms were therefore bought up. But by the end of the 1960s this conviction was waning. Other markets and other firms required other organizational approaches, other management policies and different marketing approaches. Moreover, conflicting cultures in firms caused organizational problems. The theory behind this policy, which had been inspired by H.A. Ansoff, failed. Ansoff pleaded for a conglomerate strategy because 'by putting more eggs into the same end-product basket the firm's dependence increased on a particular segment of economic demand' (Ansoff 1965: 134). Recently the conglomerate strategy, or horizontal merger, was replaced by a strategy of vertical integration. This means that the control of production from raw material to end-products was emphasized. The new strategy was accompanied by a policy of creating business units responsible for the production of a single product from beginning to end, and placing it all, including its selling activities, in one hand. (In the next subsection, I will return to this.)

As for the trend towards cooperation with companies that in other areas were the strongest competitors, cooperation must be seen as the coordination of decisions. Top managers of giant corporations describe this situation as 'everybody cooperates with everybody'. The motives for this are fourfold:

(1) to gain enough capital for new developments without taking all the risks involved in new experiments,
(2) to create a pool of scarce human resources,
(3) to create world-wide standards,
(4) to gain entrance into the three main markets: Japan, the United States and Europe (Tolsma 1986).

These two general trends throw light on the actual manifestation of the process of concentration.

Specific developments
The empirical information in this subsection is drawn from research on the policy of restructuring and of automation in the production of TV sets and in research on the R. & D. policy of a Dutch multinational corporation in electronics.

Long before the reduction of production costs had been given high priority in this and other companies, 'know-how' about the firms' production processes was to a large extent available. The various product divisions had their own maintenance departments. The product division 'lighting' could for some time produce profitability because of the specific knowledge of how to produce electric bulbs very cheaply. So 'maintenance' has to be defined quite widely. Maintenance departments operated autonomously. Their activities were directed to ameliorate the production process in their own individual divisions. In the 1970s, however, with regard to new production technology a policy was initiated to coordinate production manufacturing knowledge for the entire company. Until that time manufacturing technology was a department of the company's research laboratory. Since the 1970s this department has become autonomous. The new Centre for Manufacturing Technology (CFT) was given the task of generating production-technological know-how to support the maintenance departments of the product divisions. The increasing importance of this centre, and the shift in its tasks during the 1970s is the essential point of this section. To begin with, it is necessary to give a short historical overview about the production philosophy of the company. The relevance of this is that recent trends in production seem very much like the Tayloristic organization which was widespread in the 1950s and 1960s.

The era of flow production
In the 1960s the increasing markets for TVs was accompanied by a favourable level of profits. The advantage of economies of scale were fully utilized. Huge batches of TVs could be produced in a short time. The variety of types was low in comparison with the 1,000 types available nowadays. Under these circumstances of a 'sellers' market, there was no need to worry about sales. The market for electronic products increased from 10 to 20 per cent per year. There was also little need to worry about the production techniques. The hardware-controlled means of production were very well fitted to produce large batches of components for TV sets. It is true that the learning time for workers was relatively long (two months) and that it took a lot of time to rebuild an assembly-line for producing new types or changing old

ones, but once the initial problems were solved, the line could work for years. The lead time was good, the flexibility was bad, but that didn't cause serious problems. The increase in the volume of production and the safe continuity in production were achieved at that time by organizational measures. The assembly of TVs was organized in a flow production. For example about eighty workers, mainly women, did their hand-assembling job on sixteen lines, each line producing a different type. The means of production were brought to the market by specialized firms.

'Island' automation
By the end of the 1960s as a result of the prolonged labour-shortage, a solution for the vulnerable production processes was looked for in the automation of dirty and physically difficult work. But above all quality-testing activities were automated. Testing the components of a TV set is a critical activity. In this way the management hoped to solve the problems of the labour shortage and to improve the quality of products. However, with the introduction of automated test-machines, other problems appeared. The work capacity of automated test-machines was too large for only a single assembly-line. To make full use of them, the production of three lines had to be tested automatically by a single test-machine. This was the reason why *buffers* were created. It was the organization of buffers in the production process which started the tendency which would characterize the organization of production during the 1970s. The policy responsible for this tendency may be called the *policy of island automation*, or the policy of sub-optimalization. With it started the function-oriented organization of production which replaced the production-oriented flow organization. The result of this policy was a bad lead time and poor flexibility. The lead time increased but the work content of a TV set rapidly diminished. The so called work-in-progress time was several weeks, whereas the work content took no more than about two hours.

At the start of the period of 'island automation' the advantage for the company was a short pay-back time of investments. Otherwise the reduction in work content was but partly the result of automation. It was 20 per cent. The main reason was the improved materials technology, in semi conductor materials in particular.

Computer-aided manufacturing
During the period of 'island automation' the possibility of computer-aided manufacturing (cam), computer-aided testing (cat) and computer-aided logistics (cal) gradually emerged. On the one hand, this was made possible by technological progress in micro-electronics; on the other hand, the company was forced in this direction by the product-package market situation. The market had altered. From a 'sellers' it had become a 'buyers' market. In the second half of the 1970s the TV market stagnated while capacity had enormously increased. Furthermore, consumers had become aware of the variety of features they could choose from. For the company this meant that large batches of one type of TVs were no longer easily sellable. This had a great impact on production process. The company missed the flexibility to produce small orders. Consequently, stocks of outdated sets amassed; costs increased and re-emballage activities had to be renewed. More often than not, the company was urged to resort to dumping. The lack of flexibility was due to the policy of sub-optimalization. The increasing complexity of a TV set imposed an increase in the number of specialized departments. To a certain degree all departments were autonomous with regard to the sequence by which the batches of the various types were produced. For this reason stocks had to be held to assure the continuity of production in the entire plant.

In summary, it can be said that the function-oriented organization of production had given rise to a plant within a plant.

To cope with the coordination problems, a main-frame computer was introduced. The first requirement was to create a data transmission system to control the total flow of production. Before this was done the need arose for combining the data for the total flow of production with computer-controlled machines and assembling and transport systems. For this purpose more 'know-how' for production technology was required. At the beginning of the 1970s this was the task of the CFT. It had already been installed in the mid 1960s. It was in fact the autonomization of a sub-department of the Research and Development Laboratory. Until then it had been the task of the CFT to support the various production divisions and to test and pre-develop new techniques on metal forming, welding, soldering, tribology and so on. Until 1974, the activities of the CFT, with regard to manufacturing techniques, were mainly directed towards the automation of separate functions, that is transporting, griping, handling. Much knowledge was available outside the CFT. The product divisions (Lighting, Audio, Video, Consumer-electronics, etc.) had their separate plant-mechanization departments. The impact on the production process of these departments was quite large. Their activities were not in a strict sense maintenance work but development of new machine parts. The mechanization department of the product division of Lighting even constructed complete machinery. For fear of competition, the machines for producing electric bulbs were kept secret.

Computer-integrated manufacturing
In its new form one of the first subjects to be studied by the CFT was industrial robots and manipulators. The robots in the market at that time did not achieve the degree of accuracy that the production of TV sets needed. Moreover, the progress on micro- and mini-computers raised questions about their integration into the production equipment. Advanced knowledge was available about testing and inspection. The problem there, was how to create a structure for a computerized testing systems. Not much later a steering group was set up to deal with the combined control of machines and processes. The main problem to be solved was how in complex computer-controlled production systems the hardware and software should be defined and structured. Flexible automation, industrial measuring techniques and electronic mechanization, became the key words. The formal motivations for starting the steering group was 'the result of the changing product mix, the requirements of the market and the changing constraints'. Gradually, the

activities of the Centre shifted from NC programming systems for drilling, boring, reaming, tapping and milling to flexible automation and process control. Especially the sub-department of the CFT, the computer-aided manufacturing department, was to carry out pre-development and to build up know-how on the effective utilization of computer technology. Two fundamental innovations resulted from these attempts: the standardized building systems for machines, and the modular construction systems for the various functions of the elements of production. With the help of a standardized building system, it was easy to construct and to reconstruct prototype machines. The use of modules saved much production time in assembling. Both these developments played an important role in the way of thinking about the production process. A further important activity was the study of servo-techniques. This is a control technique used in programmable production equipment as well as in products. With the help of this technique it is possible to steer separate functions of a production machine.

Lately the stress of research concentrates on the designs for automation or design for assembly. *This is accompanied by the development of a new production philosophy.* In thinking about design for automation, the conclusion was reached that the philosophy of function-oriented automation had to be abandoned. The starting point for the new philosophy was the idea that production has to be organized in a way that enables it to react immediately ('Just in Time') to the changing requirements of the market. Stocks had to be reduced to facilitate economies of scope. The era of the economies of scale is approaching its end. The philosophy is the result of the study of how the Japanese corporations could do their job on the audio and video market better than European and American giant companies. It led to two 'actions'. The first was an analysis of the relationship between the costs of production and the selling costs; the second was a trip to Japan by many managers to learn something about the Japanese way of production. The goals were clear: the lead time had to be shortened, the volume-flexibility had to be increased and the time to rearrange machines had to be drastically reduced. Although the trips to Japan did not provide the final solution, a number of new ideas learnt there were applied to the production process. The Japanese factories produced a very specialized part of a product. Non-critical and labour-intensive work was farmed out to 'co-makers' or subcontractors within 50 miles of the 'mother' factory. It is likely that the idea of co-makership will become very popular to European managers.

At the moment, giant corporations buy (but to a limited extent) components for their products from small enterprises. These firms have to be located within a range of about 100 kilometres. The reason is that the transport lines to the 'mother' factory must be short to obtain quick delivery when necessary. Another characteristic is that the mother factory dictates the prices of the products that the small enterprises have to supply. The advantage for the small firms is that they can sell a guaranteed quantity of their products. Occasionally, the mother factory supplies test-machines to ensure the high quality of the products of the co-makers. Legally, this is a type of cooperation. The small firms are legally and financially independent. In fact, economically these firms are completely dependent on the mother factory. For this reason we can label this process 'concentration'. For the management the main conclusion of the two 'actions' was that the earlier situation, when a plant functioned within a plant, severely hindered the reconstruction of the production process. The achievement of the earlier-mentioned goals required an integrated organization of the product design, the production process, the equipment and the design of the plant. Organizationally, this could be achieved by the installation of business units. This is a product-oriented type of organization. The management of a business unit is responsible for a product, from design and production to the selling of the product. The new philosophy held that the function-oriented organization had to be abandoned in favour of a product-oriented organization. The ultimate result was a production process that realized a production process that is flexible enough to produce the product which is demanded at that very moment. *Obviously, in the new philosophy the product design is no longer the starting point but the production process.*

In the last chapter I will show the impact of these developments on the concentration-process and on the distribution theory in general.

9.3 PRODUCTION TECHNOLOGY AND DISTRIBUTION THEORY: SOME CONCLUSIONS

Although the empirical information is restricted to a single company, it is possible to formulate several general conclusions. In other giant corporations, identical developments have taken place. For example, Hitachi started in 1971 a Production Engineering Research Laboratory, and Toshiba installed in 1970 a Manufacturing Engineering Laboratory. Moreover, it is evident that the developments in giant corporations exceed the limits of these corporations.

Not surprisingly, especially electronics companies increased their research efforts in production technology. If data comunication is the product, then it is but a small step to interfaces between information about stocks and selling figures, on the one hand, and direct orders to production machines on the other. Nevertheless, the conclusions are of limited character. It goes no further than to indicate a trend. The impact of this trend is not yet very clear.

The first conclusion is that the captains of industry are convinced that a period is breaking in which the major sphere of competition is in the region of production processes. The important key words here are flexible computer-integrated manufacturing, short through-put times, quick switching from one product to another. This conviction, accompanied by the autonomous developments in micro electronics, have placed production technology into the forefront of the process. Although the activities were initially exploited for internal goals, they led to the recognition that an external market existed for an integrated view on the production process, that is for interfaces between data communication and production equipment. This led to an extension of the traditional products; know-how on production technology was commercialized. This means not only the selling of equipment but, more important, the selling of a philosophy. This philosophy resembles the Tayloristic production philosophy of the 1950s but is now concentrated in the hands of a small number of giant corporations. With this development, the monopoly power, already present with regard to a large part of consumer products, is extended to the industry making the means of production. Although the *availability* of monopoly power does not necessarily imply its use, it is permissible to suppose here that monopoly power is actually used. Hence the development in production technology can be seen as an enlargement of the process of industrial concentration in industry.

This process manifests itself in the phenomenon of co-makership or subcontracting, described in the previous section. As I have said, from a legal point of view we cannot speak of dependency, yet economically the co-maker is totally dependent on the mother plant. We can thus speak of concentration.

The second conclusion is that one of the factors which can hinder concentration, namely the trade-unions, becomes less and less significant with the application of the new strategy of the firms. To be sure, the position of the trade unions has come under pressure due to the loss of employment, resulting from the spreading of automation. As important as that may be the fact that the trade unions were unable to formulate requirements that maintain the interest of labour against new production technology. By bargaining 'technology agreements' one is opting for a defensive strategy. Moreover, trade unions are confronted with the fact that the new technology needs higher-qualified labour. It is common knowledge that the percentage in trade unions of people with higher salaries, is low. It is likely that this trend will go on. Manifestations in the Netherlands of the decreasing power of the trade unions can be found in the recent bargaining attitude of such giant companies as Philips, Akzo and the Banks. The relevance for distribution theory of the developments as pictured above is the process of concentration by means of the increased influence of giant corporations on manufacturing industry and the decreasing influence of trade unions. In the first section I mentioned the Degree of Monopoly Theory on these subjects. Here I have tried to highlight these aspects with the help of empirical information and to elaborate their consequences for income distribution. Concentration is a manifestation of the degree of monopoly. It points to an increasing distortion in the distribution of Gross National Product in favour of profits. Recent figures in the Netherlands demonstrate this dramatically. Indeed, profits have increased sharply since 1983 (van Empel 1986).

In sum, concentration received new impulses from the developments in new production technology which resulted in a change in the production relations. For income distribution this may imply a long-term diminution of the share of wages in the National Product.

10 Insights from Ancient Views on Distribution*

S. Todd Lowry:

The relentless commitment of the ancient Greeks to philosophical speculation and theoretical abstraction has provided both stimulus and guidance for most subsequent European thought. Beginning with natural philosophy, the Greeks accepted a materialist premise of a total quantifiable natural base, often conceived as a process in either an anthropomorphic or a physical sense. When formally structured in ideal or mathematical terms, the assumption that there was a predetermined quantitative reference base had an enduring influence, shaping subsequent deductive treatments of the distribution of material goods. Ultimately, the idea of novation or the creation of new or additional quantities was contradictory to the assumption that all potential material quantities are already implicit. This latter assumption provided the point of departure for rigorous deductive analysis and served as the basis for the premise of rational consistency.

The ancients approached the problem of acquiring material income in three ways. First, they assumed that income or wealth could be appropriated by capture (raiding for booty and the hunt); second, that it could be acquired from the bounty of nature (agriculture); and, lastly, that the potential inherent in material quantity could be more

---

* The issues dealt with in this paper are developed in a broader context in the author's *The Archaeology of Economic Ideas*, Durham, NC: Duke University Press, 1988.

226

fully realized by improvements in the organization of human activities (planning, coordinating and the division of labour). These formulations framed the issues in terms of which the ancient Greeks viewed the social problem of the allocation of distributive shares among members of a group and the individual problem of the allocation of income to the hierarchy of concerns reflecting a sequence of different personal needs and desires.

10.1 THE DIVISION OF SHARES: BOOTY AND THE HUNT

It is of some interest that a basic concept of distribution among participating individuals was first structured in a non-commercial setting. Outside of the distributive institutions of family, clan or tribe, individuals participating in the joint hunt or the raid in search of booty had to find ways to divide the 'income' from their venture. The ancient formula for the distribution of such gains was suggested in Hesiod's eighth century B.C. description (*Theogony*, 535–560) of the division of a slaughtered ox between Prometheus and Zeus and in some of Aesop's fables. These accounts present a simple and fair solution to the problem of two or more hunters dividing the meat resulting from the hunt or from some other joint venture. According to the ancient custom, one party first divided the meat as equally as possible. The other party or parties then chose their shares, leaving the divider to take the last portion. Knowing that he would have last choice naturally impelled the divider to make the division as equal as possible since he knew that any unequal share would inevitably be his. This arrangement created a social mechanism for mutual voluntary choice in the division of 'income' about which none of the parties could justifiably complain since the divider had a free choice in fixing the portions to his or her own point of subjective indifference, and each choosing party had the freedom to choose any portion.

Of course, the Greeks recognized that deception and power could be corrupting influences upon such a system of voluntary distribution. That raw power might take precedence over the social mechanism in the absence of group enforcement of the sharing process, or the authoritative administration of the system among subjects was traditionally represented in Aesop's fable of the 'lion's share.' According to one version of this story, the lion participated in a hunt with three other animals. After one of the other animals divided the kill into four equal portions and invited the others to choose, the lion placed his paw on a portion and announced. 'This is my share as leader of the hunt.' He then placed his paw on a second portion and claimed, 'This is my share as king of the beasts'. Placing his paw on the third portion, he roared, 'This is my share as a participant in the hunt'. Finally, claiming the last portion, he began, 'This is my share ...' Unable to come up with yet another nominal justification, he finally said, 'Well, I dare anyone to try and take this away from me!'

The ideas implicit in this cynical commentary on the reality of power were repeated often enough in anecdotes and in formal philosophical works to establish that the Greeks did not seriously entertain a concept of a negotiated distributive process (a self-regulating mechanism) immune from arbitrary power unless it was protected by either a democratic public tradition or an administrative authority. Aristotle's theory of natural restraints imposed by utilities, to be discussed below, assumed pressures that required intervention.

10.2 THE DISTRIBUTION OF AGRICULTURAL INCOME

The backbone of the ancient Mediterranean economy was the extended agrarian household, and this agricultural unit dominated the social and political outlook. Despite the development of a few conspicuous political centres which aggregated tribute and served as extensive entrepôts through which much trade was funnelled, the idealized Greek state was a small agrarian community controlled by citizen freeholders living in extended households. In their economic writings, both Xenophon and Aristotle treated land as a source of wealth to be garnered and directed to its proper uses by the responsible citizen, the head of the household (Lowry 1965). Their observations were based on the self-sufficient, extended household (*oikos*) of the Greek world. In this semi-subsistance agricultural economy, production was primarily for use rather than exchange and was limited by specific needs or utilities. The market served only as an auxiliary system for the exchange of surpluses to satisfy incremental needs. Since what was to be produced on the land was what was to be consumed, distribution decisions in ancient Greece encompassed the choices that we today would characterize as *production* decisions. Schumpeter's contention that Aristotle did not have a theory of distribution (Schumpeter 1954: 60) reflects a misunderstanding of this fact and a thrusting of modern market analysis upon Aristotle's explanation of production for use in the *oikos*. The idea of rent as a distributive share distinct from the use values distributed to family members by the head of the household or citizen freeholder was not emphasized by the Greeks as it was by later thinkers who had in mind the institution of feudal tenures which required money rents or shares to be paid to landlords.

In the *Politics* (Aristotle 1948:1266a–7a) discussed Phaleas of Chalcedon's proposal for the equalization of property in land. Although many had recognized inequality as one of the main causes of civic discord as well as of 'ordinary crimes', he said, proposals to eliminate inequality could only be effective if the number of children permitted each family, and access to 'office' or political power, were also regulated. Moreover, he added, 'want is not the only cause of crimes' (1267a), and he suggested that 'It is more necessary to equalize men's desires than their properties' (1266b).

In the *Laws*, Plato cautioned that 'there must be no place for penury in any section of the population, nor yet for opulence (Plato 1961:744) in a properly administered city, and he recommended that no one should have less than a standard allotment of land nor more than four times the value of an allotment acquired 'from treasure trove,

donation, or business, or by any other similar chance'
(744e). Any excess would be appropriated by the state
(745a). To enforce this provision, all property other than
original allotments would be required to be publicly
recorded.

The Greeks conceived of a tripartite distribution of goods
or income to the members of the household in accordance
with the needs for sustenance, amenities, and leisure. This
distribution reflected an ordinal hierarchy of needs satisfied
by corresponding goods. Thus 'goods of the body' satisfied
physical needs, 'external goods' provided certain amenities
of life, while 'goods of the soul' or psychic values provided
the leisure and aesthetic values necessary for the cultivation
of the mind required for the performance of the duties of
the free citizen. Since the Greeks thought the agricultural
labourer or slave could utilize only the first order of goods,
his or her distributive share consisted only in subsistence,
while the share of the artisan or specialized craftsman
included both 'goods of the body' and 'external goods'.
Only the free Greek citizen was thought to have the capacity
to use and appreciate all of the classes of goods. As
planner, supervisor and moral and intellectual leader of the
household, he directed production choices and distributed
income to members of the extended family. His proper
functioning in society required that his share include goods
of the body, external goods and psychic goods.

The social distribution of income in ancient Greece was
thus deduced from a pattern of natural utilities thought to
govern the natural needs of individuals, with the productive
activities of the household organized to provide goods for
the satisfaction of the needs or 'demands' of its members.
The ordinal hierarchy of both needs and 'goods' involved
a priority of concern, first, for sustenance. It was recognized,
however, that one could become sated with any 'good of
the body', implying diminishing utility. Beyond this, natural
need shifted to amenities or external goods. As satiation
approached, the diminishing utility of external goods was
replaced by a desire for psychic values on the part of the
true freeman and citizen but could be extended into gluttony
and excessive luxury if permitted to the debased individual.

In his *Politics* Aristotle (1948:1323) described the limiting force of subjective utility, but he restricted his analysis to individual conduct and did not extend it into the commercial realm (Lowry 1974). The Greek perspective was echoed in Adam Smith's *Moral Sentiments* (1813:IV.1) where it is suggested that the rich, constrained 'in spite of their natural selfishness and rapacity' by their limited need for comsumption goods, would be 'led by an invisible hand to make nearly the same distribution of the necessaries of life' as would have been made 'had the earth been divided into equal portions among all its inhabitants.' The idea of the diminishing utility of goods of the body came to be known as 'Engel's Law' in nineteenth-century economic thought.

10.3 EFFICIENT COMBINATION AND INCREASED RETURNS

After capture and agriculture, the third facet of the Greek view of wealth was the realization that a finite natural potential might be more fully realized by harmonizing human activities directed toward given goals with the patterns implicit in nature. To the extent that humans were natural elements, their propensities and skills could be adjusted and combined to fit together to effect an improved combination that would more fully exploit this existing potential. That the Greeks held such a view is illustrated by the strict division of labour not only suggested but required of the citizens of Plato's *Republic* and the explicit description of the division of labour in the assembly-line production of shoes in Xenophon's Cyropaedia (VIII.2. 5–6). In his *Oeconomicus*, Xenophon illustrated his essentially geometrical view of efficient combination by references to, for example, the effectiveness of order in a military body and in a chorus (VIII.3.4) and the efficient order of a Phoenician galley (VIII.9). Extending his concept of efficient order as an element of success from the physical arrangement of things to effective leadership, he also used a quantitative ratio of 2 : 1 in his description (XXI.3) of the success of a well-led crew of a ship as opposed to a poorly led one. The Greek view of efficient combination might be likened to the combining of pieces in a puzzle to approximate the best approach to the natural ideal picture.

This approach to production is described in Aristotle's *Politics* (Books I and VII) in terms of the elements of the ideal *polis*, and he emphasizes the role of the administrator or head of the household who, by developing his intellect, would be in the best position to guide the less intelligent in a mutually beneficial way to produce a greater yield. The combination of master and slave, for example, permitted the master to exercise his supervisory acumen while the slave was able to use his physical powers more efficiently under the master's supervision. The potential of both the slave's efforts and the master's intelligence were thus more fully exploited, and the resulting increase in returns from nature permitted them both to be better off. A perceptive slave would, from this point of view, choose to be guided by a master and share in the increased income to be distributed even though his utilities would primarily limit him to an interest in goods of the body, that is the simple pleasures of the flesh.

10.4 BARTER, MONEY, EXCHANGE AND THE METICS

The ancient Greek approach to the acquisition and distribution of wealth posited a system in which the administrative distribution of income to the appropriate sequence of individual needs and to the different categories of individuals in society was guided by a naturally self-limiting pattern of utilities which would lead to a stable, natural political economy. The parallels with eighteenth-century Physiocracy are suggestive. A conspicuous feature of the ancient economy was that most commercial activity was controlled by *metics* (resident aliens) since, for the Greek citizen, wealth and status were traditionally derived from the management of agricultural estates and civic activities.

Working within this frame of reference, Aristotle (Politics,

I) had to expand his restricted view of the *oikos* (extended household) and the *polis* by incorporating barter and money exchange. He did this by stressing that *use* is the purpose for which goods exist and the only justification for their production in the natural scheme of things. Exchange, he asserted, would lead to an unnatural or secondary use of goods. However, he granted that if the ultimate purpose of barter is to obtain other goods for use, the process would still be subject to the natural limits of utility and would therefore be stable and desirable. Even the exchange of goods for money, although involving an unnatural use of the goods, would ultimately be subjected to a natural limit if the purpose of the exchange was to spend the money for consumption goods. This pattern of exchange was characterized by Marx as commodities-money-commodities (C–M–C), to be distinguished from money-commodities-money (M–C–M).

Aristotle's view of monetary exchange carried on by the professional trader who used money to buy goods for the purpose of exchanging them for money (rather than for other goods for use) was that it was not only an 'unnatural' use of goods but also that, since it occurred outside the system of natural limits which controlled the distribution of income in the primarily agrarian *polis* or traditional Greek community, it would be 'unlimited'. The merchant, he noted, would not be constrained by the satiation of needs which guided other participants in the exchange process. The objective of the 'limited' kind of exchange is primarily the sharing and distribution of goods produced for use, with goods flowing from producer to user unimpeded by individual accumulations of stores of money. The merchant's motivation, on the other hand, would be to garner a surplus unhampered by the limitations of natural utility. This analysis was reinforced by the historical reality of the fourth century BC when most traders, being *metics*, did not necessarily share the same cultural values or institutional restraints to which the native members of the closely knit communities were subject. These outsiders, he thought, would be prone to extort and carry off a surplus in the form of either money or goods which properly belonged to the natural potential of the community to expand its population at the established standard of living (Lowry 1974);.

The idea is clearly presented in the first book of Aristotle's *Politics* that money exchange carries with it the dangerous possibility of a misdirection of income, particularly when *metics* or foreigners are involved, since they are not committed to psychic values in the community. This is the source of the frequent charge that Aristotle was hostile to trade. The confusion arises when his insistence on the unnaturalness of exchange as a *use* of goods produced for consumption is taken as a blanket disapproval of exchange itself. Aristotle *did* condemn what he considered the pernicious kind of trade which was unrestricted by a natural utility limit on the trader, for whom money or accumulation, rather than consumption or leisure, is the object.

The measures introduced by Lycurgus, the legendary Spartan law giver, to reduce the 'dreadful inequality' in ancient Sparta, provide incontrovertible evidence that the ancient Greeks understood very clearly some of the deleterious social effects of the maldistribution of wealth and also monetary and other measures to deal with it. According to Plutarch, (1914; VII–X), 'the city was heavily burdened with indigent and helpless people' because 'wealth was wholly concentrated in the hands of a few'. To remedy the resulting inequities, Lycurgus first convinced the Spartans of the need for a total redistribution of the land. Next, he advanced the idea of redistributing all movable property to remove 'every vestige of unevenness and inequality'. When the propertied citizens objected, he 'took another course, and overcame their avarice by political devices'. Declaring a new iron money quenched with vinegar to destroy its commodity value the only legal tender, he withdrew gold and silver money from circulation. The domestic economy was insulated from foreign trade when he assigned so 'trifling' a value to the iron money that 'a large storeroom' was needed to keep 'ten minas' worth' and a 'yoke of cattle' required to transport it. Obviously no foreign trader would bring iron into Sparta to be used as money nor accept the tainted iron which had lost its commodity value. In his 1755 *Essai sur la nature du commerce en général* (I.xvii), Cantillon cited Lycurgus' iron money as an example of a fiat money system, but he failed to understand that the possibility of counterfeiting had been eliminated by Lycurgus' policy of setting prices lower than the commodity value of iron.

Plutarch's account of this ancient use of monetary policy as part of an overall plan to effect a redistribution of wealth was circulated in England as early as 1579 in Sir Thomas North's translation of a French edition of Plutarch. His starkly beautiful description of the effectiveness of Lycurgus' monetary policy in stemming the flow of Spartan wealth to foreigners to pay for luxury imports and redirecting it to the support of local craftsmen and utilitarian domestic production, is instructive. 'No merchant-seaman', he reported, 'brought freight into their harbours: no rhetoric teacher set foot on Laconian soil, no vagabond soothsayer, no keeper of harlots, no gold- or silver-smith, since there was no money there.' Luxury, 'gradually deprived of that which stimulated and supported it, died away'. This is how it happened that Spartan craftsmen, 'freed . . . from useless tasks', began to make 'common and necessary utensils' of such extraordinary quality they were widely sought after. The Laconian *kothon* or drinking-cup became part of the kit of every soldier because its colour 'concealed the disagreeable appearance of the water . . . they were often compelled to drink, and its curving lips caught the muddy sediment and held it inside, so that only the purer part reached the mouth of the drinker'.

10.5 THE DISTRIBUTION OF THE BENEFITS OF EXCHANGE

The primary way in which Xenophon and Aristotle perceived the possibility of something approximating our modern notion of productivity was in terms of increases in utility gained from combinations or exchanges.

Although, from a materialist point of view, the total quantity of wealth or natural values cannot be increased, exchanges and combinations may permit two individuals to surrender items they each value less for things they each value more so that the resulting sum of *utility* will be greater than before the exchange. This is, in effect, a theory of the efficient distribution of value deduced from the ability of individuals to adjust to natural potential. Xenophon approached the matter from an administrative point of view, and his notions of efficient combination parallel modern notions of efficiency and programming.

Aristotle, however, thought of negotiated transactions as functioning in a setting of what we would now call isolated exchange, where the area of mutual benefit is subject to bargained distribution between the participants. Ultimately, however, since, as is generally recognized, the proper division of a potential mutual benefit is moot, Aristotle considered it to be a proper subject for judicial determination if the parties could not agree between themselves. In ancient Greece, public arbitration seems to have been the preferred institution for distributing disputed benefits from exchange. A juridical interpretation of the exchange discussion in Book V of Aristotle's *Nicomachean Ethics* (Lowry 1969) is consistent with much other Greek literature. In the case of imperfect markets, the potential benefits from trade can be distributed in any of a number of ways, all of which are fair in the sense that both parties are better off than they would have been in the absence of an exchange. In another sense, the division of any surplus utility generated by exchange above the minimum benefit necessary to induce trade is a zero-sum game, that is, a relationship in which *any* gain to one is a loss to the other. This, however, is a perception that arises *after* the commitment to exchange is made but while the exchange rate is still subject to negotiation.

In either event, whether this mutual benefit from trade is conceived as a surplus to be divided according to some social principle of distribution or as an anticipatable profit or surplus to which each party may presume a prior claim, the ancients tended to deduce it from the social process of interaction and not from some concept of production of natural values. While Aristotle seemed to be inclined to distribute this subjectively defined surplus administratively, he did not clearly distinguish it from the objectively defined material surplus that could support the growth of population or be carried off by outsiders. In any case, the Athenians maintained a complex system of public regulation of the grain trade, upon which their concentrated population had come to rely, an approach which must have appeared obvious and reasonable to them since this important trade was primarily controlled by *metics*.

The ideal *polis* described in Aristotle's *Politics* was a closed economy in which income was distributed in a way which contributed to community stability and self-sufficiency. Although propertied Greek citizens might assimilate material benefits from agricultural production, their larger distributive share was not viewed as a 'surplus' lost to the community since, rather than being carried away by 'outsiders', the Greek citizen would 'spend' the benefits in public service, intellectual pursuits and civic enrichment. The ancient Greeks did not have a well-developed system of public finance, but citizens with the greatest material wealth were obliged to finance liturgies, festivals and other civic events.

The importance of the attempt of the ancient Greeks to structure a concept of surplus in terms of subjective utilities within the deductive confines of a self-sufficient economy, is indicated by the fact that, in contemporary theory, surplus is still defined as a mutual aggregation of utilities in a general equilibrium system. Allais writes:

'A long approach going back over a century has made possible an increasingly precise grasp of the vague and blurred concept of the 'advantages' drawn from the functioning of the economy. The concept of surplus, properly worked out, provides us with an operational definition of these advantages which in no way implies resort to the concept of cardinal utility, and is free of all considerations of prices, and any hypothesis of continuity, derivability or convexity.' (Allais 1986: 136)

Although Aristotle's writings suggest an ordinal and subjective utility approach to surplus in both macroeconomic and microeconomic contexts, it is clear that he was unable to separate the pure theory of a self-contained whole—an isolated economy—from the realities of outside involvements with parties (the *metics*) who did not necessarily play by the accepted institutional and moral rules. This facet of the ancient concern for the distribution of a potential material surplus is relevant today, particularly for the less-developed countries. Trade between the developed and less-developed countries generates a subjectively defined 'advantage' or surplus that can be divided fairly between the participating parties within the confines of a wide range of terms of trade. However, as Aristotle was aware, outsiders tend to 'march to a different drummer' and, unless the distribution of the surplus is guided by public policy in cases where there is a seriously uneven distribution of bargaining power, a material outflow of the natural potential of the state and a loss of the birthright of future generations may be involved, with a 'lion's share' going to the economically advanced nation.

In general, the ancient Greek emphasis upon leadership and administrative control in the development of subjective values and the allocation of material resources provides little support for later hypotheses of natural laws of economic process or growth.

References

Adelman, I. and Morris, C. (1973) *Economic Growth and Social Equity in Developing Countries*, Palo Alto: Standford University Press

Ahluwalia, M. (1976) 'Income distribution and development: some stylized facts', *American Economic Review* 66 (May), pp. 307–42

Ahluwalia, M. (1978) 'Dimensions of the problem', in H. Chenery *et al.* (eds) *Redistribution with Growth*, New York: Oxford University Press

Allais, M. (1986) 'The concepts of surplus and loss and the reformulation of the theories of stable general economic equilibrium and maximum efficiency, in: M. Pananzini and R. Scazzieri, (eds) *Foundations of Economics: Structures of Inquiry and Economic Theory*, Oxford: Basil Blackwell, pp. 135–74

Andrews, P.W.S. (1949) *Manufacturing Business*, London: Macmillan

Andrews, M.J. *et al.* (1985) 'Models of the UK economy and the real wage–employment debate', *National Institute Economic Review,* May, pp. 41–52

Ansoff, H.I. (1965) *Corporate Strategy*, New York: McGraw-Hill

Appels, A. (1986) *Political Economy and Enterprise Subsidies*, Tilburg: Tilburg University Press

Aristotle (1948) *Politics*, trans. Ernest Barker, Oxford: Clarendon Press

Arndt, H.W. (1963) *The Economic Lessons of the 1930s*, London: Cass

Arrow, K.J. *et al.* (1961) 'Capital–Labour substitution and economic efficiency', *Review of Economics and Statistics* 43 (August), p. 225–50

Atkinson, A.B. (1972) *Unequal Shares*. London: Allen Lane

Atkinson, A.B. and Stiglitz, J.E. (1980) *Lectures on Public Economics*, London: McGraw-Hill

Bartlett, R.L. and Poulton-Calahan, C. (1982) 'Changing family structures and the distribution of family income: 1951–1976', *Social Science Quarterly* 63 (March), pp. 28–38

Bauer, O. (1913) 'The accumulation of capital', *History of Political Economy* 18, 1986, pp. 82–110

Bonnell, S.M. (1979) 'The "real wage overhang" and the wage share of output', *Australian Bulletin of Labour* 5, (4), pp. 27–47

Bonnell, S.M. (1981) 'Real wages and employment in the Great Depression', *Economic Record* 57 (157), pp. 277–81

Brenner, Y.S. (1969) *A Short History of Economic Progress*, London: Cass

Brenner, Y.S. (1971) *Agriculture and the Economic Development of Low Income Countries*, The Hague: Mouton

Brenner, Y.S. (1984) *Capitalism, Competition and Economic Crisis*, Brighton: Harvester Press

Brenner, Y.S., *et al. (1986) Visies op Verdeling* (Perspectives on Distribution), 's-Gravenhage: Vuga

Bronfenbrenner, M. (1960) 'A note on relative shares and the elasticity of substitution', *Journal of Political Economy* 68, pp. 284–7

Bronfenbrenner, M, (1971) *Income Distribution*, London: Macmillan

Butlin, N.G. (1984) *Source Papers in Economic History*, Source Paper No. 4, Canberra: Australian National University

CAER (1978) *Real Wages and Unemployment*, CAER Paper No. 4, University of New South Wales

Cautillon, R. (1892) *Essay upon the Nature of Commerce in General*, first published in 1755, reprint for Harvard University, G.H. Ellis: Boston

CBS (1966a–86a) *Nationale Rekeningen* 1965 t/m 1985 (National Accounts 1965–1985), 's-Gravenhage: Staatsuitgeverij

CBS (1980b) *De Personele Inkomensverdeling 1975 dl.1* (The Personal Income Distribution), 's-Gravenhage: Staatsuitgeverij

CBS (1982b) *De Personele Inkomensverdeling 1977, Kerncijfers* (The Personal Income Distribution, Main data), Heerlen: CBS

Champernowne, D.G. (1974) (A comparison of measures of inequality of income distribution', *Economic Journal* 84, pp. 787–816

Chapman, A.L. (1953) *Wages and Salaries in the United Kingdom*, Cambridge: Cambridge University Press

Chase, R.X. (1979) 'Production theory', in A.S. Eichner (ed.), *A Guide to Post-Keynesian Economics*, New York: Sharpe

Chenery, H. and Syrguin, M. 1975) *Patterns of Development, 1950–1970*, New York: Oxford University Press

Chenery, H. *et al.* (eds) (1978) *Redistribution with Growth*, New York: Oxford University Press

Cline, W. (1975) 'Distribution and development: a survey of the literature' *Journal of Development Economics* 2, pp. 359–400

Coe, D. (1985) 'Nominal wages, the NAIRU and wage flexibility', in OECD *Economic Studies*, no. 5, Paris: OECD

Corden, W.M. (1979) 'Wages and unemployment in Australia', *Economic Record*, 55, pp. 1–19

Cowling, K. (1982) *Monopoly Capitalism*, London: Macmillan

CPB (1956, 1965–85) *Centraal Economisch Plan* (Central Economic Plan), 's-Gravenhage: Staatsuitgeverij

Dalton (1920) 'The measurement of the inequality of incomes' *Economic Journal*, September, pp. 348–61

Domar, E.D. (1957) *Essays in the Theory of Economic Growth*, New York: Oxford University Press

Duijn, J. van (1983) *The Long-Wave of Economic Life*, London: Allen & Unwin

Dutt, C. (1964) *Fundamentals of Marxism-Leninism*, Moscow: Progress Publishers

Eichner, A.S. (1976) *The Megacorp and Oligopoly: Micro Foundations of Macro Dynamics*, Cambridge: Cambridge University Press

Eichner, A.S. (1979) *A Guide to Post-Keynesian Economics*, New York: Sharpe

Eklund, K. (1980) 'Long waves in the development of capitalism' *Kyklos* 33, pp. 383–419

Empel, F. van (1986) 'Een Rendementsexplosie' (A profit explosion), *Intermediair*, 30 May

Ewijk, C. van (1981) 'The long wave — a real phenomenon?' *De Economist* 129, pp. 324–72

Fei, J., Ranis, G. and Kuo, S. (1979) *Growth with Equity: The Taiwan Case*, New York: Oxford University Press

Feinstein, C.H. (1968) 'Changes in the distribution of the national income in the United Kingdom Since 1860', in J. Marchal and B. Ducros (eds) *The Distribution of National Income*, London: Macmillan

Ferguson, C.E. (1969) *The Neoclassical Theory of Production and Distribution*, Cambridge: Cambridge University Press

Fields, G.S. (1980) *Poverty, Inequality and Development*, Cambridge: Cambridge University Press

Fisher, F.M. (1969) 'The existence of aggregate production functions', *Econometrica* 37, pp. 553–77

Forrester, J.W. (1977) 'Growth cycles', *De Economist* 125, pp. 525–43

Freeman, C. *et al.* (1982) *Unemployment and Technical Innovation: A Study of Long Waves and Economic Development*, London: Frances Pinter

Fuchs, V.R. (1963) 'Capital–labor substitution: a note', *Review of Economics and Statistics* 45, pp. 436–8

Garegnani, P. (1970) 'Heterogeneous capital and production function and the theory of distribution' *Review of Economic Studies* 37 (June), pp. 407–36

Ginneken, W. van (1982) 'Generating international comparable income distribution data', *The Review of Income and Wealth* 28, pp. 365–79

Ginneken, W. van and Park, J. (1984) *Generating Internationally Comparable Income Distribution Estimates*, Geneva: ILO

Glyn, A. and Sutcliffe, B. (1972) *British Capitalism, Workers and the Profits Squeeze*, Harmondsworth: Penguin

Goodwin, R.M. (1983) 'A note on wages, profits and fluctuating growth rates', *Cambridge Journal of Economics* 7, pp. 305–9

Grossmann, H. (1929) *Das Akkumulations- und Zusammenbruchsgesetz des Kapitalistischen Systems* (The Law of Accumulation and Collapse of Capitalism), Leipzig: Hirschfeld

Gruen, F.H. (1978) 'Some thoughts on real wages and unemployment', in CAER, *Real Wages and Unemployment*, CAER Paper No. 4, University of New South Wales

Hahn, F.H. (1972) *The Share of Wages in the National Income*, London: Weidenfeld and Nicolson

Hahnel, R. and Sherman, H.J. (1982) 'Income distribution and the business cycle: three conflicting hypotheses', *Journal of Economic Issues* 16, pp. 49–73

Harcourt, G.C. (1972) *Some Cambridge Controversies in the Theory of Capital*, Cambridge: Cambridge University Press

Harrod, R.F. (1948) *Towards a Dynamic Economics*, London: Macmillan

Hartog, J. (1981) 'Inkomstenbelasting en Herverdeling 1914–1973' (Income taxes and redistribution), *Economisch Statistische Berichten* 66 pp. 680–2

Hartog, J. (1983) (Inequality reduction by income taxes: just how much? An investigation for the Netherlands, 1914–1973', *Empirical Economics* 8, pp. 9–13

Hartog (1987) 'Labour market policies from a neoclassical perspective: implementing the trinity,' in K. Groenveld *et al.* (eds) *Economic Policy in the Market Process Success or Failure*, Amsterdam: North-Holland

Hartog, J. and Veenbergen, J.G. (1978) 'Long-run changes in personal income distribution', *De Economist* 126, pp. 521–49

Haveman, R.H. (1985) *Does the Welfare State Increase Welfare?* (Inaugural Lecture), Leiden: Stenfert Kroese

Hibbert, J. (1975) 'Measuring changes in the nation's real income', *Economic Trends*, No. 255, pp. xxvii–xxxv

Hicks, J.R. (1932) *The Theory of Wages*, London: Macmillan

Hicks, J.R. (1939) *Value and Capital*, Oxford: Oxford University Press

Hicks, J.R. (1950) *A Contribution to the Theory of the Trade Cycle*, Oxford: Clarendon Press

HMSO (1985 and 1986) *UK National Accounts; National Income and Expenditure Accounts*, London

Hodgson, G. (1982) 'Theoretical and policy implications of variable productivity', *Cambridge Journal of Economics* 6, pp. 213–26

Howard, M.C. and King, J.E. (1985) *The Political Economy of Marx*, 2nd ed, Harlow: Longman

ILO (1940) *Year Book of Labour Statistics*, 5th year of issue, International Labour Office

ILO (1943) *International Labour Review* 47 (5)

ILO (1945) *International Labour Review* 51 (1)

IMF (International Monetary Fund) (1985) *World Economic Outlook*, A Survey by the Staff of the International Monetary Fund, Washington, DC: IMF

Jaffe, W. (1979) 'The normative bias', *Quarterly Journal of Economics* 91 (August), pp. 371–87

Jain, S. (1975) *Size Distribution of Income: A Compilation of Data*, Washington, DC (World Bank)

Japanese Economic Planning Agency (1977) *Annual Report on National Income Statistics*, Tokyo: Ministry of Finance Printing Bureau

Japanese Economic Planning Agency (1984) *Annual Report on National Income Statistics*, Tokyo: Ministry of Finance Printing Bureau

Kakwani, N. (1980) *Income Equality and Poverty*, New York:

Oxford University Press, ch. 16

Kaldor, N. (1955–6) 'Alternative theories of distribution', *Review of Economic Studies* 23, pp. 83–100

Kaldor, N. (1960) *Essays on Value and Distribution*, London: Free Press

Kaldor, N. (1966) 'Alternative studies of distribution', *Review of Economic Studies* 33, pp. 309–19

Kaldor, N. (1972) 'The irrelevance of equilibrium economics', *The Economic Journal* 82 (Dec.), pp. 1237–55

Kaldor, N. and Mirrlees, J.A. (1962) 'A new model of economic growth', *The Review of Economic Studies* 29 (June), pp. 306–22

Kalecki, M. (1971) *Selected Essays on the Dynamics of the Capitalist Economy, 1933–1970*, Cambridge: Cambridge University Press

Kenyon, P. (1979) 'Pricing' in A.S. Eichner (ed.), *A Guide to Post-Keynesian Economics*, London: Sharpe, pp. 34–5

Keynes, J.M. (1936) *The General Theory of Employment, Interest and Money*, London: Macmillan

Keynes, J.M. (1939) 'Relative movements of real wages and output', *Economic Journal*, XLIX, pp. 34–51

Khan, S. and Knight, M.D. (1985) *Fund-Supported Adjustment Programs and Economic Growth*, Occasional Paper 41, Washington, DC: IMF

Killick, T. (1984) *The Quest for Economic Stabilisation: The IMF and the Third World*, London: Heinemann Educational Books with the Overseas Development Institute

Kindleberger, Ch. P. (1973) *The World in Depression 1929–1939*, London: Allen Lane

King, J.E. and Regan, P. (1976) *Relative Income Shares*, London: Macmillan Press

King, J.E. (1986) 'P.W.S. Andrews', mimeo, University of Lancaster

Kleinknecht, A. (1984) *Innovation patterns in crisis and prosperity: Schumpeter's long cycle reconsidered*, Amsterdam, thesis Free University Amsterdam

Klundert, Th. van der (1970) 'Inflatie en Werkloosheid', (Inflation and Unemployment), *Economisch Statistische Berichten*, 18 November 1970, p. 1119

Kondratieff, N.D. (1926) 'Die langen Wellen der Konjunktur', *Archiv für Sozialwissenschaft und Sozialpolitik* 56, pp. 573–610

Kondratieff, N.D. (1928) 'Die Preisdynamik der industriellen und landwirtschaftlichen Waren', *Archiv für Sozialwissenschaft und Sozialpolitik* 60, pp. 1–86

Kondratieff, N.D. (1935) 'The long waves in economic life', *Review of Economic Statistics*, vol. 17, pp. 105–15 (abbreviated translation of Kondratieff 1926)

Kondratieff, N.D. (1979) 'The Long Waves in Economic Life', *The Review* (Fernand Braudel Center), vol. 17, pp. 519–62 (complete translation of Kondratieff 1926)

Kondratieff, N.D. (1984) *The Long Wave Cycle*, New York: Richardson & Snyder (complete translation of Kondratieff's contribution to Oparin 1928)

Kravis, I.B. (1962) *The Structure of Income: Some Quantitative Essays*, Philadelphia: University of Pennsylvania

Kravis, I.B. (1968) 'Income distribution', in D.L. Sills (ed.) *International Encyclopaedia of the Social Sciences* 7, New York: Macmillan and Free Press

Kregel, J.A. (1972) *The Theory of Economic Growth*, London: Macmillan

Kregel, J.A. (1979) 'Income Distribution' in: A.S. Eichner (ed.) *A guide to Post-Keynesian Economics*, London: Sharpe

Kuh, E. (1965) 'Income distribution and employment over the business cycle', in J. Duesenberry (ed.), *The Brookings Quarterly Econometric Model of the US*, Chicago: Rand, McNally

Kuznets, S. (1940) 'Schumpeter's business cycles', *American Economic Review* 30, pp. 257–71

Kuznets, S. (1955) 'Economic growth and income inequality', *American Economic Review* 45 (March), pp. 18–20

Kuznets, S. (1959) 'Quantitative aspects of the economic growth of nations: IV distribution of national income by factor shares', *Economic Development and Cultural Change* 7 (April), pp. 1–100

Kuznets, S. (1963) 'Quantitative aspects of the economic growth of nations: VIII, distribution of income by size', *Economic Development and Cultural Change* 12 (October)

Lecaillon, P., Morrisson, C. and Germidis, D. (1984) *Income Distribution and Economic Development: An analytical survey*, Geneva: ILO

Lowry, S. Todd (1965) 'The classical Greek theory of natural resource economics', *Land Economics* 41, pp. 204–8

Lowry, S. Todd (1969) 'Aristotle's mathematical analysis of exchange', *History of Political Economy* 1, pp. 44–66

Lowry, S. Todd (1974) 'Aristotle's 'natural limit' and the economics of price regulation', *Greek, Roman and Byzantine*

Studies 15, pp. 57–63

Lydall, H. (1977) *Income Distribution during the Process of Development*, ILO World Employment Programme Research Working Paper no. 52 (February)

Maddison, A. (1982) *Phases of Capitalist Development*, Oxford: Oxford University Press

Mandel, E. (1975) *Late Capitalism*, London: New Left Books

Mandel, E. (1980) *Long Waves of Capitalist Economic Development: The Marxist Interpretation*, Cambridge: Cambridge University Press

Marx, K. (1962) 'Wage, price and profit', in K. Marx and F. Engels, *Selected Works*, Volume I (first published in 1867), Moscow: Foreign Languages Publishing House

Marx, K. (1969) *Capital*, Volume I (first published in 1867), Moscow: Progress Publishers

Meek, R.L. (1967) *Economics and Ideology and Other Essays*, London: Chapman & Hall

Mensch, G. (1979) *Stalemate in Technology*, Cambridge: Ballinger

Miljoenennota (1972–84) *Miljoenennota* (State of the Dutch Government Budget), 1972–1984, Ministery of Finance, 's-Gravenhage: Staatsuitgeverij

Mitchell, B.R. (1975) *European Historical Statistics 1750–1970*, London: Macmillan Press

Morley, R. (1979) 'Profit, relative, prices and unemployment', *Economic Journal* 89, pp. 582–600

Moseley, F. (1985) 'The rate of surplus value in the postwar US economy: a critique of Weisskopf's estimates', *Cambridge Journal of Economics* 9, pp. 57–79

Neville, J.W. (1967) 'The share of wages in income in Australia', *Economic Society of Australia and New Zealand, New South Wales Branch, Economic Monograph* 286, pp. 1–4

Nieuwkerk, H. van, en R.P. Sparling (1985) *De Internationale Investeringspositie van Nederland* (The International Investment Position of the Netherlands), Monetaire Monografieën No. 4, Amsterdam/Deventer: De Nederlandsche Bank/Kluwer

Nieuwkerk, M. van (1986) 'De Internationalisering van de Nederlandse Economie', (The Internationalisation of the Dutch Economy), *Economisch Statistische Berichten*, 12 November 1986, pp. 1088–93

NIO-Vereniging (1985) *Harde Heelmeester Maakt Stinkende Wonden; Effecten van IMF-beleid in de Derde Wereld* (Tough Medics Make Hard Wounds: The Effects of IMF Policies in the Third World), Amsterdam: NIO

Odink, J.G. (1983) 'Inkomensherverdeling door Belastingen en andere Overdrachten' (Income Redistribution by Taxes and Transfers), *Maandschrift Economie* 47, pp. 66–73

Odink, J.G. (1985) *Inkomensherverdeling* (Income Redistribution), Groningen: Wolters-Noordhoff

Odink, J.G. (1987) 'Herverdeling van Individuele- en van Huishoudinkomens; Wat Maakt Dat Uit?' (Redistribution of Individual and of Household Incomes. Does it Matter?), *Maandschrift Economie* 51

OECD (1977) *Economic Outlook*, Volume 21 (July), Paris: OECD

OECD (1978) *Australia*, Economic Survey, Paris: OECD

Okhawa, K. (1968) 'Changes in national income distribution by factor share in Japan', in J. Marchal and B. Ducros (eds) *The Distribution of National Income*, London: Macmillan Press

Oparin, D.I. *et al.* (1928) *Bol'shie tsikly kon'iunktury* (Major Economic Cyclus), Moscow: Krasnaia Presnia

Oshima, H. (1962) 'The international comparison of size distribution of family incomes with special reference to Asia', *Review of Economics and Statistics* 44 (November), pp. 439–45

Otani, I. (1978) 'Real wages and business cycles revisited', *The Review of Economics and Statistics* LX, pp. 301–4

Pasinetti, L.L. (1962) 'The rate of profit and income distribution in relation to the rate of economic growth', *Review of Economic Studies* 29 (Oct.), pp. 267–79

Pasinetti, L.L. (1972) *Growth and Income Distribution: Essays in Economic Theory*, Cambridge: Cambridge University Press

Paukert, F. (1973) 'Income distribution at different levels of development: A survey of evidence', *International Labor Review* 108 (August–September)

Pearce, D.W. (ed.) (1981) *Dictionary of Economics*, London: Macmillan

Pen, J. (1971) *Income Distribution*, Harmondsworth: Penguin

Phelps Brown, E.H. and Hart, P. (1952) 'The share of wages in national income', *Economic Journal* 62 (June), pp, 253–77

Phelps Brown, E.G. and Browne, M.H. (1968) *A Century of Pay*, London: Macmillan

Plato (1961) *Laws*, in E. Hamilton, E. and H. Cairns, (eds), *The Complete Dialogues of Plato*, trans. A.F. Taylor, Princeton, NJ: Princeton University Press

Plutarch (1914) *Lives*, I. Lycurgus, Loeb (ed.) Bernadotte Perrin (transl.), New York: G.P. Putnam's Sons

Rees, A. (1983) 'Discussion', *Brookings Papers on Economic Activity*, pp. 446–8

Reijnders, J. (1984) 'Perspectivistic distortion: a note on the approximation of trends and trend-cycles', *Social Science Information* 23, pp. 411–26

Riach, P.A. (1986) 'The share of wages and economic activity, Sweden 1960–1966', mimeo, Monash University

Ricardo, D. (1962) *Principles of Political Economy and Taxation*, Harmondsworth: Penguin

Robinson, J. 1949 *An Essay on Marxian Economics*, London: Macmillan

Robinson, J. (1962) *Essays in the Theory of Economic Growth*, London: Macmillan

Sachs, J.D. (1983) 'Real wages and unemployment in the OECD countries', *Brookings Papers on Economic Activity* 1, pp. 255–304

Saint-Etienne, Ch. (1984) *The Great Depression, 1929–1938: Lessons for the 1980s*, Stanford: Hoover Institution Press

Salverda, W (1978) 'Haalt de Arbeidsinkomensquote de 100 Procent? (en Wat Dan Nog...) (Will Labour's Income Share Reach the Hundred Per Cent?), *Tijdschrift voor Politieke Ekonomie* 1 (4), pp. 66–94

Samuelson, P. (1939) 'On the interaction between the multiplier analysis and the principle of acceleration', *Review of Economics and Statistics* 31, pp. 75–8

Schedvin, C.B. (1970) *Australia and the Great Depression*, Sydney: Sydney University Press

SCP (1981) *Profijt van de Overheid in 1977* (Benefits in Kind from the State), Sociale en Culturele Studies No. 1, 's-Gravenhage: Staatsuitgeverij

Sen, A.K. (1973) *On Economic Equality*, New York: Norton

Shaikh, A. (1980) 'Laws of production and laws of algebra' in E.J. Nell, *Growth of Profits and Property*, Cambridge: Cambridge University Press

Sisson, C.A. (1986) 'Fund-supported programs and income distribution in LDCs', *Finance and Development*, March, pp. 33–6

Smith, A. (1813) *The Theory of Moral Sentiments*, 2 vols, Edinburgh: J. Hay & Co.

Snape, Richard H. (1981) 'Wages policy and the economy in the seventies and beyond', in K. Hancock (ed.) *Incomes Policy in Australia*, Sydney: Harcourt Brace Jovanovich

Solow, R.M. (1958) 'A sceptical note on the consistency of

relative shares', *American Economic Review* 48, pp. 618–31

St Cyr, E.D.A. (1972) 'Notes on the behaviour of profit shares in British manufacturing industries', *Manchester School*, June, pp. 165–75

Sraffa, P. (1960) *Production of Commodities by Means of Commodities*, Cambridge: Cambridge University Press

Suppes, P. (1967) 'Decision theory', in: *The Encyclopedia of Philosophy*, vol. 2, New York: Macmillan & Free Press, pp. 310–14

Tobin, J. (1984) 'Impasse of the 1980s: locomotives who can't or won't', *The World Economy* 7 (1), pp. 5–21

Tolsma, H. (1986) 'Concurreren en Samenwerken' (Competing and cooperating), *Intermediair*, 16 May

UN (1948) *United Nations Statistical Year Book*, first issue, New York: Lake Success

UN (1950) *United Nations Year Book of International Trade Statistics*, first issue, New York: Lake Success

Urquhart, M.C. (ed.) (1965) *Historical Statistics of Canada*, Toronto: Macmillan

US Bureau of the Census (1975) *Historical Statistics of the United States, Colonial times to 1970. Bicentennial Edition*, Part 1, Washington, DC

US Bureau of the Census (1978) *Statistical Abstract of the United States*, Washington, DC

US Bureau of the Census (1985) *Statistical Abstract of the United States*, Washington, DC

Wattenburg, B.J. (1976) *Statistical History of the US from Colonial Times to the Present*, New York: Basic Books

Weintraub, S. (1956) 'A macroeconomic approach to the theory of wages, *American Economic Review* 46 (Dec.), pp. 835–57

Weisskopf, T.E. (1979) 'Marxian crisis theory and the rate of profit in the postwar US economy', *Cambridge Journal of Economics* 3, pp. 341–78

Weisskopf, T.E., Bowles, S. and Gordon, D.M. (1983) 'Hearts and minds: a social model of US productivity growth, *Brookings Papers on Economic Activity* 2, pp. 331–441

Wolff, P. de, and Driehuis, W. (1980) 'A description of postwar economic developments and economic policy in the Netherlands', in R.T. Griffiths (ed.) *The Economy and Politics in the Netherlands since 1945)*,´s-Gravenhage: Martinus Nijhof

World Bank (1985) *The World Bank Annual Report 1985)*, Washington, DC World Bank

World Bank (1986) *World Development Report 1986*, New York: Oxford University Press

Yotopoulos, P. and Lau, L. (1970) 'A test for balanced and unbalanced growth', *Review of Economics and Statistics* 52, pp. 376–83

Youngson, A.J. (1960) *The British Economy 1920–1957*, Cambridge, Mass: Harvard University Press

Zwan, A. ver der (1980) 'On the assessment of the Kondratieff Cycle and related issues', in S.K. Kuipers and G.J. Lanjouw, (eds), *Prospects of Economic Growth*, Amsterdam: North-Holland

The Authors

SHEILA MARY BONNELL is Senior Lecturer in Economics at La Trobe University in Australia. Her published work includes 'Real wages and employment in the Great Depression,' *Economic Record*, September 1981; 'A measure of the incidence of the cost of structural change', written together with T.C. Chew and P.B. Dixon, *Economic Record*, December 1982; 'The real wage overhang and the wage share of output', in Chapman, Isaac and Niland (eds) *Australian Labour Economics Readings*, Melbourne, 1979; and 'Modelling the effects of changes in junior wage rates on Structural change and teenage employment' in Paul Volker (ed.) *Structural Change and Unemployment*, Canberra, 1985. Her present research is on the effectiveness of labour market programmes for young people.

Y.S. BRENNER is Professor of Economics at the University of Utrecht in the Netherlands. His books published in English include *Theories of Economics Development and Growth,* London, 1966; *A Short History of Economic Progress*, London, 1969; *Agriculture and the Development of Low Income-Countries*, The Hague, 1971; *Looking into the Seeds of Time*, Assen, 1979; and *Capitalism, Competition and Economic Crisis*, Brighton, 1984. His current research deals with the relationship between economic growth and distribution in historical perspective

J. HARTOG is Professor of Economics at the University of Amsterdam. His work includes *Personal Income Distribution: A Multicapability Theory,* Boston, 1981; 'Earnings

251

and capability requirements', *Review of Economics and Statistics 2*, 1980; and 'The emergence of the working wife in Holland', written together with J. Theeuwes in *Journal of Labour Economics,* January 1986 (supplement). His current research is concerned with labour economics: earning functions, the role of education, of the efficiency of the labour market and the position of ethnic minorities.

J.E. KING is Senior Lecturer in Economics at the University of Lancaster in England. His writings include *Labour Economics,* London, 1972; *The Political Economy of Marx,* together with M.C. Howard, Harlow, 1975, revised 1985; *Relative Income Shares* with P. Regan, London, 1976; *Ten Per Cent and No Surrender: The Present Strike, 1853–4,* Cambridge, 1981; and *Economic Exiles,* London, 1988. His current interest is in Marxian economics since 1883.

SUK-MO KOO is Vice-President of the Korea Economic Research Institute. He published 'Effect of quarterly earnings announcements on analysts' forecasts' (with Edwin J. Elton and Martin J. Gruber) in *Research in Finance* Volume 6, 1986 New York. His current research is on monetary policy and financial markets in the developing countries.

JAE WON LEE is Associate Professor of Economics at Baruch College and the Graduate Center of City University New York. His publications include (Determinants of the changes in relative factor share', *Review of Economics and Statistics,* August 1970; 'A dynamic analysis of the relative share of production labour to capital', *Applied Economics,* August 1976; and together with Charles Kao. 'An empirical analysis of China's brain drain into the United States', in *Economic Development and Cultural Change,* April 1973; and 'Projected demand for higher education: 1970–80', *Journal of Literature of Social Studies,* September 1971; 'A re-examination of the Phillips Curve,' in B.J. Whang (ed.) *Essays in Economic Theory, Application and Practice,* Seoul, 1974. His current research interests are economic growth and income distribution; ownership structure of firms and their performances; impact of external debts on income distribution; implications of external debts on the relationships between the industrial nations and the Third World countries.

S. TODD LOWRY is Professor of Economics and Administration at Washington and Lee University in Lexington, Virginia. His work includes *Pre-Classical Political Economy*, Boston, 1987, and *The Archaeology of Economics Ideas*, Durham, NC, 1987. Among his articles are 'The roots of hedonism; an ancient analysis of quantity and time', *History of Political Economy* 13, 1981; 'Recent literature on ancient Greek economic thought', *Journal of Economic Literature* 17, 1979; 'Bargain and contract theory in law and economics', *Journal of Economic Issues* 10, 1979; 'The Archaeology of the circulation concept in economic theory', *Journal of the History of Ideas* 35, 1974; 'Aristotle's 'Natural Limit' and the economics of price regulation', *Greek, Roman and Byzantine Studies* 15, 1974; 'Aristotle's mathematical analysis of exchange', *History of Political Economy* 1, 1969; and 'The classical Greek theory of natural resource economics, *Land Economics* 41, 1965. His current research interests are ancient economic thought and the development of administrative and legal principles relevant to economic ideas.

A.J.C. MANDERS teaches economics at the University of Utrecht. Among his publications in English are 'Automation and the quality of working life', *Asian Journal of Economics*, Delhi, 1983; 'Market structure and the labour process', *International Journal of Manpower*, Bradford, 1987; His current research is on decision-making on new production technology in a multinational microelectronics company.

J.G. ODINK is Associate Professor of Economics at the University of Amsterdam. Most of his published work is in Dutch. Included here was his chapter on income redistribution in the second edition of J.S. Schoorl (ed.) *Inleiding tot micro-economie* (Introduction to Micro-economics) Groningen, 1985; 'Prices of used cars in West Germany before and after W.W.II', together with E. van Imhoff, *De Economist*, 1982; and 'True versus measured Theil inequality', also with E. Van Imhoff, in *Statistica Neerlandica*, 38, 1984. His research interests are in income distribution: the equity–efficiency trade-off; optimal income brackets; and household versus individual incomes.

P. REGAN teaches economics graduate studies at the University of Lancaster in England. His publications incude: *Relative Income Shares*, with J. King, London 1976; and a contribution to M. Robertson (ed.) *The History of Lancashire Country Council* London, 1977. His research interest is in labour economics.

R.J. RIMMER is lecturing in the Department of Mathematics and Operations Research at the Footscray Institute of Technology in Australia. Among other works he published together with Dixon and Parmenter, 'Sensitivity or ORANI projections of the short run effects of increases in protection to variations in the values adopted for export demand elasticities', in D.C. Hague (ed.) *Structural Adjustment in Trade Dependent Advanced Economics,* London, 1983; also together with Meagher, Parmenter and Clements, 'Special purpose versions of a general multisectoral model: tax issues and the Australian wine industry', *Review of Marketing in Agricultural Economics* V, 1985; with Pearson, 'An efficient method for the solution of large computable general equilibrium models', *Journal of the International Association for Mathematics and Computers in Simulation*, 27 1985; and with S.M. Bonnell, Parmenter and Scorgie, 'Modelling the effects of changes in junior wage rates on teenage employment: how far can we go with the available data?, in P.A. Volker (ed.) *The Structure and Duration of Unemployment*, Canberra, 1985. Presently, he is investigating Kaldorian distribution theory; reviewing recent contributions by Post-Keynesian economists on income distribution; and building a short-run model in the spirit of Kaldor's neo-Pasinetti theory.

JAN P.G. REIJNDERS is lecturer in economics at the University of Utrecht. His main publications are *Herstructurering automatisering en gevolgen voor de arbeid* (Restructuring, Automation and the Consequences for Working life) (Dutch), Utrecht, 1981; 'Backgrounds of the restructuring process in the video sector', in M. Bouwman (ed.) *Philips'*

International Reorganisations and Worker's Resistance, Eindhoven, 1982 (Dutch); 'Werkstructurering in beeld' (Focus on Work Structuring), in W. Doorewaard *et al.* (eds) *Stratego op bedrijfsnivo* (Strategy on the Company Level) (Dutch), Eindhoven, 1983; 'Perspectivistic distortion: a note on the approximation of trends and trend-cycles', *Social Science Information* 23/2, 1984; and 'De verzorgingsstaat en lange termijn stabiliteit' (The welfare state and long-term stability) in *Visies op verdeling* (Perspectives on Distribution) (Dutch) 's-Gravenhage, 1986, which he edited together with Y.S. Brenner and P. van Wijngaarden. Presently his main interest is economic development in the long run. His book *'The Enigma of the Long Waves'* is forthcoming in 1988.

A.H.G.M. SPITHOVEN is a research worker at the University of Utrecht. Among other works, he contributed to Y.S. Brenner *et al.* (eds) *Bezuinigen is geen Werk* (Frugality Creates no Work), Amsterdam, 1981; 'Business cycles and absenteeism' (Dutch), in *Economisch Statistische Berichten*, May 1982; 'Job perspectives for people aged 55–65 years' (Dutch), in *Tijdschrift voor Gerontologie*, October 1986; and 'Unemployment, investment in depth and Oligopolies' (Dutch), in Y.S. Brenner *et al.* (eds) *Visies op Verdeling* (Perspectives on Distribution), 's-Gravenhage, 1986. He is working on his PhD, 'Cyclical and structural unemployment in the Netherlands'.

J. TINBERGEN was Professor of Economics at *de Nederlandse Hogeschool* (NEH) in Rotterdam (now the Erasmus University). Together with R. Frisch, he was awarded the Nobel Prize for Economics in 1969. He considers his main books to be: *Economic Policy, Principles and Design*, Amsterdam, 1956; *Income Distribution: Analysis and Policies*, Amsterdam, 1975; (together with D. Fischer) *Warfare and Welfare*, Brighton 1987.

J.K. VERKOOIJEN is lecturer in development economics at the University of Utrecht. Most of his work appeared in the form of research reports, among these were 'Land reform and debt in Peru', University of Tilburg, 1975;

'Socio-economic diagnoses and development plans for several provinces in Cusco, Peru', Government of Peru, 1983; and 'Micro-regional integrated rural development in the southern Andes of Peru', *Proceedings of the Dutch Geographical Association*, 1988. His major research is on rural development in Latin America where he spent five years as economic planner and five years as economic planner and five years on a Dutch Government development mission.

Name Index

Subject Index

structure 12, 40
Classification of persons 36
Co-makership 222
Cobb-Douglas function, 92,
204
Coefficient of variation 199,
201
Collusion between giant
corporations xii
Columbia 164
Comparative advantages,
Ricardo's law of 43
Competition 21, 27, 39, 46
international 35
perfect 20, 25, 34, 56, 90,
212
Composite commodity
theorem 24
Conglomerate-strategy 216
Consumption x, 3, 51, 119,
130
habits 188
parasitical 32
Cost x, 12, 22, 35, 95
Cost-benefit techniques 17
Costa Rica 164
Counter-cyclical fluctuations
38, 56, 67, 81
CPB (Centraal Planbureau;
Central Planning Office)
50, 117–20, 123, 128, 129,
131, 141, 144, 145, 241
Credit 186
Creditworthiness 180, 181,
184, 185
Crowding out effect 22, 147

Debt problems xi, 150, 180,
184, 186–9
Decision Theory 24
Demand 12–14, 18–21, 23, 25,
38, 41, 42, 89, 142
aggregate (*see also* effective
demand) 18, 28, 30, 52,
56

derived 49, 134, 135
elasticities 49
Mill's law of reciprocal 43
Democratic euphoria 20
Denmark 91, 164
Depression 45, 47, 48, 85,
ideology of 144
prolonged viii, 62
Developing countries xi, 3, 33
Development xiii
historical 16
plans 32, 33
technological 1
Diminishing marginal
returns 117
Diminishing Returns,
law of 14, 49
Disequilibrium 19, 29, 56
Distribution ix–xi, 11, 28, 185,
187, 189, 191, 196
between Investment and
Consumption ix
functional 11, 48, 52, 119
personal 11, 48
primary 119, 123
theories xiii, 21
Dividend 2, 31, 35, 41
Double switching 24
Drawing Right, Special 161
Dual market hypothesis 17, 18
Dutch Disease 124

Economic
growth x, 11, 42, 134, 184,
185
laws 33
legislation 41
stability 147, 149, 151
thought, fundamental
critique of
mainstream 20
Economizing 132
Effective demand (*see also*
demand, aggregate) viii,
17, 19, 21, 26, 31, 39, 40,